WELL I'LL BE A BLUE-NOSED GOPHER...

Practicing Happiness Now!

Dr. John C. Webb ©
Sarah Bausinger, Illustrator

Well I'll Be A Blue-Nosed Gopher…Practicing Happiness Now! © 2020
This is a work of non-fiction.
Text set in Gill Sans.
Copyright © 2020 PRACTICING HAPPINESS NOW LLC
Cover and book design by Mae I Design & Photography
Edited by Sarah Fox
Illustrated by Sarah Bausinger
ISBN: 978-0-578-65734-9

All rights reserved.
No part of this book may be reproduced in any form or by any electronic or mechanical means, including information storage and retrieval systems, without written permission from the author, except for the use of brief quotations in a book review.

"The Times They Are a-Changin'." Words and music by Bob Dylan. Copyright © 1963, 1964 by Warner Bros. Inc.; renewed 1991, 1992 by Special Rider Music. All rights reserved.
International copyright secured. Reprinted by permission.
Excerpts from "GARFIELD © 1982 Paws, Inc." Reprinted with permission of ANDREWS McMEEL SYNDICATION. All rights reserved.
Excerpts from "The Adventures of Spin & Marty." Copyright © 1955.
Reprinted with permission of Disney Enterprises, Inc. All rights reserved.

CONTENTS

Be a Blue-Nosed Gopher! 1

Introduction: Why Do We Need a Book on Practicing Happiness? 5
    Why Me? 7

Section One: Who the Heck Am I? 11

Chapter One: Happiness Is...What? 13
    A Mood or a State of Mind? 13
    What "Creates" Happiness? 15
    What Does Happiness Feel Like? 17
    Myths of Enlightenment and Bliss 19
    Addictions? Not Me! 21

Chapter Two: Taking the Time to Connect 25
    Quiet Time Is Essential Time 25
    Setting Up Your Quiet Time to Work for You 29
    About Practicing! 31
    Happiness Step One - Meditations 32

Chapter Three: Knowing Who You Really Are 35
    Connecting to Our Higher Purposes 35
    Who Am I? The Higher Self 38
    Happiness Step Two - Discovering Your True Nature 42
    Happiness Step Three - The Real You 44

Chapter Four: Letting Go... 49
    Loving and Forgiving Yourself 49
    Happiness Step Four - Letting Go of the Baggage 56
    The Emotional Nature 58
    Happiness Step Five - Releasing Negative Emotions from Childhood 60

Chapter Five: Being Your Higher Self 61
    What Do You <u>Love</u> to Do? 61
    Happiness Step Six - Doing What You Love 63
    Happiness Step Seven - Keeping Score 67
    A Perfect Day—A Perfect Life 68
    Happiness Step Eight - Have a Perfect Day 71

Section Two: Thought + Action = Transformation 73

Chapter Six: Thought Management—Who's in Control? 75
    Elegant Mansion or Garbage Dump? 75
    Happiness Step Nine - What Are You Thinking? 79
    Happiness Step Ten - Positive or Negative Thoughts? 81
    Unlimited Thinking Brings Unlimited Results! 83
    Happiness Step Eleven - What I Want More of in Life 89

Chapter Seven: Trusting Your Thoughts! 91
    Intuition—Use it or Abuse it? 91
    Acting on Your Intuition 92
    Happiness Step Twelve - Practicing Intuition 97

Chapter Eight: Get a Life — The Way <u>You</u> Want It! 99
    Personal Goals: Defining What You Really Want in Life 99
    Working Hard or Hardly Working? 102
    Too Much of a Good Thing 104
    Making Space vs. Taking Up Space 105
    Happiness Step Thirteen - What I Really Want 108

Chapter Nine: Turning Dust into Gold 111
    Our "Perfect" Imperfections 111
    The Champion Procrastinator 113
    Happiness Step Fourteen - The Truth Is... 115

    Transforming the "Fairy Tale" 116
    Happiness Step Fifteen - Prioritizing 119
    What If? 121
    For Your Wallet or Purse 123

Chapter Ten: You Can Get There from Here (Sooner Than You Might Think) 125
    Shortcuts to Your Goals. 125
    Happiness Step Sixteen - Shortcuts! Getting There Sooner 129
    Additional Goal Time-Savers 130
    Happiness Step Seventeen - Follow Through with your Goals! 135

Section Three: Put Time on <u>Your</u> Side! 137

Chapter Eleven: Time Passes and Time's Past 139
    The Nature of Time 139
    Happiness Step Eighteen - Time-Saving or Squandering? 142
    Freeing Ourselves from the Past 143
    Happiness Step Nineteen - Movin' On 148

Chapter Twelve: Is the Present "Now" or Is Now the "Present"? .. 149
    "Well I'll Be a Blue-Nosed Gopher!" 149
    Choosing Now 150
    Enjoy Your "Present" 155
    Happiness Step Twenty - Your "Now" Moments 158
    Indian Time 159
    Quality Time 163

Chapter Thirteen: The Uncertain Future 165
    Whose Agenda are We Following, Anyway? 165
    Happiness Step Twenty-One - Good Riddance to Weak Verbiage! 173
    Uncertainty Shouldn't Be Uncomfortable 174
    Happiness Step Twenty-Two - A Happier Future 177

Section Four: Embracing Endless Energy 179

Chapter Fourteen: Energy—Got Some?. 181
    The Energy around Us. 181
    How's Your Energy Level?. 183
    Happiness Step Twenty-Three - Energy Check! 185
    Directing and Exchanging Energy. 187

Chapter Fifteen: Overcoming Energy Blockers and Drainers. . 193
    Meteor Showers and Black Holes 193
    Unnecessary Activities 194
    Poor Pacing or Timing of Your Energy. 196
    Here's to Your Health. 197

Chapter Sixteen: Subtle Energy-Zappers 203
    Fear and Doubt (Again!) 203
    How Attachments Rob Energy 208
    The Energy Void 209
    Happiness Step Twenty-Four - Unclogging the Drain!. 212

Chapter Seventeen: Are We Having "Fun" Yet?. 215
    Relearning How to Have Fun. 215
    Humor Yourself! 217
    No Time for Fun? R.I.P. 219
    Happiness Step Twenty-Five - Lightin' the Fire or Chillin' Out?. 223

Section Five: Ego Check! 225

Chapter Eighteen: I'm <u>Not</u> an Egomaniac! (Now Get Out of My Way!) 227
    Seeing Ego for What It Really Is. 227
    Fear of Losing Control. 229
    Did I "Win" or "Lose"?. 231

Chapter Nineteen: More Ego Tricks 239
    The Know-It-All. 239
    Pity 243
    Our Image vs. Who We <u>Really</u> Are. 244

The "Need" for Praise 246
Taming the Beast 248
Happiness Step Twenty-Six - Ego Check!. 249
Happiness Step Twenty-Seven - Happiness Weather Report . . . 252

Chapter Twenty: Rising Above the Muck 255
Chasing Happiness or Running From it? 255
Discovering "Enoughness" 256
Compassion 257
Happiness Step Twenty-Eight - Ego-Squelching Activities 262

Chapter Twenty-One: Perfect Life—Perfect Problems 263
Abundance 263
Happiness Step Twenty-Nine - Facing Adversity 272

Chapter Twenty-Two: More Garbage to the Dumpster 273
Lightening the Load 273
Happiness Step Thirty - Morphing Attachments into Preferences 280
Happiness Step Thirty-One - Don't Worry! 287

Chapter Twenty-Three: Judge Not, Want Not 289
Impartiality 289
Happiness Step Thirty-Two - Just Being 293
Happiness Step Thirty-Three - Erasing Disappointment 296

Chapter Twenty-Four: Seeing the Big Picture 299
Unity 299
Happiness Step Thirty-Four - Showing Compassion and Love   301
Happiness Step Thirty-Five - Saying Thanks 307
Happiness Step Thirty-Six - A Little Self-Analysis 309

Section Six: Casting Off the Chains of Negativity ... 313

Chapter Twenty-Five: Potential Wreckage ... 315
- Battling the Negative Emotions ... 315
- Hatred ... 317
- Anger, Impatience ... 321
- Happiness Step Thirty-Seven - Dousing the Fire ... 326

Chapter Twenty-Six: Subtle Trickiness ... 329
- Sadness ... 329
- Guilt ... 332
- Greed ... 333
- Pride ... 334
- Low Self-Esteem ... 336
- Jealousy ... 336
- Happiness Step Thirty-Eight - Overcoming ... 338

Chapter Twenty-Seven: Turning the Light Back On ... 339
- Fear and Doubt ... 339
- Stress ... 345
- Happiness Step Thirty-Nine - Washing Away the Dirt ... 348
- Collecting Tumbleweeds? ... 349

Chapter Twenty-Eight: We Don't Have Forever.... ... 353
- Our Certain Future ... 353
- The Nature of Death ... 355

Chapter Twenty-Nine: Let's Face It... ... 361
- Fear of Death ... 361
- Happiness Step Forty - It's Your Funeral ... 365
- Consequences of Ignoring Death ... 366

Chapter Thirty: Have a Good Journey... ... 371
- Preparing for Death ... 371
- Happiness Step Forty-One - Meditations about That Exceptional Moment ... 375
- First Meditation ... 375
- Second Meditation ... 376
- Third Meditation ... 377

    Fourth Meditation 377
    Before Birth/After Death. 377
    Happiness Step Forty-Two - Remember Me! 381

Section Seven: Happiness Matters! 385

Chapter Thirty-One: Practicing Happiness Makes a Difference!. .387
    Collective Happiness 387
    Taking Care of Each Other 389
    Peace—More than a Word. 391

Chapter Thirty-Two: The Quest for Reality 395
    Getting Closer to Reality. 395
    Happiness Step Forty-Three - Making a Difference 399
    Happiness Steps Locator 401

Acknowledgments. 403

References. 407

About the Author. 419

A NOTE FROM THE AUTHOR

Practicing Happiness in a Pandemic?

As this book goes to print, the COVID-19 (coronavirus) rages on, dramatically affecting the lives of nearly everyone on the planet. Since I wrote the manuscript before the pandemic began, it's easy to ask: how can one practice happiness when there is so much sickness, loss of loved ones, unemployment, and a complete upheaval of the world we once knew?

I sincerely believe we need this book now more than ever. Or at least some of you will because I'll never pretend one book works for everyone. Practicing happiness and being a "blue-nosed gopher" (as explained in the next few pages) is about discovering ways to stay grounded and get through these times of hardship. Face it: there have been plagues, hunger, wars, and natural disasters throughout our history. Even in the face of inconceivable suffering, we've seen the best of human nature come forward. Adversity helps us realize and act upon what is most important: loving and helping our neighbors, our families, our friends, and those in need.

Difficult times create more urgency for us to seek our true purpose here on Earth, to find and be our higher selves, and do what's most important in life. We can either allow the challenges we face to overcome us, or we can choose to rise above them, no matter how difficult. And, yes, all of us do have the right to choose happiness, a sense of humor, and to be positive, even in troubled times. That is how we will get through this. So read on! Practicing happiness will make a difference, and I absolutely wish for you to be happy and healthy in better times ahead!

BE A BLUE-NOSED GOPHER!

There is nothing wrong with your eyes. You read correctly. Yes, a **blue-nosed gopher!** A mutant rodent has **what** to do with happiness? How did this cute but pesky little varmint give me so much more than giant holes in my backyard?

I'd just finished what I thought was my final version of the book you are now reading. I've always advocated that a big part of being happy is the ability to cope with adversity. Suddenly, that idea was given a major test.

I was trying to incorporate a writing career along with being a university professor and a jazz musician when Toni, my wife and soul mate, suffered a major bipolar episode. If you've ever had a friend or family member with a mental disorder, you know that can literally turn your entire world upside down. That's exactly what happened. As wonderful as my wife was when she was healthy, she literally became a danger to herself and required hospitalization. When she was released, she was still not well, was on too much medication, and would wander off to parts unknown. One night, she did not come home at all, and at six a.m. the next morning, I got a phone call from the hospital that no one ever wants to get.

A nurse gravely informed me that Toni had been hit by a fast-moving car while she was walking. She was in critical condition, and I had better get to the hospital ASAP. The next few days were a complete blur. Toni was in a coma with a broken femur, broken arm, punctured lung, several large wounds, and—worst of all—a traumatic brain injury that would change her forever.

It's far easier to be "happy" when things are going well, isn't it? To keep my head above water, I was literally forced to follow my own words. During our ordeal, I was reminded daily that **we were not alone** in our suffering. Every day, the waiting rooms outside the intensive care unit (ICU) were filled with grim-faced relatives and friends of people going through hardships like ours. How heart-wrenching is it to see families stagger out of the ICU after having just lost a loved one? How does one talk about happiness to them?

I cannot begin to express how thankful I am Toni was not taken from our lives that fateful night. Through the nine months of ICU, rehab hospitals, and a special NeuroRestorative unit for traumatic brain injury patients, I watched with awe as Toni slowly relearned how to breathe, talk, eat, and walk with a walker. Her courage was remarkable. Toni's memory of her life remains pretty much wiped clean, and her short-term memory is also severely challenged. But, three months after the accident, an amazing change occurred.

Her personality kicked in, and she became a "cheerful little earful," laughing over the least little thing and singing songs. When we would tell her something, she started responding, "Well, I'll be a blue-nosed gopher!" This was followed by her unique laugh, which would make everyone around her laugh. When she began saying this dozens of times a day, I asked everyone at the hospital if they had taught her that saying. No one stepped forward. For several months, Toni rattled off her "blue-nosed gopher" proclamation on a daily basis until I could stand it no more. So, I searched online to see if there was such a saying anywhere in the world.

Lo and behold, on the 1950s TV show *The Mickey Mouse Club*, there was a series of short episodes called "Spin and Marty." One of the supporting characters would exclaim, "Well I'll be a blue-nosed gopher!" *The Mickey Mouse Club* was Toni's favorite show when she was a little girl. Nestled in her long-term memory, the saying stuck in her brain.

Toni, devoid of her past, has become one of the happiest people I've ever known. Toni still says that phrase a number of times each day, and no matter what frame of mind I may be in, it reminds me to be happy **now.** Waiting for something to make us happy makes our happiness depend on something or someone else.

Practicing happiness is more than something nice to do; it's a necessity. Working on our well-being daily not only helps us enjoy life more, but it gets us through our toughest times. With even a little practice, happier days and the best future are possible. It turned out I had a few changes to make in my book, including how Toni teaches and inspires me (and others!) about happiness every single day. Laugh at the little things—**now!** Have fun—**now!** And be a blue-nosed gopher!

INTRODUCTION

Why Do We Need a Book on Practicing Happiness?

Do you ride up and down the mood "roller-coaster"? Does that little, dark, rain cloud follow you even on sunny days? Do you long to be that happy kid again? Do you have food, shelter, a job, and a family, but finding happiness is like chasing the end of a rainbow you never find? Maybe something's missing in your life, or you're suffering from a recent trauma or adverse situation. Well, welcome to the real world, filled with land mines capable of blowing your good mood into ash! How is it that our so-called happiness can be here one moment and then disappear faster than our cash at the grocery store?

I've encountered this saying about happiness a number of times: "You either have it or you don't." But that motto just doesn't cut it anymore. We experience happiness, but then we ruin the party with "I'm happy as long as (this or that happens)." Then, the minute it **doesn't** happen, our well-being spirals down the garbage disposal!

It's simple, really. Happiness has to be **practiced!** And your happiness will improve dramatically the second you're ready to work on your "state of happiness." Then you can still stand up to the plate after life throws a fastball at your head! Why not give your well-being the same attention medical, business, or other professionals would to their jobs?

Think of something you're good at. Don't be modest now! What you do best is usually what you've done **often**.

> During seminars, I conduct a shoelace-tying contest. Everyone unties one shoelace completely. Whoever doesn't have laces can referee. Everyone with laces puts both feet flat on the ground. On cue, they tie one shoe as fast as possible, and the first to finish and raise his or her hand wins. What a mad scramble! It's hard to declare a winner because it's so close. But a winner is found, and a prize is given (shoelaces or maybe some calming herbal tea). I then interview the shoelace speedster. "Hi! What's your name? Wow, you were soooo fast! Amazing! Congratulations! You are soooo talented! Tell us, how did you get so good at this?" The winner usually says something like: "Well, you know, I've done it all my life…"

Let's speculate. Let's say our winner is twenty-four years old and started tying shoes at age four. That's twenty years of shoelace tying. My remedial math guru says that only two shoelace ties a day for twenty years is 14,600 times, and that's not counting leap years! Folks, I promise, if you do **anything** that many times, you will be two hair-lengths away from becoming a Zen master at it! With that many repetitions, the difference between the "talents" of each individual is about half a millisecond.

For classical saxophone recitals, there are some difficult runs I've needed to practice nearly 50,000 times. Oh, save the medal! That's spread out over months, so it's not so bad, really. After the recital, people would compliment my talent. I thanked them politely, but I knew that **practice,** not talent (and maybe a good reed), was 99 percent responsible for my ability to play those runs.

Everyone knows something about happiness. But, what we know means nothing unless we PRACTICE what we know. Then, an idea struck me! Why can't we actually **practice** to improve aspects of our own precious well-being? Instead, we practice anger, sadness, or fearfulness and become quite accomplished at them! Why would we want that when we can begin practicing happiness?

Throughout the book, I've included "happiness steps," which are designed to improve your overall well-being. You don't have to go to the top of a mountain, give up all your material possessions, or put your life on hold to do these steps. You don't need to be a counselor or psychologist to understand them either. If you're currently under a doctor's care, by all means continue it. **This book is not intended to be a substitute for medical treatment.** The goal here is to create positive changes in your life. The happiness steps included can be practiced at any time, and you won't even need your shoelaces!

Why Me?

In education, there is an urgent need for more emphasis on well-being, compassion, and wisdom rather than accumulating information. It's time to take the study of happiness seriously. It makes little difference how much is taught or learned if no attention is paid to how to live a happy and meaningful life, which is intricately related to our purpose here on Earth. Whether we're on the job, vacationing, going to the grocery store, or even reading this book, happiness matters in a big way!

I retired early from my job as a professor of music and university administrator in order to spend more time writing, playing jazz, and caring for my favorite blue-nosed gopher. Since I am not a psychiatrist or paid counselor, I offer unique perspectives and experiences that I hope will help you. Plus, my wife Toni shows and lives happiness every day despite her severe brain injury and other physical impairments. Thankfully, she has helped me reduce my long-winded tendencies for a "plethora of excessively-inordinate, superfluous, professorial diatribes!" Toni helps me keep it simple and real!

In our household, the subject of happiness comes up fairly often. Toni has a way of simplifying complex issues:

"I want to be happy. I **don't** want to be sad!"

Ding ding! If you really want to be happy, you have to first **admit you want it!** Bury your pride for one moment and repeat that line!

Or maybe you need to shout this one:

"I'm sick and tired of the BS in my life!"

Feel better? Congratulations! This means your well-being **means** something to you. If I only had two seconds with you, I would say:

Happiness is a **decision,** not a condition. The end.

If it's that simple, then why are there gazillions of books on happiness (counting mine)? Are they all scams? "Happy" is such a simple word, so it ought to be easy to accomplish, right? Instead, our state of being can be as confusing as the State of the Union! The billions of dollars spent on mental health and related drugs to "up" our well-being in the U.S. every year confirm this. In today's challenging world, we need inspiration on a continuing, daily basis (Happiness Steps!) to help us improve one or more facets of our lives.

WELL I'LL BE A BLUE-NOSED GOPHER

I don't pretend to be a "happiness guru"—a supreme model of perfection who holds all of the secrets to the known universe. My quest began because I, too, was sick and tired of the BS! I **did** want more happiness!

Let's face it. We're **all** a work in progress. I've been immature, angry, bored, and self-centered. I've been silent when I should have spoken, and I've spoken when I shouldn't have. I've had hangovers, been lied to, been cheated on, been beat up, and been fired from jobs. (There's a country tune in there somewhere!) I've worked with every kind of student imaginable, and they **all** loved me (cough!). As a musician, I've played for every kind of crowd from a drunken brawl (where they should have put up a chain-link fence to protect the band) to high-society balls where the wealth in the room could buy an entire state. I've laughed until I've almost suffocated, and, yes, I cried when I saw *Titanic*. I'm not a saint, and I'm a fairly mediocre softball player.

The book you're about to read is far bigger than me. There's no deep mystery here. Anyone can be a happier human being, but it requires regular practice! Practicing happiness **works**, but the way it works differs for each of us. My wife, Toni, loves to do jigsaw puzzles, but the way she does them is unique because she rarely looks at the picture of the puzzle! Sometimes she'll assemble the puzzle very quickly— upside down! But it's still a completed puzzle. In the same way, you can…

- read the book from cover to cover,
- select a chapter you seem drawn to, OR
- randomly pick a paragraph or page and apply it to your life!

However you decide to use this book, the goal is to unlock the door to happiness with ideas to put into practice in order to better ourselves and, consequently, our well-being. Now, are you ready to start practicing?

Given with abundant love on this beautiful day,
JOHN

SECTION ONE
Who the Heck Am I?

CHAPTER ONE
HAPPINESS IS...WHAT?

A Mood or a State of Mind?

In the introduction we stated (or screamed!) that we wanted more happiness. But what is this "happiness" we want? We get that "yessss!" feeling when things are going well, but then "life" comes along, and it seems our happiness disappears faster than Grandma's last oatmeal raisin cookie in the kitchen. (In our house, it was always the "ghost" that stole it.)

How is it that our happiness can pull a disappearing act? That's because it was our **mood** that changed! Good moods are nice, but happiness has to hold up when the toilet overflows and creates a cataclysmic flash flood on your new carpet two minutes before you need to leave for work. I wouldn't expect anyone to be smiley or happy about it at all. Allow yourself an expletive or two, but then you have to clean the crap and move on! Good moods come and go, but the happiness we want has to be able to float our boat even in a hurricane.

Today, people who are often happy, bubbly, or cheerful are often made fun of by those who do not share the same mindset:

"I think her real name is Mary Juana."
"There could be a few loose screws somewhere..."
"He's probably from another planet!"

Well, welcome to **Earth.** There's a strange comfort in the idea that we should have a miserable life sprinkled with some happiness on weekends or vacations.

> *"Happiness? For everyone? Ha! Take a reality pill!"*
> **-I.B. CYNICAL-**

The media is no help because they only run positive events as "special interest" stories. After ten minutes of the nightly news, I feel like I've been run over ten times by an SUV! The little happy story between the bombings, fires, accidents, and murders just doesn't cut it. The constant focus on the "bad boys and girls" of the world is not a true picture of how most people live their lives. It's time to shatter the idea that misery, doom, and gloom is what "should be"! Happiness is **<u>not</u>** a luxury or for special occasions! *Au contraire.*

Happiness is...
- a fundamental right for everyone,
- a basic necessity for our health, and
- critical for the survival of humanity!

It's not a "pipe dream" to say that happiness makes a difference. If your happiness factor is raised, it will spread to others, which ultimately makes a significant difference in human behavior worldwide. We may not all be joining hands and singing Pharrell Williams's tune "Happy" just yet, but we **can** start with our own lives.

What "Creates" Happiness?

Man is born to enjoy, to create, and to radiate happiness.
-MAHARISHI MAHESH YOGI-

What's really ironic to me is how little attention humanity has paid to this statement. It's not selfish to be happy; it's part of our very purpose in life. Of course, I'll add this disclaimer: No one's "happiness" should infringe upon the rights of others or cause suffering to others.

A mind that is happy and contented produces health in the body. A mind that is angry or fearful ultimately produces illnesses in the body. That alone is enough to warrant a "serious" look at how to increase happiness and cope with suffering.

I created and taught a number of freshman seminars called "Practicing Happiness" at The University of Texas at Tyler, and during the first week, most students would rate their overall happiness level as high or very high. As the semester progressed, their writings revealed major happiness issues. The cause was deeper than my "spectacular" lectures or the required research paper. We're typically reluctant to admit our unhappiness to others and to ourselves! Mihaly Csikszentmihalyi, a renowned researcher on happiness, states:

> *Self-reported happiness is not a very good indicator of the quality of a person's life. Some people say they are "happy" even when they dislike their jobs, when their home life is nonexistent, when they spend all their time in meaningless activities.*

He also mentions that while extroverted people appear to be happier because they socialize more, that is not necessarily an indication of inner happiness. While social relationships are important, a happy life is one filled with **meaningful** activities in work and leisure.

The life most of us want (with health, abundance, and happiness) is created through positive thoughts and actions. Our mental state can be capable of overcoming physical problems, so the best solution is to "train" our minds to be happy—for our health! A healthy, positive mind is the utmost priority.

Q. Thank you, oh Swami, but I cannot go to the top of a mountain for twenty years to reach such a nirvana. How can I ever attain this mind?

A. No need to be a mountain climber. Besides, it's freezing up there. Whatever quality of human experience you desire is available **right here, right now,** through your own thoughts.

Pick your title:

Director of Happiness, Peace, and Serenity

Or...

CEO of Perpetual Suffering and the—

Think about it. Are you happier with negative thoughts or positive thoughts? The mind is a **powerful** entity! Placebo studies have shown that positive thinking and expectation of a positive result can greatly influence our physiological health. Positive thoughts influence the body to be more immune to illnesses and the effects of stress. For the most part, our minds influence our health far more than outside factors!

Unfortunately, we look for outside influences to change our thoughts, so then we depend on **outside factors** for our happiness. The reality is...

No one can make you unhappy without **your** permission!

Are you giving out permission slips? Maybe it's too hot outside, or your brother makes you angry enough to bend a crowbar into a horseshoe. You can let those things control your happiness, or you can take charge of your life.

> *The source of the word happiness is the Icelandic word happ, which means "luck" or "chance," the same source of the words haphazard and happenstance. I did not want to leave the experience of happiness to chance and therefore sought to define and understand it.*
> -TAL BEN SHAHAR, PH.D.-

What Does Happiness Feel Like?

Happiness feels different for everyone. The perception of happiness (or lack of it) is based on our attitude. One person's treasure is another's trash. A good saxophone reed at $4.95 means everything to me before a recital, but it is no good to an accountant! Eating a big cheeseburger is a delightful treat for someone who's ravenous and loves cheeseburgers, but to a vegan who has just eaten dinner—not so much.

Happy people...
- usually have good dispositions;
- are cheerful, smile, and laugh a lot;
- may not always exhibit outward signs of happiness (hello, me!);
- feel good about themselves most of the time;
- function well in relationships;
- enjoy learning;

- enjoy helping others;
- have inner peace and tranquility most of the time;
- feel they have freedom in their lives;
- are willing to make changes; and
- feel life is a learning process.

Now, back to the real world, where we're light years from perfect. As a performer, I'm always making mistakes (can you believe it?). I try not to cuss, and sometimes I succeed! I cover the mistake up as best I can, vow to do better next time, and move on! With happiness issues, it's pretty much the same.

When it comes to being good-natured, we've all seen glimpses of what humanity is capable of:

On Christmas day, to visit family, we would drive 90 miles from Orange County to Ventura, California. We traversed through Los Angeles and the San Fernando Valley, which is usually a traffic catastrophe. It was unbelievable how polite all the drivers were on Christmas! People were friendlier, and they'd wave and wish a merry Christmas to a perfect stranger. Great! I love it! What about the other 364 days?

Humans have an extraordinary capability to exhibit politeness and respect **under certain conditions.** Toni reminds me how to remember the other 364 days.

While Toni's long- and short-term memory is severely compromised, the part of her brain that recalls music and lyrics is amazing. She remembers lyrics better than I do and often just starts singing a song that pops into her head. The most frequent song she sings all year long is "Deck the Halls." Whether I'm balancing the checkbook (a Herculean feat for me) or if we're going out to eat, she'll suddenly start the tune and sing it exactly like this: "Don-da-da-da-da-da-da-dah fa-la-la-la-lah-la-la-la-lah!"

Then she'll laugh three laughs: "ha-ha-HA!" It's impossible not to smile and remember that the Christmas spirit should stay with us all year!

It's time to declare **every** day a holiday! If you work in a Monday through Friday environment, notice the moods in the workplace on a Monday morning versus a Friday afternoon. Wouldn't it be great if Monday moods were just as good as Friday's? My mood on Sunday nights, anticipating Monday, would make Al Bundy look like a giggling tooth fairy. If you only live for vacations, then you're always in anticipation of it, and when you're finally on a vacation, you start anticipating having to go back to work! That's no way to live. Happiness and fun are not "bankable" or to be reserved only for certain days. Every day is a special day. For me, no more TGIF. It's TGIA: Thank God I'm **Alive!**

Myths of Enlightenment and Bliss

So, if you're happy, you live a life of continuous bliss with no problems, gain enlightenment, and live happily ever after, right? A five-year old won't even buy into that one. The more someone claims they are officially "enlightened," the faster I suggest you run the other direction.

An enlightened person doesn't ride around on a magic carpet, nor are there radiant beams of light emanating from his or her (probably too big) head!

Enlightenment doesn't come about by words or accomplishments:

*Inside yourself or outside, you never have to change
what you see, only the way you see it.*
-THADDEUS GOLAS-

As you see in the next two illustrations, our outer world may not noticeably change, but our inner world can.

Before enlightenment: doing the dishes and taking out the trash.

After enlightenment: doing the dishes and taking out the trash.

-ZEN PHILOSOPHY (ALTERED A BIT BY *MOI*)-

As we grow spiritually, we still have to eat, do chores, and, yes, go to the bathroom! We'll have problems, too. We can act like a gnarly troll on steroids or play that sad ol' country tune again, but we can choose not to. Well-being is a decision that can be made at any time.

I don't claim to know to what enlightenment is, but I can tell when

I'm moving in the right direction. It's like shining a light into a dark room. We gradually learn more about ourselves and work on having a positive attitude toward our spirituality. The more spiritual work we do, the better we feel.

> *We can easily forgive a child who is afraid of the dark. The real tragedy of life is when an adult is afraid of the light.*
> **-PLATO-**

Enlightenment is not something to seek; it's something to **be**.

Addictions? Not Me!

Nearly everyone at one time or another has longed for an instant shot of bliss of some kind. We want a rush of incredible, powerful feeling. If only there were a magical happiness pill to take us to bubbling ecstasy with no side effects! If I find one, I'll be the first to let you know! If we're unhappy with the environment we've created for ourselves, it's tempting to look for outside stimulation for happiness. Alcohol and drugs (including an abundant amount of legal prescription drugs) entice us with the bliss we think we want. Specific neurons in the brain are temporarily activated, bringing a feeling of pleasure. Unfortunately, the "bliss" is temporary and is often accompanied by harmful side effects when the indulgence is overdone or repeated over and over, which creates more suffering than the temporary bliss was worth.

This brings us to a powerful point: **We really do want happiness**! We want it so badly that we can be lured into addictive habits to achieve short-term bliss. No one says, "When I grow up, I want to be an addict." Yet addiction does exist for millions who are chained to harmful habits they cannot stop.

It's like licking honey off of a sharp knife. The reward of the sweet taste lasts only as long as you have a tongue! Few people realize an addiction until it's too late and will trade their entire futures for it at the expense of themselves and others. Why? Addicts are really seeking a high that external substances or circumstances can't give them: their own spirituality.

Another reason for an addiction is to escape one or more crappy situations, but once the "bliss" wears off, old thought patterns take over again. There was a saying (the escapist's national anthem): "Beam me up, Scottie. This planet sucks!" Then there was: "Just say no," which really didn't work because the minute you focus on what **not** to do, you're twice as likely to do it! In order to not do what's bad for us, we have to have a better alternative that eliminates the thought that these substances will do us any good.

Indulging our senses and drinking salt water are alike: the more we partake, the more our desire and thirst grow.
–INDIAN PHILOSOPHY-

Ironically, alcohol, a legal substance, may be the most formidable foe of all for those prone to addiction. I don't proselytize to my students (some of whom are going to be performing in nightclubs or bars) about the evils of this and that. Those who preach total abstinence may have a point—for themselves. But prohibition didn't work; people drank more than ever before (at least according to my dad!). I try to be realistic. Substances and all sorts of temptations have been and always will be around. Addiction is possible! What I tell my students is:

- make sure you don't put yourself in a situation where you could do harm to yourself or others and
- make sure that drugs and alcohol never matter. They should have no significant or negative effect on your life whatsoever.

Fortunately, there are healthy ways to achieve an altered state of consciousness that can bring a feeling of bliss. If you become absorbed with an activity you love, you've likely experienced a relaxed feeling called "flow," where time seems to fly by. Long distance runners get a "runner's high." Musicians performing a piece they love go into a relaxed state. Meditators achieve varying degrees of altered consciousness. When we return from being in "flow," we're able to better cope with day-to-day situations without harmful side effects.

In the early 1960s, at Harvard University, Timothy Leary and Richard Alpert researched the effect of psychedelic drugs, especially LSD. A few years later, Alpert studied in India with guru Neem Karoli Baba, whom Alpert called *Maharaj-ji*. *Maharaj-ji* gave Alpert the name "Ram Dass" (servant of God). Under that name, Ram Dass has written a number of thought-provoking books dealing with spirituality and consciousness.

> Ram Dass (RD) took a bag of LSD to India to find someone who could give some insights as to what this new, mysterious drug was all about. Then he realized that his own guru, Maharaj-ji, would be perfect for the task. The next day, his guru summoned him, asking for the "medicine," even though RD hadn't even mentioned a thing to him yet! He offered him 300 micrograms of LSD, but his teacher requested 900! RD stayed with him all day, and there was no effect on his guru whatsoever.
>
> Several years later, on a return trip to India, the two reunited, and *Maharaj-ji* told RD to bring more of the "medicine." The guru ended up taking an astounding 1,500 micrograms (over a triple dose), and as he did, he asked RD if it would make him crazy. When RD answered the affirmative, the guru began to act completely crazy, and when RD panicked, the guru stopped and told him he was just joking. There was never any visible effect on the guru from this huge dose!
>
> Maharaj-ji later commented that LSD could be useful **if** someone is at peace and his or her mind is turned toward God.

But one cannot stay on the "trip" forever! In a later reference, he stated, "LSD is like visiting Christ, but you can't stay there. You know, it would be much better to become (like) Christ than to just visit with him. But your medicine (LSD) won't do that, because it's a false Samadhi (path)."

Drugs show you the possibility, but they don't allow you to BE the possibility. Rather than only being able to "visit" a state of happiness, isn't it better to "be" happiness?

CHAPTER TWO
TAKING THE TIME TO CONNECT

Quiet Time Is Essential Time

A man does not seek to see himself in running water, but in still water. For only what is itself still can impart stillness upon others...
-CHUANG TSE-

It's so easy to believe there's not enough time to work on happiness. Life is hectic and can easily whip us into a psychotic frenzy. A few seconds of driving in any major city will give you a sense of urgency verrrrry quickly! Why are we in such a rush? Unless we're constantly busy or in a hurry, we aren't doing enough or accumulating enough, right? This is nothing new. My wife's grandfather José Jaramillo used to say (translated from Spanish), "Everyone's in such a hurry...to get one foot in the grave!"

With new technology at our fingertips, we're not only getting busier, but we multitask obsessively.

Joseph is talking on his cell phone while having coffee and a bagel at a local restaurant with a business associate who is texting multiple clients. Joe's iPad is playing downloaded favorites when he discovers an online banking error, which delays him from finishing his report for work. As he resumes his report, he stops to check his emails, Facebook, and Instagram. He's flying to Chicago in three hours, and as he checks the weather conditions, he realizes he will need his heavy jacket. An old friend walks in he has not seen in over a year, but as he socializes for a few moments, he begins to get frustrated that his report is taking longer than he had anticipated. Also, he needs to run home to get his jacket.

Meanwhile, Joseph's wife, Tasha, interrupts her graduate writing assignment to answer the home phone when her cell phone also rings. She turns down her music and takes care of both calls when she realizes she's running late to pick up her son from choir practice, take her daughter to a soccer game, and then go to the store and the post office. She hurriedly turns off her big screen TV she'd had on with the sound down, grabs her iPad, and dashes out the door, all the while talking to a real estate client on her cell phone. She continues on the phone while driving and gobbles half of a sandwich from lunch she hadn't had time to finish. After picking up the kids, she'll rush to take them to a friend's house and then pick up her husband and drive him to the airport for his business trip. She'll get back just in time to show a new home to a prospective buyer, go to her son's choir concert, and then come home and finish her graduate project due tomorrow at eight a.m.

Is this a little like your day?

There's no law against being busy, but too much busyness causes us to forget a very important commodity—ourselves! Heroically, we protest: "I don't have **time** to think about myself when I've got a million **other** things to do!" One question:

If **you're** not living your life, who is?

Excess busyness comes with a price. It consumes our valuable time to the point that we don't spend **one single minute** toward what's most important: our well-being! In the story, Joseph might make a crucial error on his report, or Tasha might neglect something in her real estate deal because she was driving and eating while conducting business on her cell phone. Worse, she could have gotten in a car wreck! Joseph and Tasha may also be too busy to eat nutritious food, exercise properly, or have a good relationship with their kids, let alone each other.

To practice happiness, we have to spend some time **daily** to sort out our most essential issues; rediscover what's most important to us; and get ourselves mentally, emotionally, physically, and spiritually in balance. This is best accomplished when we are alone in a quiet place. In this noisy world, it's easy to be afraid of quietness. Even a **few minutes** of uninterrupted quiet time will work wonders. Some of us have been knee-deep in busyness for so long that we're not even sure what we'd do if we had a few minutes of quiet time, except maybe fall asleep! So, instead of allowing circumstances to slap us around like a beach ball in a tidal wave, it's time to give ourselves a moment or two to start changing all that.

I recommend using quiet time for prayer and/or meditation. There are two basic categories of meditation techniques: those designed for contemplation and concentration practice and those designed for relaxation and deep rest. Contemplation and concentration practice brings an important issue to our minds in order to make decisions in a calm atmosphere. Since important issues won't be solved in a single day, it's essential to make quiet time part of a regular practice.

The second category of meditation (relaxation and deep rest) is designed to temporarily shut down the thought process. Sometimes the mind just rambles on and on with negative or useless thoughts, so I finally told mine to shuuuuut up! Relaxation meditations, such as transcendental meditation, are designed to free us from this constant "mind chatter." This allows the mind to go into a deeper brain-wave activity than sleep provides. It's a perfect opposite to contemplation because sometimes we simply need to relax and get our minds away from thoughts! Techniques include mantras, breathing exercises, creative visualizations, or concentrating only on the present moment. We want thoughts to fade away into the background, and even stop for a while, so the mind is essentially quiet or free from conscious thought. This is not a trancelike state or hypnosis, but it is a very relaxed state of deep rest, like diving below the ocean waves to find the stillness on the ocean floor.

I've found both techniques to be successful. Ultimately you'll know which style you're drawn to most often. If you have an inclination to pray, by all means, incorporate it during contemplation and just before or right after relaxation techniques. There are many types of meditations, all with specific explanations for the process. My wife and I greatly benefited from transcendental meditation, which requires a teacher initially, but the first two Happiness Steps coming up in this book are meditations that require no training.

Reserve some time for yourself on a regular basis, even if it's only ten minutes a day. Consistent practice will bring an increase in creativity, overall energy, and an ability to remain calmer in difficult situations. It can be life changing. Without my meditation practice, this book would not exist.

> *When you practice prayer or meditation, as when you practice an instrument, you do something both creative and collaborative. You forge your own spiritual path, you engage in a dialogue with the divine, and you invite a greater reality into your consciousness. In stating your readiness to be open to Spirit, you prepare yourself to receive whatever comes...*
> -MARCIA MENTER-

Setting Up Your Quiet Time to Work for You

Meditation is easy to do. You don't have to change your religious beliefs, become a vegetarian, sit in awkward positions, get up at 4 a.m., wander off into the desert, or even wear sandals! Select a time each day when interruptions are not likely. Contemplation meditations work well in the morning before a lot of activity begins or before bedtime. Relaxation meditations work best in the early morning and late afternoons. The latter time usually allows for a regeneration of energy for the evening. If it is done too close to bedtime, you might fall asleep! Choose the same time each day, if possible. Start with twenty minutes or a little less. That's long enough to either provide a short, deep rest or some contemplation without becoming bored or discouraged. Later on, you can increase the time of meditation if you like.

Where to meditate? If your living room resembles Grand Central Station or a NASCAR race, don't meditate there! Find a favorite quiet spot either inside or outside. Make your spot meaningful, and place a significant religious or spiritual item or two around. A nice outside setting can inspire you for creative thought if there aren't lots of distractions. Locate a place you are drawn to.

Silence your cell phone and home phone, put your computers to sleep, close the door, turn off the TV, and ask for no interruptions until you come out. If you want music, make sure the volume is low enough to not disturb you. Avoid radio with any talking or commercials.

Usually, the eyes are closed for relaxation meditations and can be open or closed for contemplation. Sit comfortably on something with good support for your back, but don't get too comfortable or you might end up with a power nap instead of a meditation! Some meditations involve merely sitting comfortably, while others give more detailed instructions on to how to sit. Do what works for you. Take a few deep breaths, relax, and allow your mind to settle down before beginning.

Sometimes contemplation meditations can be done while walking, running, or with any repetitive activity that does not require intense mental concentration—sort of like "meditation in action." After some experience, you can meditate anywhere. The goal is to bring the best ideas and positive feelings from your quiet time into daily life.

> When I was music department chair, I would shut the door to my university administrative office around 5 p.m., turn out the lights, and meditate for twenty minutes. After coming out of the meditation, I had renewed energy to get done what I needed to. I got a few strange looks when I would open my door back up, but it was worth it!

I also recommend doing a relaxation meditation before that all-important meeting, exam, interview, speech, or performance in any venue. After some practice, you can even do a very short version (ten seconds) when you really need it! This has worked with my university music students about to perform in front of an audience.

Finding others to meditate with strengthens your practice and your commitment. Meditation groups offer readings, discussions, and companionship with people also interested in transforming their lives. The energy coming from a meditating group can be powerful. I especially encourage the whole family to spend quiet time together.

> *For where there are two or three gathered together*
> *in my name, there am I in the midst of them.*
> **-JESUS-**

Meditation is like tasting a juicy watermelon; a mere description can't substitute the experience of that first bite! By getting to the core of your most important issues in contemplation, you will save yourself far more time than it takes to <u>do</u> the quiet time! In relaxation meditations, you will get closer to your true self and bring more of that self back into your world of activity. Quiet time will help you stay in balance and is the first important step in practicing happiness! Are you ready to open the door for some profound changes in your life?

> *Be still, and know that I am God*
> **-THE BIBLE-**

About Practicing!

Imagine standing before a beautiful pond with large, flat, stepping stones scattered throughout that are easy to walk to and comfortable to stand on. You can start wherever you want and go to whichever steps beckon to you. There's no destination in particular; just enjoy being out in the pond! The happiness steps in this book are much the same. Do them as often as you feel you need to. The pond is different for everyone. You don't have to walk on all the steps to be happy! See the "Happiness Step Locator" at the end of the book to shop around!

Happiness Step One
Meditations

Contemplation Meditation

Choose a method of sitting that suits you, and take a few moments to get calm. When you feel ready, ask yourself:

What is the most important issue in my life right now? To be happier and feel better about this, I will do the following things…

As you ponder, be relaxed but alert too. Thoughts will come and go. Notice the silence between your thoughts because it will help you remain calm. Don't force answers, and be open for surprises. Avoid judging your thoughts or worrying about what others might think. Ask for the highest thoughts possible from God or your higher being of choice. If negative thoughts arise, simply let them blow away like the wind. Focus on positive, loving thoughts, which repeatedly raise your energy vibration. When you're through, jot down or remember your positive thoughts. When you feel ready, move on to another issue, but only when you feel a sense of satisfaction that you've covered what you could on that issue for the day. You can always revisit difficult issues because some may take days or weeks before you get a clear sense of a course of action. Repeat your contemplations for twenty minutes daily as often as you like.

Relaxation Meditation

Sit quietly and take a few deep, relaxing breaths. Closing the eyes aids the process of relaxation and helps lower the brain-wave activity. Once you begin, allow a couple minutes to get relaxed.

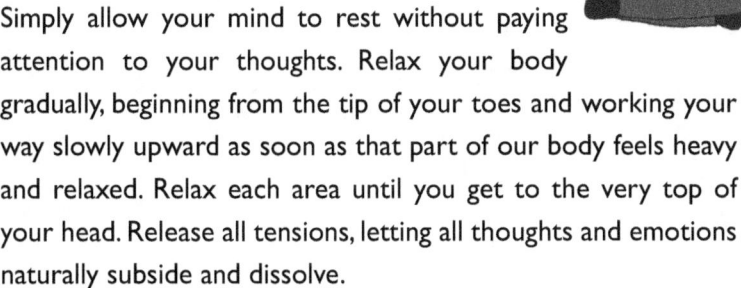

Simply allow your mind to rest without paying attention to your thoughts. Relax your body gradually, beginning from the tip of your toes and working your way slowly upward as soon as that part of our body feels heavy and relaxed. Relax each area until you get to the very top of your head. Release all tensions, letting all thoughts and emotions naturally subside and dissolve.

Once you're relaxed, go to a beautiful place in your mind. It can be a place you've been to, or you can think of the most beautiful place you can possibly imagine. It's restful, peaceful, and everything is always okay. There are no worries, negative emotions, or judgments. There is unlimited love and compassion, and you're free to be the way you truly want to be. Everything is perfect. Stay there as long as you'd like.

When you're through, take a couple of minutes to wake up to allow your mind and body to adjust. Remember your positive feelings throughout the day, and do your best to bring this relaxed feel into your everyday life.

Repeat this meditation for twenty minutes daily as often as you like.

CHAPTER THREE
KNOWING WHO YOU <u>REALLY</u> ARE

Connecting to Our Higher Purposes

Let's go back to our busyness for a moment. Being really busy can be good sometimes, but not if we're spending all our time with what isn't right for us. In reality, we're happier when more of our busyness is spent fulfilling our higher purposes in life versus living the life of Freddie Fender's "Wasted Days and Wasted Nights."

Your higher purposes often involve what **you** love and are drawn to do, and you've probably known most of them since childhood. Unfortunately, a lot of us neglect our true purpose(s) in favor of busying ourselves with what may seem important but isn't what tugs at our heart and soul. If others don't approve of our direction, we might live our lives just to gain approval. Why does this happen? It's because we don't take time to think about who we really are, and as any sage will tell us: In order to fulfill our higher purposes, we will need to make some changes.

In the grand scheme of things, we're here to do more than occupy space. We each have a "curriculum" of sorts to fulfill, and I believe we have an obligation to figure out what the **heck** that is!

> *We have what we seek. It is there all the time, and if*
> *we give it time it will make itself known to us.*
> **-THOMAS MERTON-**

How do we dredge this information to the surface of our conscious minds? We start **looking** for the answers! Don't expect them to be delivered with your pizza, but if you begin searching, your higher purposes will begin to come to you. Ideas that arrive about why you're here and what you should be doing may not seem rational and sometimes will be flat-out crazy (which is actually a good sign!). You'll begin to see your life in terms of the big picture. If you're building a car, you want to picture the entire automobile so you can see how the parts relate to the whole.

And now for the warning label: It doesn't work to merely **know** your higher purposes. Begin to **live** them the best you can, especially when the going gets rough, and it often does. Overwhelmed? Just begin with one idea and work on it. You can take on another one later. Signs you are doing something toward one of your higher purposes is when you lose track of time and you seem to have boundless energy doing what you love to do.

Some good folks plan their life's direction about as well as a riding lawn mower without a driver.

> Leslie brought home her fiancé to meet her parents, so her father invited the young man into his study to find out more about him. "What are your plans?" he asked George.
>
> "I'm a scholar of God," George replied.
>
> "Well, that's admirable," Leslie's father replied. "But what will you do to provide a nice house for my daughter?"

"I will study, and God will surely provide for us," George explained.

"And how will you buy her a nice engagement ring?"

"I will study hard, and God will provide for us."

"And children?" asked the father. "How will you support children?"

"Don't worry, sir. God will provide," replied the fiancé.

The conversation continued in much the same manner. After George and Leslie had left, her mother asked her father what he found out. The father answered, "Well, there's bad news and good news. The bad news is he doesn't have a **clue** about how to provide for our daughter. But the good news is that he thinks I'm God!"

Then there are those who have a plan, but greatly underestimate the time and effort it will take to make it happen.

Jennifer is a fine saxophonist who has successfully performed several pieces in front of judges in high school and in public performance. In her first year at university, her saxophone professor assigned a concerto for her to play. It was twenty minutes long and in three movements. Jennifer practiced as she always had, but her performance was a disaster, and she had left the stage in tears. Why did she "bomb"? She had practiced…

Or so she thought! The problem was that the more difficult concerto required far more practice than what she was used to. What used to work for her easier pieces didn't come close to what she needed to perform at this new level. Our life's plans are like a concerto or even a symphony; they require serious **planning!**

Because we have been given the treasure of life, we are here in large part to love and serve humanity to the best of our ability. By identifying our higher purposes, we can bring the best of who we are to the world. When one of our unique higher purposes is matched with others who need what we have to offer, great things happen!

> *I am going to venture that the man who sat on the ground in his tipi meditating on life and its meaning, accepting the kinship of all creatures and acknowledging unity with the universe of things was infusing into his being the true essence of civilization...*
> **-LUTHER STANDING BEAR, OGLALA SIOUX-**

Who Am I? The Higher Self

When we think or talk about who we are, we usually associate ourselves with our:
- name;
- gender;
- physical features;
- heritage and citizenship;
- age;
- geographical location;
- family and friends;
- marital or dating status;
- health;
- education;
- religion, philosophy, and political beliefs;
- job, status, economic condition, and possessions;
- hobbies; and
- membership in organizations.

Now prepare to toss these aside!

It's time to look behind the mask of our labels. The question "Who am I?" helps us discover more about our "higher selves," which are our divine connections guiding us toward our purposes here. The higher self is also known as our "true nature" and houses our best qualities.

The higher self remains consistent, unlike one's personality, which is usually attached to our labels and roller-coaster emotions. It's the "steering wheel" for a positive future. The meditation exercises are a great way to connect to the creativity, imagination, and passion from your higher self.

Have you ever heard someone say, "He knows me better than me?" That's cute but sad. If **you** don't get to know yourself, who will?

> *You got to be careful if you don't know where you're going, because you might not get there.*
> **-YOGI BERRA-**

Our higher selves exist long before we develop any of our cultural labels. When I think of babies or toddlers, I ask why it seems that everyone but the wicked witch of the west goes gaga over them. After all, they cry and wet the bed! I conclude it's because they have just arrived here, and in them, we see their purity. They are closest to the source of where we came from. The way a baby's laugh lights up an entire room is a marvelous example of the higher self in action!

> *When we arrived here we were FINE. Then we were de-fined. Now we must be re-fined.*
> **-SWAMI SATCHIDANANDA-**

Who you really are is more than your name, age, education, political beliefs, etc. It's about your deeper purpose.

> *You are what your deep, driving desire is.*
> *As your desire is, so is your will.*
> *As your will is, so is your deed.*
> *As your deed is, so is your destiny.*
> **-BRIHADARANYAKA UPANISHAD IV.4.5-**

Following your higher self prevents the need for excessive money, power, or validation from others to dictate your life's direction. Money, power, and status without higher purpose bring insecurity and incompleteness. When you **are** your higher self, you will attract the people and things you need for a happier life.

It's not unusual to ask, "What if my higher self or true nature is a bad one?" Unless you are Damien Omen, 99.99 percent of our innate human nature is naturally peaceful. Despite what we hear on the nightly news, people prefer love to hate. Our hands are more suitable for hugging than hitting! Even people who committed the most evil deeds in history didn't start out that way. Our faults are learned and reinforced over time. The good news is that they can be unlearned!

> *A monk once went to his master teacher and said,*
> *"O wise one, I have a problem. I have this bad temper.*
> *I get mad and have tantrums. What can I do?"*
> *The wise teacher replied, "This bad temper*
> *you have—let me see it now."*

WELL I'LL BE A BLUE-NOSED GOPHER

*The monk responded, "I can't be mad just at
any time, and I'm not angry right now."
The teacher said, "That's because the anger is not your true
nature. Follow your true nature, and your temper will go away."*
-ZEN-

Your higher self is above anything physical, mental, or emotional; it never changes or dies, and it is **always good.** That's everything you are. At the same time, your physical self is how you actively do constructive things. Putting the two together is one powerful combination!

Happiness Step Two
Discovering Your True Nature

To discover as much as we can about our higher selves, we need to recall some vital aspects about what our true nature feels like. I recommend that you write these down, as you may want to refer back to them in the future.

- Recollect a happy childhood memory or two.
- What makes you feel very creative?
- What gets you really excited about something?
- Recall a time when you felt relaxed and carefree.
- Remember when you simply did something you wanted to do without worrying about the approval of others.
- Name at least two things you like about yourself in the present day.
- What would motivate you to get out of bed in the morning and charge into the day?

Notice how you feel when you think of these things. They represent aspects of your true nature, which contains an inexhaustible amount of abundance and happiness.

Author and Hay House founder, Louise Hay, used affirmations as an effective tool for life transformation and to overcome her own cancer. Affirmations help us project ourselves into the future as if we already have achieved our goal. To summon these feelings into your daily life, I've created some affirmations to say to yourself or out loud:

- *I recall my favorite childhood memories and bring these positive feelings into my life right now.*
- *I am very creative and bring this creativity into whatever I do.*
- *I do what excites me and brings me energy.*
- *I feel relaxed and free to express my true self.*
- *I follow my higher self without the need of approval from others.*
- *I recognize and honor the qualities I like about myself.*
- *I do what makes me want to charge into the day.*

Repeat these affirmations for as many days as it helps you. Bring these feelings into your life **now.** You can pick a different affirmation each day, using all seven in one week, or pick one or two affirmations and work on them as long as you need to. This week, in your daily planner, list the activities that…
- were similar to favorite childhood memories,
- were creative,
- brought excitement and energy,
- brought out what you like about yourself,
- you did without the need for approval,
- made you want to get out of bed and charge into the day.

Happiness Step Three
The Real You

Will the "real you" please stand up? It's time to stop and reflect about who you **really** are. That's why this happiness step is more detailed than the others.

In your quiet time, take a few deep breaths, and be at peace. Put your fears away, listen with a quiet mind, and connect with your deeper self.

List at least ten positive qualities that define what your true self is like, even if you do not always have these attributes. Here's the challenging part: absolutely avoid using **any** of the items listed below in your definitions.

- Name
- Gender
- Physical features
- Heritage and citizenship
- Age
- Geographical location
- Family and friends
- Marital or dating status
- Health
- Education
- Religion, philosophy, and political beliefs

WELL I'LL BE A BLUE-NOSED GOPHER

- Job, status, economic condition, and possessions
- Hobbies
- Membership in organizations

Positive qualities I have are:

1. _____   6. _____

2. _____   7. _____

3. _____   8. _____

4. _____   9. _____

5. _____   10. _____

Now for the "Who am I?" question! Avoid writing **any** negative statements you might be tempted to say about yourself. Positive affirmations about your best qualities come from your higher self. Negative judgments do not. Statements like "I always get mad when…" or "I'm not very good at…" tend to bind us to these definitions. If you're having trouble, dig a little and add anything positive you can think of. Honoring yourself and your higher nature is not the same as having a big head. In your response lies your destiny; it's the best of what you bring to the table here on Earth. It's time to describe the real you.

Ask and it shall be given you; seek and ye shall find; knock and it shall be opened unto you. Everyone that asketh receiveth; and he that seeketh findeth.
-JESUS-

To jump-start you on the "Who am I?" question, answer the below question by writing what first comes to your mind.

I believe I am here on Earth to accomplish…

_____   _____

_____   _____

_____   _____

_____   _____

What special talents and gifts do I have to offer? Think of at least four. Put a star by the items you think are close to your higher purposes.

_____   _____

_____   _____

_____   _____

_____   _____

_____   _____

Now, review your positive qualities, higher purposes, and special talents/gifts and then answer these questions: Who am I? What is my nature?

_____

_____

WELL I'LL BE A BLUE-NOSED GOPHER

_____

_____

_____

_____

_____

_____

_____

_____

Each day, select one of your positive qualities, talents, gifts, or higher purposes, and keep that quality in the forefront of your mind as often as possible throughout the day. Affirm that quality, gift, or purpose in your mind and say it out loud when you're feeling brave. When you're ready, pick another one until you've gone through them all. It helps to write down how you used these qualities.

- The quality, gift, or higher purpose I chose to focus on today was....
- Something I did to put that thought into action today was...

CHAPTER FOUR
LETTING GO...

Loving and Forgiving Yourself

Taking a good look at ourselves is not easy (especially for me early in the morning!). While I can ultimately get myself presentable for the human race, I've found that confronting my inner problems is even scarier than my $19.99 Halloween mask! Looking inward, it's easy to deny or reject what we need to change, clinging to the comfort of what we've always done before. When we finally realize personal changes are necessary, a period of feeling worthless or angry will likely hit too, and we often project those feelings outward to those who help and love us the most. That's why the statement "you always hurt the one you love" is all too true! Or we can act like a singer sent home on *American Idol:*

DENIAL   "No way! You don't know what you're doing! I rocked!"

ANGER   "You *&^%$#! My four-year-old can judge better than you!"

BLAME   "Your stupid comments from last time messed me up this time. This is **your** fault!"

It's easy to blame everyone else for our problems, isn't it? That removes any responsibility we could possibly have! Except then we've flunked the truest test of strength, which is to know our inner self, learn who we are, and why we're here.

> *He who knows men is clever.*
> *He who knows himself has insight.*
> *He who conquers men has force.*
> *He who conquers himself is truly strong.*
> **-THE TAO –**

Besides getting to know ourselves, we also have to learn to love ourselves as we are **right now,** with all of our imperfections! The ability to love and forgive ourselves is indispensable for our happiness and spiritual growth.

Your higher self loves you no matter what. The compassion, understanding, and love we want from others is always in our higher selves, so when we use those qualities, we are being our higher selves. If we fail to recognize our good traits, we beat up ourselves for our faults and depend on the approval of others. This feeds the fuel for our perennial unwanted partners, **fear and doubt,** which stop us dead in our tracks. Fear and doubt are like Cinderella's wicked stepsisters—we see them daily and battle them often!

The movie *A Beautiful Mind* provides another comparison:

Based on the true story of a legendary mathematical genius battling schizophrenia, Professor John Nash (played by Russell Crowe) was constantly followed by two imaginary people throughout his life. After many years, he finally realized they were figments of his powerful imagination enhanced by his illness, so he decided to render them insignificant by ignoring them. The imaginary characters still followed him around, blabbing to him, but they no longer had any power over him.

Like Nash's imaginary characters, it's up to us to shatter fear and doubt, and although they may not go away, we can at least shove them aside and move forward!

Fear and doubt can also knock on our door due to guilt from the past and the lack of ability to forgive ourselves. If you ever want to overcome obstacles, **forgive yourself**, even if you don't think you deserve it. Remove this huge block to progress, even if you have to use some mental dynamite!

We often feel shame over something we've done in the past and then project it into who we think we are today. Many of us have given ourselves incredible guilt trips for even minor things:

> I once shoplifted some pencils from a drugstore in seventh grade and felt terrible for days. Finally, I couldn't stand it any longer. I took them back to the store and nearly got caught returning them! But I might as well have robbed a bank because I still felt guilty!

If I had that much guilt for lifting a few pencils, then the sum total of my stored guilt dwarfs a supernova! Luckily, we don't remember all of the bad things we've done. Still, we rarely realize the impact of stored guilt. Maybe you've done something in the past you're not proud of. Does that mean you deserve floggings for all eternity? I think not! You have to let it go!

Do you often take a guilt trip? If so, it's time to cancel that cheap bus ticket! Don't expect to forget the past, but you do have to forgive it. Rather than deny the dark part of your past, lead it toward the light. Darkness cannot survive in light. So forgive. Forgiving is our ticket to the good life that is naturally ours to have if only we will have it!

Fact: **Your past cannot be changed,** so it behooves you to forgive yourself for all of your transgressions. You don't need an eye exam; you read this correctly—I said **all** of them! This doesn't free ourselves of the responsibility for our past actions, but it does free us from allowing fear, doubt, and guilt to freeze our commitment toward a happier future. Are you going to let your past ruin your today and tomorrows?

By forgiving, we render our negative past powerless!
(You may cheer now!)

You **are** worthwhile. To think you have no value paralyzes your potential for progress. Beware of thoughts that say, "I'm always wrong" or "My efforts aren't good enough (and they never will be)." Put the handkerchief down. We often sabotage ourselves with unreasonable deadlines and then chastise ourselves for not living up to our own brutal criteria! That's a "lose-lose" proposition! You are human. Think of your "mistakes" or "sins" as misdirected actions moving temporarily away from God. After all, the word "sin" comes from the Greek term used in archery meaning "to miss the mark," and believe me, if I'm at the archery line, run in the other direction! We all make lots of mistakes, so recognize them as necessary teachers; learn from them, and don't stay stuck with regret. Simply vow to do better and direct your energy toward the positive and toward God.

> When I was fourteen, my first teacher on the organ was a jolly fellow named Mr. Harold Grimes. He always smiled, and he reminded me of Santa Claus without the white beard. He was very encouraging, and when I would screw up *ad nauseum,* he would smile and say, "Just try it again—a little slower." When I would finally play a song that resembled music, he would place a little sticky star on my music. I didn't always deserve the star, but he motivated me to do better next time without fear. If I really nailed a tune, he'd put up a gold star, and I'd feel almost good enough to play ice skating rinks. It must have worked because I'm still playing (but skating rinks were spared). I was too young and immature to realize his impact on me until much later in life. Thanks, Harold.

Why not encourage ourselves this way, too, whether or not we have all of what we think we want or need? Your physical body is influenced by your feelings. When you love and accept yourself, you raise the vibration of your energy and create a strong potential for more good into your life. Think about it: wouldn't you rather be around a positive, energetic person? Be that person! Walk and talk with confidence and self-assurance. Trust that whatever good you're trying to do will ultimately work out. Problems are opportunities for spiritual growth, and setbacks are only temporary. Your power of thought, aligned with your higher purposes, creates greatness. You are your own master. No one else is!

Think of the grudges you have toward yourself and others as a giant mountain blocking your ability to travel forward in life. Over the years, blames, grudges, and guilt trips pile up. Meet "Mt. Some Flung Dung." This "Heap O' Refuse" stinks, so shovel it out! Forgiving peels off grudges one layer at a time.

...And forgive us for our debts, as we also have forgiven our debtors... For if you forgive men their trespasses, your heavenly Father also will forgive you...
-MATTHEW 6:12, 6:14-

What's the cost of **not** forgiving? Only that it creates stress, which accumulates over time, causing short-term and long-term negative behaviors. Nearly any doctor will tell you that stress, especially over a long period of time, is a major contributor to illnesses galore, heart problems, strokes, cancer, depression, migraines, ulcers, obesity, and other health problems. No big deal, right? Mark my words...

Stress is a killer.

Potentially stressful events **will** occur in our lives, so it's up to us to train ourselves to not allow stress to accumulate and get the best of us. How do we do that?

In Charles Dickens' *The Christmas Carol*, Scrooge's friend Jacob Marley's ghost carries around heavy chains that represent the baggage of his past deeds. Like Marley, we'll build our own chains link by link if we allow it! The forgiving process is a giant stress-reliever and frees you from the heavy chains of the past.

Learning to love and forgive ourselves creates the ability to love and forgive others. When you forgive someone who has wronged you in some way, it doesn't mean you condone what he or she did or that you are weak. You're choosing love over hate. This can be done instantly, but in many circumstances, forgiveness will take time and effort. The payoff? A happier, healthier, and freer future!

The inability to forgive is like carrying a huge sack of "garbagy" grudges while trying to climb that all-too-familiar mountain of self-loathing—every day! Who has time for that? For the major hurts in your life committed by others, let the higher powers bear the responsibility of judgment because **you** have to move on. Use your valuable energy toward better things. It's time to move the mountain, cut the chains, and throw out the garbage!

Forgiveness is the fragrance the violet sheds
on the heel that crushed it.
-MARK TWAIN-

Happiness Step Four
Letting Go of the Baggage

Begin by doing the relaxation meditation from Happiness Step One, where you progressively relax your muscles and go to your favorite beautiful place. Once you're there, take a moment to think of the very worst thing you've ever done in the past. Don't take much time choosing it. Usually, it's the first idea that pops into your mind.

Next, take a deep breath before thinking or saying the first sentence of each pair of sentences below. Then, go to the second sentence, and visualize what it says as you repeat the line in your mind several times to help your visualization. It may help if you see a picture of your mountain of grudges getting smaller, your chains getting fewer, your garbage sack getting lighter, or your unforgiving feelings flying away like birds. Move on to the next pair when you're ready.

- *(Say) I now forgive myself unconditionally for my worst deeds without reservation, no matter what they were.*
- (Visualize) I let my worst deeds go…let them go…let them go…

- *(Say) I now forgive myself unconditionally for all my past faults without reservation.*
- (Visualize) I let all of my past faults go…let them go…let them go…

- *(Say) I now stop beating up and chastising myself for the past I cannot change.*
- *(Visualize) I let go of my past that I cannot change…let it go… let it go…*

- *(Say) I now stop repeating my negative past behaviors.*
- *(Visualize) I let go of negative behaviors…let them go…let them go…*

- *(Say) I am no longer stuck in a spiritual rut, and now open the doors to progress.*
- *(Visualize) I open doors…open doors…open doors…*

- *(Say) I now forgive myself unconditionally for all of the times I have mistreated loved ones, others, and myself.*
- *(Visualize) I forgive myself…forgive…forgive…*

- *(Say) I now love myself unconditionally, as I am, right now.*
- *(Visualize) I love myself…love myself…love myself…*

- *(Say) I now forgive my loved ones, family members, and friends who have ever mistreated me in any way, no matter how bad the situation may have seemed.*
- *(Visualize) I forgive loved ones, family, and friends…forgive… forgive…*

- *(Say) I realize that everyone wants happiness just like I do and that they suffer from faults like myself. I now forgive unconditionally **everyone** who has **ever** mistreated me in any way, no matter what.*
- *(Visualize) I forgive all others…forgive…forgive…*

- (Say) I realize that the past has given me what I have needed for my growth and that everything about my past is okay now, no matter what.
- (Visualize) My past was necessary. It's okay...okay....

- (Say) I practice forgiveness daily and repeat these affirmations until they become a natural part of me.
- (Visualize) I forgive daily...forgive...forgive...

You've completed a major and difficult process with this meditation. Repeat as often as you need to, especially the toughest ones. Some of these can take months or even years. Sometimes I would think I had forgiven someone or a situation, only to have it resurface in the form of anger, so I would come back and rework the affirmation until I could truly let go without emotional attachment. Good luck, forgivers!

The Emotional Nature

Another way to get to know yourself is by looking at your emotional nature, which can be described by the feelings you had most often when you recall your early childhood. Whether you were happy, angry, carefree, or afraid, your strongest and most common emotions from that time clue you in to what your emotional nature was like then. Your emotional nature from that time may be similar to your emotional nature now.

However, your emotional nature may or may not be the same as your higher nature. Maybe your childhood wasn't *Lifestyles of the Rich and Famous*, but more like *Oliver Twist* meets *Little Orphan Annie*. Still, no childhood is all bad. Think of the most common positive emotion you carried with you from that time. That is a part of your higher nature, which can override any negative emotions from the past.

Feelings of unworthiness often come (sometimes unintentionally) from loved ones (parents, relatives, and friends). Those feelings can also come from your schooling, church, and any other authority figures. But you just forgave them in the last Happiness Step, right? In order to overcome negative emotions from childhood, we'll have to forgive **everyone** we think contributed to our thoughts of shame, including ourselves. Forgiveness helps long-standing negative emotions to be less powerful and occur less often. If you're angry, instead of slamming the door so hard it causes a 5.2 magnitude earthquake, you might settle for a huge sigh and go work out!

Remembering your childhood emotions helps you understand what is within your nature to do and what isn't. That way, you'll know if and when you're getting out of balance with your nature, which creates unhappiness. Let's say you are not one to show a lot of enthusiasm. You know you can be more enthusiastic if you work on it, but you're not the next Tony Robbins either. That doesn't matter. You are simply being you. If you're quiet and prefer places like libraries and monasteries, don't take a job at Chuck E. Cheese! Perhaps you're the adventuresome, outdoorsy type, so sitting in a cubicle staring cross-eyed at a computer screen all day might just drive you bonkers.

How happy we believe ourselves to be is related to genetics, brain chemistry, and our childhood environment, which determine how much of our programming might need some tweaking. While our emotional nature becomes more solid with adolescence, it is absolutely possible to reduce negative feelings. How? You guessed it—**practice!**

Happiness Step Five
Releasing Negative Emotions from Childhood

Recall a strong negative emotion you often had when you were a small child. Then recall a strong positive emotion from that time. Say the following affirmation:

> *I now release this negative emotion from my childhood. It's in the past and does me no good. If I feel this negative emotion coming back, I will replace it with my strong positive emotion.*

You may find yourself needing to apply this several times a day, depending on your situation. Repeat this with your other negative and positive feelings from childhood, and repeat this as often as necessary.

CHAPTER FIVE
BEING YOUR HIGHER SELF

What Do You <u>Love</u> to Do?

Hopefully, by now you're tuning in to yourself and finding out what's going on in that marvelous mind of yours! Now it's time to remind yourself of what you love to do.

As an administrator, my days were filled with job-related activities that allowed for little time to do anything else. So, when I first filled out my "things I love to do" list, I thought the list was someone else's because

I **never did those things!** After this sorry revelation, I vowed to make sure I accomplished at least **one** thing from the list daily! Sometimes that was a walk at two a.m., but I discovered that even though I was tired due to less sleep, I actually felt better! I quickly realized that doing just one thing I love to do felt like a baseball team scoring one run in a game. It wasn't good enough! Why not do a bunch of things I love to do every day?

When we first think about what we love to do, we usually list leisure activities. We need some of those! If you enjoy relaxing on a sunny tropical beach, great! There are also enjoyable activities that benefit yourself and others in some way. If you like playing sports, there is the exercise benefit. Ideally, what we love to do goes into our daily work as well. I love playing and singing jazz in a nice club setting, and (hopefully!) it brings enjoyment to others. At the university, I enjoyed helping students find out what they really want in their lives and future careers. And I got paid! You can't beat that!

What you love doing reveals your true nature and is an indication of how you need to spend a good portion of your time (as long as it's not harmful to yourself or others, of course). The more you do what you love, the more your "happiness meter" will go up!

Happiness Step Six
Doing What You Love

Before affirming what you love to do now, first recall what you loved to do in the past.

Think about when you were a child up to about age twelve. **Quickly** jot down a list of everything you loved to do back then. Leave some space between each item. Try for five, ten, even twenty things! If you don't get to twenty, don't worry about it. You can add them later. Next, in the space between each item, using just a few keywords, write down the benefit(s) of that activity. Next, as a grownup, write a related activity that you can do **very soon** to bring you those same feelings you experienced as a kid. Here are two examples from my journal:

- As a kid, I loved to: roll around and play in the leaves.
- Benefits were: being outside, feeling exhilarated and carefree, not worrying about getting insanely dirty!
- To do soon: hike in the woods this fall, play softball on a muddy field.
- As a kid, I loved to: play with stuffed animals and put on shows with my sister.
- Benefits were: creativity with music/comedy, entertaining others, relationship-building.
- To do soon: add comedy and creativity to one of my next classroom presentations or performances.

Ready, go!

- As a kid, I loved to:
- Benefits were:
- To do soon:

Did you get to twenty? Either way, before going on, look at your "to do soon" ideas and **literally** enter them into your schedule (on the device of your choice) on a specific day and time! And when you actually do one, if you enjoyed it, schedule a repeat of that activity for as long as it remains meaningful!

Next, create a list of things you loved to do as a teenager. Like before, leave a space for the "benefits were" and the "to do soon" activity. Some activities may be repeats from childhood, and others may be slightly different. Go for it!

- What I loved to do ages 12-19:
- Benefits were:
- To do soon:

Next, plug your "to do soon" items into your schedule so they don't become a "maybe someday in the not-foreseeable future" kind of thing! Repeat those activities as often as you feel good about doing them.

Now to the present. What do you love to do **now**? List a minimum of seven things, in any order. Write what comes to your mind right away, and leave some space between each one. Don't ponder over this one too long because you already know the answers! Are you ready?

- I love to:
- Benefits are (optional if it helps you to continue to list these):
- To do soon:

Once more with feeling—schedule these into your preferred device, even if it's a paper calendar!

Once you've listed all the things you love to do, ask yourself which activity do you want to do more often. Is there a hobby or a major activity in your life you've left behind? Complete this sentence:

I will make the following CHANGE(S) in order to do this item I love more often:
Remember, **no change=no gain!** Write down a change you are going to make!

_____

_____

Plug into your schedule what you'll do **soon** to begin that change!

These lists give you very strong clues as to who you are, what you're about, and the kinds of things you should be bringing into your life more often, especially with what you do for a living. Unhappiness runs abound because so many of us are out of alignment with the life we really want. For example:

- A forester, hiker, and mountain biker who is an accountant in Illinois.
- A mathematician and cross-country skier who is building houses in Florida.
- You?

It's shocking to realize how many of us live an unfulfilling life. Don't put off awakening your passion. Do more of what you love!

As you do more of the things you love, be sure to hang out with people who share the same interests you do. Surround your living and working environment with meaningful objects, too. Call or visit an old friend, place an object of meaning in the room you sleep or work in, buy a favorite plant for your workplace, or rearrange your living room. I periodically go on an anti-clutter campaign and clean out stuff I haven't used that occupies space. The more you create an environment filled with what you love, the more positive energy you'll create around you.

To complete this happiness step, do **one** thing that improves some aspect of your environment. If you feel inspired, keep it going every day until you feel really good about your surroundings!

_____

More? _____

_____

_____

Happiness Step Seven
Keeping Score

Keep score for a week. It only takes a few seconds a day. Here's how you do it: With your to-do list, give yourself one "point" each time you do **one thing** you love or even do something toward accomplishing it. For instance, your vacation isn't until summer, but you tucked away $100 or perhaps you read an article about your destination. That's a point! You want your house painted, so you selected the color today—that's another point! At the end of the week, count your total points. Be creative! Include **anything** you did to improve your home or work environment as well (one point each!). Even the smallest steps toward a happier future will increase your well-being now!

Daily Activities

- Things I love to do that I did today were:
- Things I did to make my environment more meaningful today were:
- Daily Point Total = _____

Do this each day for one week. Then, add up all your points for the week! Continue doing this exercise for as long as you feel it is beneficial for you. How did you do?

1-2	A start!
3-4	A **better** start!
5-6	Getting somewhere!
7-10	On the way for sure!
11-14	Catching on!
15+	The happiness train is rollin' now!

A Perfect Day—A Perfect Life

While you're doing things you love, let's do one better. What if you had a day that you could honestly call "perfect"? Take a second, and imagine what that perfect day would be like. Have fun with it. Perhaps you'd like to relax on a sunny beach while sipping margaritas or hike up to the top of a mountain.

What you imagine your perfect day to be reveals more about your true nature. If you choose all leisure activities as a perfect day, it's an indication you need more of those days in your life! Even then, after a certain number of leisurely days, our higher purposes will tug at us, and we'll get tired of margaritas every day or of hiking after a few dozen treks up the mountain.

Do we really want a life of leisure? In 1919, psychoanalyst Sandor Ferenczi introduced the term "Sunday neurosis," citing that patients exhibited more neurotic behavior on weekends. Since then, the continuing pattern of people experiencing more

loneliness, depression, and anxiety on holidays and weekends indicates that humans are ill-equipped to be idle for long. In the mid-twentieth century, it was predicted that future humans would have lots of leisure time. **That** got shot full of holes, didn't it? Why? Despite new technology, we have more work nowadays because **people like to be productive!**

A perfect day of leisure? No problemo! But "perfect" days can be accomplished through meaningful work that we love to do. For example, retired people typically engage in activities that are altruistic or for personal growth, even though they no longer work in the traditional sense. We need to have fun in our lives, which is precisely the point. When you are fulfilling your higher purposes, the difference between work and play is less apparent because...

> Every day is a perfect day when you are
> fulfilling your higher purposes.

Here's another spin on "perfection." Observe nature. There's a balance of day and night that averages out in equal numbers of light and dark hours. There is cold and warm weather relative to seasons and location, each with its own unique beauty. Nature teaches us the balance of activity and rest and of pleasantness and harshness. The universe is a dichotomy. In addition, nothing physical stays the same. Stars are born, go through changes, blow up into a supernova, and wither away. The balance of opposites in a constantly changing universe is in itself perfection.

So it is with our lives. We were not placed on this planet to enjoy only pleasantries nor to endure only hardships. And we're not here forever. That's why **every day is perfect** for us in that we're learning what we need to learn. In that way, we are "perfect in our imperfections." Our colossal screw-ups help us learn and grow.

Try this. Find a nice, green lawn; maybe it's your lawn (certainly not mine!). Get down on your knees, and look closely at each blade of grass. If your neighbors are staring, just act like a lawn expert. Notice how some blades are fully green, some may have a little brown, some are smooth, and others were munched on as some hungry creature's lunch. The lawn is full of "imperfections," yet the end result is beautiful when you look at the whole yard. If the yard starts looking unsightly, you water and fertilize it, hopefully before you take your lawn off the list of your town's "parade of homes" tour. So, whether your days (or your lawn!) are "I Feel Pretty" or "I'm So Lonesome I Could Cry," they are all perfect for growth. So when does the perfect day arrive? It is already here. It is **today** and every day!

Happiness Step Eight
Have a Perfect Day

What would be a perfect day for you? What would you do? Who would you spend your day with? What would you like to happen? By all means, use some items from Happiness Step Six, "Doing What You Love." If there are any activities in your perfect day that aren't in "Doing What You Love," add them to that list!

_____

_____

_____

What from your perfect day do you want more of in your life right now?

Pick one thing from your perfect day, and **do it!** If you cannot replicate that exact activity, do something close to it. Here are some examples:

Perfect day:

"I'm in Cancun sitting on the beach sipping a cool one while reading my favorite book!"

¡Ay, caramba! You cannot go to Cancun today.

Go out in the backyard, or even your favorite room, and get your favorite book and beverage. Indulge, even if for only ten minutes!

Perfect day:

"I'm hiking through the Himalayas with my best friend!"

You're both working, plus you forgot your oxygen mask.

Find the hilliest spot in town, and hike it as many times as you like, no matter how bad the weather. After all, the Himalayan climate is brutal! Did you forget to call your best friend?

Each day, plan what you will bring into your day to make it more perfect. At the end of the day, write down what you did, and plan more perfection for tomorrow and beyond!

SECTION TWO
Thought + Action = Transformation

CHAPTER SIX
THOUGHT MANAGEMENT— WHO'S IN CONTROL?

Elegant Mansion or Garbage Dump?

Our thoughts are the driving force influencing our perceived happiness or unhappiness. Everyone marvels at the discipline of a star athlete, the skill of an accomplished surgeon, and others who've accomplished something they worked hard for. But surprisingly, research pertaining to the effect of the **quality** of our thoughts has been less popular than an ice cream truck in a blizzard.

It's that voice in your head. No, you're not going crazy. Introduce yourself to your thoughts. Who is it that's doing the thinking? Hopefully, it's you! If **you're** not in charge of your thoughts, who is? Improving the quality of what you think activates a higher level of consciousness, producing positive inner changes that ultimately create outer changes. The cost of **not** noticing how you use your mind is like blindly investing your life savings in some random stock you know nothing about.

Notice your repeating thought patterns. Do they come from the gods or the goblins? The **quality** of your thoughts cannot be underestimated because…

What we expect to get in life, we very often get!

Put another way…

> *For as [a man] thinketh in his heart, so is he.*
> **-PROVERBS 23.7-**

We need to pay **close attention** to how and what we're thinking. While we all endure stressful events, reliving them in our minds creates accumulated stress, which negatively affects our health. So, if you don't like a certain thought, make every attempt to **get rid of it**! Refuse mind-polluting thoughts, such as jealousy, guilt, or judgment toward others. Ask yourself why you're allowing this negativity. We tend to see thoughts as "our little secrets," but we grossly underestimate their influence. Our inner thoughts are the most powerful aspects of ourselves we have!

Today's news media can vaporize any positive thinking faster than a pizza at a frat party. It requires a Herculean effort to not mentally, physiologically, and spiritually absorb the negativity from the violence, crime, and turbulence presented 24-7. It's fine to care about the world's events,

but consciously choose how much to watch for how long. If you're listening to C-R-A-P, turn it off! If there's a cause that you personally take an active interest in, then spend whatever time on it you need to. Otherwise, leave the negative news behind and move on, for your sanity!

WELL I'LL BE A BLUE-NOSED GOPHER

I will not let anyone walk through my mind with their dirty feet.
-MAHATMA GANDHI-

Take time to notice when thoughts are your own versus when they really come from someone else. You, and **only** you, control and direct your thoughts. When a negative thought arises, **stop** thinking that thought and change the subject ASAP. What you think about, you create. Thinking positive, peaceful thoughts will attract more good into your life. Thinking great thoughts about yourself and others will bring greatness.

Anyone who has ever been successful at anything at one crucial point decided to commit to the idea that he or she was **actually going to complete a goal.** Can you remember a time when you really wanted something and simply went out and got it? Anything good ever accomplished began with a thought followed by some actions. This required persistence to see it through to completion, despite challenges.

Our masterpieces lie in our thoughts. A composer begins a symphony with a single theme; an artist begins a painting with a single stroke. Future masterpieces are already in your mind right now. "Thought management" will help you manifest them because ultimately you become what you think about.

All that we are is a result of what we have thought.
- THE DHARMAPADA-

The concept of thought management led me to wonder: How many thoughts do we typically have in one day? After perusing all of my written and internet sources, the numbers fall somewhere between 40,000 and 70,000 thoughts a day. Regardless of the exact number, that's a **lot** of thinking! But how many of those thoughts are useful? If our thoughts are useless, energy-draining time-wasters, we'd be better off starting a pet rock collection. It's time to focus! If you give a really important goal only a couple of thoughts, your chance of manifesting that goal is less than winning the lottery—on Mars! Thoughts are energy, and the energy created by focused thinking is far more powerful than random thinking. When that focused thinking reaches a critical mass (say 2,000 thoughts or 4% of 50,000 thoughts in a day), the thoughts will begin to move you toward a desired goal—all with less than forty minutes of daily thought!

Every minute you spend concentrating and working on a positive future will literally manifest situations that will improve your future. There will be challenges, which are actually growth opportunities. Where would our lives be without the problems we overcame? Have you ever known someone who was handed everything on a silver platter? Was he or she a happy person?

Imagine putting your thoughts into a thought bank, where the positive thoughts go into one account and the negative thoughts go into another. The account that has the most deposits will create your reality. Neutral thoughts, such as "I'm brushing my teeth," don't go into either account. Is your thought bank in the black or in the red?

My wife has demonstrated the benefits of positive thinking over time...

When we first brought Toni to visit her family in California after her accident, they were amazed at how good she looked considering all she had been through. Besides the fine medical care she received, Toni looks so great because negative thoughts rarely enter her brain! She is a truly positive being, and years of that have given her a glow and a presence.

Over time, positive thoughts, smiles, and laughter will be much better for your appearance than years of a scowling, frowning face contorted with anger. Not to mention, you'll simply feel better too! Is your mind an elegant mansion or a garbage dump? Only you know for sure!

Happiness Step Nine
What Are You Thinking?

Before you retire for the evening, name the top five most frequent things you thought about today.

How often did you feel you controlled the thoughts that came into your mind?

_____%

How often did you feel you did not control the thoughts that came into your mind?

_____%

The two numbers above should add up to 100%.

Today's "thought bank" account:

Excluding neutral thoughts that are either positive or negative…

How often did you have **positive** thoughts of love, optimism, happiness, hope, etc.?

_____%

How often did you have **negative** thoughts of fear, doubt, anger, sadness, etc.?

_____%

The two numbers above should add up to 100%.

How did today compare to other days in the way you typically think? Affirm the following out loud or to yourself.

I want to think positive thoughts. Every time I have a negative thought, I will replace it with a positive one. I will spend more time thinking about what's important in my life and less time thinking about what is not. Daily, I will keep in the front of my mind what is most dear to me and make sure I have a meaningful day.

Repeat this step for as many days as you need to.

Happiness Step Ten
Positive or Negative Thoughts?

Write one number per line on the left side below that represents the percent you believe you exhibit the quality listed. If you place a 90 by "happy for the success of others," then that means you are 90 percent that way and 10 percent jealous and competitive. This is your own private exercise, so be honest!

<u>Characteristics of Positive Thinkers</u>   <u>Characteristics of Negative Thinkers</u>

100	90	80	70	60	50	40	30	20	10	0

(Rate yourself for each item)

	Positive	Negative
__	Happy for the success of others	Jealous and competitive
__	Emphasize good about others in speech/thought	Gossip/speak and think poorly of others
__	Confident, good self-image	Fearful, poor self-image
__	Relaxed	Tense
__	Comfortable about surroundings	Unhappy with surroundings
__	Healthy	Health problems, worried about health
__	Happy	Miserable

_	Polite	Rude
_	Full of creative ideas	Tear down ideas of others
_	Prosperous	Focus on scarcity and usually achieve it
_	Believe anything is possible	Full of doubt
_	Attract positive people and events	Attract negative people and events
_	Successful	Unsuccessful
_	Able to let go of negative past events	Cling to negative past, resentful, revengeful
_	Unselfish	Self-centered

Select one area from one of your lowest numbers that is most compelling for you to improve. Say or write your own affirmation about how you'll improve in that area.

- *I/Iam (item from left column) because I (state the change you've made).*

When you're ready, say or write additional affirmations about any item where your score was not what you'd like it to be. Don't forget to add your solutions into your calendar!

Unlimited Thinking Brings Unlimited Results!

Anyone who doesn't believe in miracles is not a realist.
-DAVID BEN-GURION-

It's easy to doubt the power of the mind and its ability to unite with our divine gifts and higher purposes. Yet, stories abound that jar even the most cynical:

> Marcus, a former student of mine, mentioned in class that while in high school, he was diagnosed with leukemia and was given six months to live. A year later, he was completely cancer-free. He told us it was because he **decided** and **believed** he would beat it despite all medical predictions. It wasn't easy for him by any means, but his conviction that he could overcome heavy odds saved his life.
>
> In Atlanta, I personally witnessed Dr. Ron Roth (a former Catholic Priest) heal ten people of chronic back problems in about half an hour before my very eyes. That completely rattled my skeptical brain molecules! There was nothing phony about what he did. He never took a cent for healing either. He told us he was simply connecting with the Holy Spirit, whose energy was there for all of us to use in a good way. If someone believes such things are not possible, then they **will be** impossible—for them!

Okay. Before your eyes completely glaze over with this power of positive thinking stuff, consider this:

Beware of the power of negative thinking!

Negative thoughts can ruin your picnic like a colony of the scariest bugs you can imagine! Can we sabotage the realization of our goals with negative thinking? We sure can! If you think negatively about your goals, your wonderful vision shatters into a million pieces. If you're always thinking about what you don't have or can't do, then what you don't have and can't do is going to expand!

Think you can and think you can't, and either way, you'll be correct.
-HENRY FORD-

How far do you think you'll get if you think: "I can't do it" or "I don't deserve it"? **Believe** good things will happen to you, and they will. Negative thoughts about the future can manifest that future, too! Is your "negative thought bank" bursting at the seams and your positive one overdrawn? Time for some good news:

No one really knows enough to be a pessimist!
-DR. WAYNE DYER-

Imagine trying to explain the internet to someone from 200 years ago. And, in 200 years, we'll be doing things we haven't even dreamed of today. The burden of proof is not to show something **can** occur, but it lies with proving something **can't** occur! Helen Keller, prolific author and the first deaf-blind person to earn a Bachelor's Degree, once stated:

No pessimist ever discovered the secrets to the stars, or sailed to an uncharted land, or opened a new heaven to the human spirit.

Every breakthrough in humankind encountered considerable doubt and persecution! My father recalled that in the 1930s, very few thought a trip to the moon would ever be possible. In less than forty years, we were on the moon! Of course, some doubt we really landed on the moon, so no matter what, doubters and pessimists will always be there!

Q. What do thoughts of fear and doubt accomplish?
A. Uh, that would be fear and doubt!

Your limited thoughts are like small children who just don't know any better. The only limitations to achieving an important goal are those you put on yourself. Ask yourself: "Am I limited because I live up to my limitations?" Give yourself permission to dream!

Okay, so maybe you know someone who wants to be president of the United States. Very few people become president of the United States. Still, every U.S. president got the notion he **could** be president at some point and stuck to it. Even presidential candidates who lost got the kind of life a presidency brings: leadership, a public life, travel, etc. In the big picture, it doesn't matter whether the exact result happens; it's the journey that we'll remember! So dream all you want, but don't get stuck in dreamland! Act on your highest visions so you can **live** them!

> *The greater danger for most of us is not that our aim is too high and we miss it, but that it is too low and we reach it.*
> **-MICHELANGELO-**

Are you an optimist or a pessimist? An optimist looks for a way to solve a problem. If a less positive result occurs, the optimist shrugs it off and goes in a different direction or tries a new angle to solve the problem. An optimist goes about solving problems by focusing on what's **right** with the world, not on what isn't.

Pessimists believe that they **should** worry about a problem, expect that it **won't** be solved, and usually achieve the result they expected, with stress as a bonus! Pessimists reason very effectively why something **can't** be done and will go to boundless effort proving it to others. Then, when the negative result is achieved, they can say, "See? I told you so," and there will be little effort to find a new solution.

There's also "Murphy's law," where devotees expect the worst that can happen will happen. We've all had "Murphy's law" types of days (or maybe weeks!), but what counts is if we continue to expect negative results or change our attitude.

> Oh, professor, I have these magnificent, expansive thoughts when things are going well, but life has dumped a mega-landslide of crap on me! What do I do?

> *This is the time you need to hang on tenaciously to your most important goals! Never give up the thought of what you are here to achieve. Hope and desire can be regained as easily as it is lost, if you allow it. And buy some extra shovels.*

If you don't like the way things are, then reconsider your "contract" with the reality you **think** you have. Tear it up, and create a better one!

WELL I'LL BE A BLUE-NOSED GOPHER

The level of thinking that got you to where you are will not get you to the level you dream of being.
–ALBERT EINSTEIN–

Our creativity and imagination can be immensely powerful. Since we sleep nearly one-third of our lives, allow your creative imagination to influence the other two-thirds. We've all had dreams or visions where we've done practically everything. Affirm this: "Anything I am capable of in the dream state I can make a part of my conscious state whenever I choose." Give yourself permission to wander into unfamiliar territory and allow your mind to become the catalyst for living an unlimited life. Like exercise, your imagination will improve through regular use. Imagine being able to manifest anything you want from your mind, letting go of all your fears and doubts. Try saying this one:

I'm here on purpose. I can accomplish anything I desire, and I do it by being in harmony with the all-pervading creative force in the universe.
-DR. WAYNE DYER-

Around this time, our logic kicks in with a "yeah, but…." Intelligence is fine to have, but it can sabotage the goals we care about. The same logic and reason we use to accomplish great things can also blow up every single creative idea we ever get! It's ironic that many "intelligent" people grossly underestimate the power of their own minds. Humans have unlimited potential, but to realize it, we have to think in terms of creative possibilities—not "yeah, buts..."

In the movie *Mr. Smith Goes to Washington*, Jimmy Stewart plays a newly elected senator from Oklahoma who is clueless about the ways of politics, let alone the "big city." His honesty and sincerity are laughed at by his cynical colleagues, along with his new plan to create a ranch for poor orphaned boys in his home state. Amid numerous scandals created by his opponents, his unbound determination eventually overcomes the cynicism and alleged superior intelligence of his fellow politicians, and he ultimately transforms himself from a laughingstock into a hero.

Sometimes you just have to bolt through that "mystery door" and go for your goal, or it may never happen for you.

Ultimately, if you can **think** it, it can be done!

Happiness Step Eleven
What I Want More of in Life

What do I want more of in my life? Think of as many things as you can. Write them down. Remember, no limitations!

Next, say the following affirmation, and repeat it as often as you wish.

- *I have abundance in my life now, and I will have it in the future. I believe that what I want more of in my life is already here; I just need to manifest it. As I work toward bringing what I want into my life, I keep in mind my higher purposes and know that staying in alignment with them will bring happiness and abundance.*

What is something I will **change** in order to get more of what I want in my life?

Now plug something you'll do **soon** into your schedule to begin that change!

CHAPTER SEVEN
TRUSTING YOUR THOUGHTS!

Intuition—Use it or Abuse it?

We choose what to do every moment of our lives. But which choice is best? We're programmed to "use our head" (hopefully for intelligent purposes), but sometimes what common sense tells us doesn't satisfy our inner souls. Intuition often whispers to us (or even yells at us!) to do something that seems irrational or foolish to our intellect. Like neglecting a leaky pipe in your home, ignoring intuition can have consequences!

Intuition is the ability to sense the truth in the absence of logical explanations. You know something, but you can't prove how or why you know it. You might get an urge to call someone for no reason, and then you find out he or she was just thinking of you, or needed your support. Maybe you're out walking and get a sudden sense not to go into a certain area. You could have a good or bad feeling about a new home purchase or business deal without any factual evidence or proof.

Your intuition also helps draw you to the things you love. In fact, the word "enthusiasm" comes from the Greek word *entheos*, meaning "God within." Paying attention to your gut feelings ultimately will guide you to do what's best, and new doorways will open. Of course, sometimes that doorway gets slammed in your face! This could mean:

- you're being tested to see how dedicated you are about what you want.
- you're being pointed in a different direction, even if you haven't figured out which way!
- you forgot to prop the door open!

If something just feels like the right thing to do, what are you waiting for? If it doesn't, or you're not sure, wait until you get a clearer message. Continue to search for answers, and don't hesitate to ask God, the universe, your higher self, or whomever you pray to, and trust that, through vigilance, you'll find the best direction. Realistically, if you like to pray, why wouldn't you believe you could get an answer **back** once in a while? It may not be a crackling bolt of lightning, but you never know! Intuitive messages can be strong or subtle, and they often come at peculiar times, seemingly out of the blue. By practicing intuition, you'll gradually develop trust in the messages that come from your higher self.

Acting on Your Intuition

Following your intuition can be hard because we're often programmed to only use the rational, intellectual mind. Intuition comes from the heart. Don't allow a mistake or two to discourage you when you're learning how to trust your intuition. When we first learned to walk, we all fell down, didn't we? We got back up and got pretty good at it, despite the occasional face-plant!

Sometimes intuition comes as an inspiring vision of a great possibility for us, but then the "doing" portion comes along, and we freeze. To have a life beyond fantasy, **act** upon your visions. Do something about those whispers before they become shouts. Attack your problems head on. You may have to make some sacrifices to achieve your highest visions. If the change you need requires dropping "plan A" and going to a new plan, so be it. By all means, learn new skills, take risks, do new things, and venture into the unknown. It'll be worth it!

You may encounter a number of big talkers who never bring their goals to fruition. Why is this? To bring your intentions to life requires confidence and persistence. When events don't happen like you want them to, be patient and hold your intuitive visions in your mind daily because the answers you seek often reveal themselves only one step at a time.

When you get a pull to do something, pay attention to it!

My wife (then my fiancée), daughter, and I were living in Orange County, California. As a junior at Cal State University Fullerton, I had been thinking about going to the University of North Texas because of their outstanding jazz program. I'd been accepted for admission and was thinking of going there in the spring. Then, in August, a major dispute arose in the band I'd been playing with for over a year, and I got this very strong feeling to go to Texas right then. I called admissions and was crestfallen to find out school had started **that day** in Texas. But this nice lady told me if I could get to Denton, Texas in six days, I could still enroll

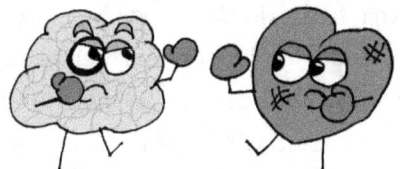

in classes (yes, this was before online registration!). My intellect (logic) and intuition (heart) had a major skirmish.

Logic: You fool. There's no earthly way you can do a cross-country move now. What are you thinking? You can't even clean the kitchen in less than a week.

Heart: Sure, you can do it. Forget the cleaning deposit. You won't get that back anyway. And, hey, you got a little truck drivin' in you! And you'll be doing what you love.

Logic: Sure, just quit the band. Lose your solid income for the last eighteen months. Move to Texas? You don't even own a pair of cowboy boots. You'll be playing in dives with a wire fence in front of you to keep the beer bottles from hitting your head. And enjoy beans for dinner every night 'cause that's all you'll be able to afford!

Heart: You've always found gigs before; you'll find them again. And you'll be learning at a university made for a "jazzer" like you. You'll be doing what you love.

Logic: You're leaving family and friends, and you don't know a single person there. Oh, and they welcome Californians from the land of fruits and nuts. They'll lasso you, brand you, and shoot you at sunrise. You don't know a blasted thing about the area except that it's ninety million degrees for five months. If you want to live more than a month, you'll need a Texas drawl, a crew cut, and a cowboy hat.

*Heart: Sure there's a little risk, fraidy-cat! You're stagnant with this band, and the huge rift that just happened is a **sign**. Go to Texas! Get that training, so you can be doing what you love.*

Logic: But what if you can't find a job? And you've never been within 200 feet of a cow. And what if your daughter hates it there and says she'd rather live in an orphanage in India? And my girlfriend has Mexican-Indian ancestry. What if there are no Mexicans there? What if she can't get a job? What if the faculty is tougher than Marine boot camp? What if my saxophone professor tells me I'd make a great accountant?

Heart: Shut upppp!! You know you need to do this to ultimately live a better life. It won't be a cakewalk. Trust your ability to adjust. They won't kick you out of school. Worst-case scenario? Accountants make good money! But you'll get a gig. Your girlfriend always finds a job. It'll work out! And you'll be doing what you love.

Six days and 1,400 miles later, we had quit our jobs, broken the lease on the apartment, and were rolling into Denton, Texas with no jobs, not knowing a single soul, and entering a new university with just enough money to last a month. It wasn't easy. At one point, I literally came within minutes of applying at the local McDonald's when a call came asking me to play in a trio six nights a week. Looking back, the move ended up being a career-changer for me, and I am grateful I did not stay and settle for the same old, same old.

Sometimes we have to "chase the mystery." You won't have to look very far to find remarkable stories of success that began when someone followed a hunch. I don't mean for you to jump off a cliff (without a parachute, at least!). Go ahead and use your intelligence (for instance, we had always been able to find employment), but you can rarely collect enough information to be absolutely sure which way to go. You have to learn to trust your heart without calling 1-800-PSYCHIC. With intuition, you're learning to use what you already have. Allow your heart and mind to work together in harmony. Treat your intuition like a wise being.

> *Trusting your intuition means tuning in as deeply as you can to the energy you feel, following that energy moment to moment, trusting that it will lead you where you want to go and bring you everything you desire.*
> **-SHAKTI GAWAIN-**

As you develop your intuition, you'll know if you're on the right path by the way you **feel.** For that reason alone, it's good to develop leadership qualities. We have to be the best possible leaders of ourselves! If we don't lead ourselves, who will? How do you get good at this? Practice, practice, practice!

Happiness Step Twelve
Practicing Intuition

First, recall a major event where following your intuition paid off. Congratulations!

Next, recall a time when you should have paid attention to your intuition but didn't.

Whoops!

Begin practicing your intuition through your simple choices. You might start with little things like what to have for breakfast, whether to go out in the evening or not, etc. As you begin to think of more important decisions, realize that sometimes decisions have to be made sooner than when we're ready, so let's cut to the chase.

Choose one important issue in your life right now. Write it down if you wish. What do you feel you should do? Think of one possible solution to the problem **quickly**.

Now, in your mind, play it forward and project what you see happening if you follow through with that idea.

Next, go back, rewind, and play it forward again, projecting what would happen by **not** following through with your idea. Which solution feels best? Do any other solutions come to mind? It may take a number of times, but repeat this process until you get a clear feeling of which action is best. When you do, follow it!

This exercise is also useful when quick decisions have to be made because imagining several possible scenarios and playing them forward can be done very quickly with practice. After all, following your intuition in an emergency can literally save your life and the lives of others!

CHAPTER EIGHT
GET A LIFE — THE WAY <u>YOU</u> WANT IT!

Personal Goals: Defining What You Really Want in Life

It's time to get specific about your higher, most important visions! Are you willing to do what it takes to make them a reality? You've identified earlier what you love to do, so let's focus on what you **really** want to be doing in your life.

> *What you do may seem insignificant, but it's very important that you do it.*
> –MAHATMA GANDHI-

Think of one of the important goals you've listed and ask yourself how badly you want it and why. Does the goal make you want to jump out of bed or hide under the covers? For some goals, the answer may be easy, but other ambitions that aren't a high priority may bring on more problems than they're worth. How to choose?

Think of the sheer volume of information: text messages, emails, tweets, pokes, physical mail, notices, ads, bills, junk, SPAM, and BS you get daily. Only a small percentage of that information is useful. The same is often true with what we do. Do you find yourself spending too much time on activities you **don't really need** in your life? That's like digging a ditch and filling it up again; it's pointless!

In Happiness Step Thirteen, you will declare what you **really want**. What you really want should contain some of the things you love to do (from Happiness Step Six). There may be no awards for playing with grandchildren, gardening, or meditation, but it's all about having balance in your life, doing what you love, and living **your** higher purposes, not what someone else thinks you should do. Think of the goals you write as **your** personal mission statement.

This isn't a "to-do" list; it's a "to-be" list. You want your goals to be inspiring to think about, like a double shot of java. If your goals are as interesting as watching moss grow, then it's time to add some healthy challenges for your growth and self-esteem. Take ownership of your responsibilities and actions. We all too often allow ourselves to go "off the air," tuning out our higher self, or we accept careers, relationships, and activities that deaden us. **Select** your goals; don't settle. The deepest longing of the human heart is the need to live for a cause greater than one's self. Listen to your heart; its wisdom never lies. It will lead you to your destiny.

What you do the most has everything to do with the quality of person you become. If you do divine things, you will become more divine. And when you do what you love to do, you will be happier. Avoid doing anything that takes a lot of time that isn't part of your higher purpose. In other words, throw out all of your **SPAM!**

Don't forget to ask yourself **why** you want a goal, or it might not work for you:

> Chris always talked about how he'd like to be on the city council to "straighten things out." After considerable urging from his friends, he ran for the office and won the seat. Once in office, he detested the politics and heavy workload for little money. He couldn't wait for the term to end. Chris had essentially gone into the political arena so his friends would look up to him. Once the excitement of winning had worn off, the harsh reality of doing a job he really didn't like set in.

Be very selective about what you do and don't do. Be careful what you wish for because the power of repeated thoughts may very well bring that goal to you, and hopefully, those thoughts are aligned with one of your higher purposes. If they're not, you either won't achieve a goal, or you'll get what you ask for and future events will teach you that the goal was not in line with your higher purpose.

Carmen wants a new love relationship to work out, but there are a lot of problems. Here are two possible scenarios:

a) The relationship fizzles because the problems would ultimately block the accomplishment of her higher purposes. Initially, Carmen is very depressed, but she eventually gets over it and meets a new love that better enables her to fulfill her higher purposes.

b) The relationship works out initially, but eventually, she becomes sorry she wished for the relationship. She and her fiancé break up, and although there was some delay, Carmen is now on the same road to her higher purposes as in scenario one. And guess what? She meets a new love, and she's very happy.

Ultimately, our higher purposes will be achieved; it's just a matter of how long it takes.

Working Hard or Hardly Working?

You need to work **hard** to achieve your goals, right? If your answer is yes, you get the game show "wrong answer" buzzer. Don't get me wrong; hard work is good— as long as it doesn't **seem like it!** When we're doing what we love, it ought to be joyful and effortless. Athletes work out hard because they love their sport. A business owner willingly goes the extra mile for his or her customers. If what you're doing feels like drudgery, there's something wrong with the picture. Ask yourself: "Do I really have to do this?" If the answer is no, **stop doing it!** If it's yes, then ask: "How could I somehow make this more fun?" If an important goal seems hard, you may be in too much of a hurry. Slow down, relax, and reflect on the goal. Remove "I'll try" and "I'm tired" from your vocabulary. T<u>ri</u>ed and ti<u>r</u>ed are very similar words, aren't they?

> As a toddler, I would drive my parents crazy by singing songs in bed at all hours of the night. When my parents gave me a flute, they enjoyed my practicing, but when I got a saxophone, my parents begged me to spare their aching ears! When I majored in music at the university, I had trouble being motivated to practice the saxophone for my lessons. I loved music, so what was wrong? I realized I didn't enjoy playing classical music on saxophone, but I could practice jazz for hours on end. Practicing classical saxophone to me was **hard work.** Classical saxophone was

someone else's agenda for me, while the jazz was my "soul."

When you do your higher work and do it often, you'll never feel like you have to work hard. Successful professionals are driven to do what they love, so their career is simply what they do. It is more of a joy and a privilege than hard work. When we do what is natural for us, we transcend effort. We call this state of mind "flow."

Human beings feel best in flow, when they are fully involved in meeting a challenge, solving a problem, discovering something new.
-MIHALY CSIKSZENTMIHALYI-

When we're in flow, things seem effortless. We forget our problems and lose track of time. Choose tasks that aren't so hard that you blow a gasket nor so easy that you are bored out of your skull. Many activities can induce flow: running, skiing, surfing, gardening, listening to music, cooking, driving, talking to friends, and if you're enjoying your job, it can happen at work! We rarely go into "flow" watching TV, or just "vegging out," for flow requires that the mind be stimulated. Being in flow doing our higher work is a sure way to be happy.

"But," growls the Grinch. "No one should achieve anything with effortless ease. We must **suffer** for our rewards!" Slap that Grinch! Suffering is not part of our higher nature, and while we all endure some suffering, it need not be part of our plan.

Take one of your higher visions and imagine that you are living the dream right now. How does it feel? If it brings you a good feeling, vow to do whatever is necessary to make it happen. If it takes some time to do, then begin preparing to enable this to happen in the future. When will be the day you stop spending too much time doing what you **don't** want to do? Don't wait 'til the end of your life to figure out what you wish you'd done! Pursuing your passion isn't selfish; it's your unique gift to the world.

Too Much of a Good Thing

Many of us have been very good at doing the work of others versus doing our own work. You might be a fine seamstress or an expert carpenter. That doesn't mean you have to make everyone's alterations or redo everyone's deck! Of course, if you love sewing and building houses and do this for a living, no problem! A lot of us can do many things well, and you may be told, "Oh, you do such a **fine** job!" But resist the temptation of trying to be the next savior of the free world by doing everything everyone wants you to do!

Sometimes we take on more than what's good for us:

Being the Music Department Chair at the University of Wisconsin-Whitewater was two jobs worth of work. Taking my duties seriously, I assumed the role of "departmental hero," spending countless extra hours at the office. As the dean, colleagues and friends patted me on the back about my hard work; my ego was stroked into continuing the circus for three years.

Now I wished they had advised me to spend more time with my family and watch my health. I didn't see my wife and daughter often enough and gained weight. I was out of balance, overworking, under stress, and tired of living in a cold, damp climate.

I literally prayed for answers. I needed a way to change my priorities, and I kept searching for solutions. Ultimately, I was guided to a higher-salaried job with less workload and a change to a warmer climate. Four years later, I resigned my administrative duties and returned to teaching. I was guided to retire early in order to take better care of my wife, move to

California, and continue doing what tugs at me the most. Had I not contemplated, meditated, and prayed, my fanatical, egotistical, "work hard 'til you drop" ethic would have led to serious consequences. Please consider these **new** statements:

No pain, no gain?

*Wrong. For a good workout, maybe, but **not** for life. Your life need not include constant pain and suffering in order for your highest goals to be realized.*

The best never rest?

*Wrong again. The best **do** rest. If you don't rest, the universe will "rest" you. Take breaks when you need to. Einstein and Edison did. Overwork, including pushing ourselves to get everything in the world done, is a form of self-abuse that will actually repel what we want to accomplish!*

For my own survival, I, Johnny Workaholic (pictured here), had to learn to accept that there would never be enough hours in the day to get every single thing done! One concept that really helped me was this: Don't think something has to be done until you've thoroughly examined its purpose.

Making Space vs. Taking Up Space

Happiness 101: **Spend the most time on what's most important!** That requires the fortitude to say no to doing things that appear to be priorities but really aren't. If you don't make the time for the goals you believe in and continue to do what you don't really want to do, your pent-up energy will eventually come out in the form of anger or frustration, and that can be costly. If what you're doing is not "it," pull the plug! Make space for what **is** important versus constantly doing what does not serve your best purpose. That's not easy because change is hard. A law of physics tells us:

> An inanimate object (your hiney) tends to stay inanimate (unless you get off of it!).

There is a fundamental resistance to change what has "always been" in our lives, even when staying the same is bad for us. Changes are inevi-table in life, but the irony is that what we need to change the most is often what we want to change the least! Our inner curmudgeon protests, "But this is the way it's always been, and I'm never gonna change it!"

A common definition of insanity is "doing the same thing repeatedly but expecting a different result." Begin by focusing on one important change at a time, and remember that for every new change you **add** to your life, you have to let something go of **equal** time commitment to allow the space in your life for the change to occur.

You can't keep adding more things to your lifeboat and expect to stay afloat. Throw something overboard! What are you willing to **give up** that will allow room for exciting changes in your life? Let some less important things go. It's simple math. Your thoughts may have infinite power, but the "space" in your life is limited by time. Any addition requires subtraction. If your parking lot holds fifty cars, don't try to park two hundred cars in it!

If you don't have room in your living room for an elephant,
don't make friends with the elephant trainer.
-SUFI SAYING-

WELL I'LL BE A BLUE-NOSED GOPHER

Stress is not caused by anything but your mind's interpretations of your busy life and its challenges, aided by an imbalance between rest and activity. Make time for rest, relaxation, and meditation. In music, it's the "silence between the notes" that makes music powerful. In art, space is as important as the design or materials in a work. Allow space and silence in your life. It will make your busy times more meaningful.

Happiness Step Thirteen
What I Really Want

What do you really want? Grab a pen or pencil, and jot your ideas down. If you get stuck, go back to Happiness Step Six, where you listed what you loved to do, and incorporate them here. Don't be shy! Have fun with it. For short-term goals, think of achieving something within a month and for long-term goals, anything over a month.

Vague goals rarely get accomplished. Avoid statements like: "I want to do better with losing weight." Be specific. A specific wish could be "I will lose two pounds this week by cutting down on my portions and exercising." Do you want to save money? How? Do you want a new job? What kind of job and where? Do you want more time to do something? What will you cut to make time for it? Do you want a vacation? A specific wish could be: "I'd like to save up to $100 this month for a two-week trip to Hawaii in January with my spouse. Within five years, we'd like to go to Australia, and I'll put $50 a month in savings for it."

For your toughest goals, take your best shot, and don't close off the possibility that it can happen. If you wrote that you'd like to travel around the world by boat, don't necessarily think: "But I'll have to win the lottery to do it." After all, you could work on a cruise ship and get paid to travel around the world! Identifying what you really want and working toward it makes life meaningful. Not all goals will come out exactly as you want, but with patience and perseverance, a lot of what you really want will manifest in unique and exciting ways! Are you ready?

___

What I really want for my HEALTH:
Long-term Goals
Short-term Goals
Rate the importance of your goals from 1 to 5 (1 being the most important)

___

What I really want for my FAMILY:
Long-term Goals
Short-term Goals
Rate the importance of your goals from 1 to 5

___

What I really want for my LOVE LIFE:
Long-term Goals
Short-term Goals
Rate the importance of your goals from 1 to 5

___

What I really want for my FRIENDSHIPS:
Long-term Goals
Short-term Goals
Rate the importance of your goals from 1 to 5

___

What I really want for my RELIGION, SPIRITUALITY, and HIGHER PURPOSE:
Long-term Goals
Short-term Goals
Rate the importance of your goals from 1 to 5

___

What I really want for my CAREER:
Long-term Goals
Short-term Goals
Rate the importance of your goals from 1 to 5

___

What I really want to do for my PEACE OF MIND and HAPPINESS:
Long-term Goals
Short-term Goals
Rate the importance of your goals from 1 to 5

___

What else do you REALLY WANT? Simply label a subject area and go with it (i.e., material things, travel, community, creativity, education, or anything else you can think of).
Long-term Goals
Short-term Goals
Rate the importance of your goals from 1 to 5

CHAPTER NINE
TURNING DUST INTO GOLD

Our "Perfect" Imperfections

Will there be major challenges to your goals? That's as certain as hot weather in Texas in July. If you walk, run, or bike outside, do you suddenly notice the **hills?** Progress toward goals has its ups and downs, too. You might be cruising downhill, and suddenly end up in "Nowheresville," driving in reverse! The growing process is like driving in the mountains with curves, steep grades, and maybe no guardrails!

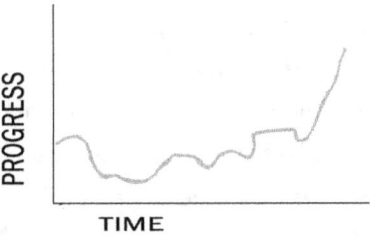

The "Imperfect" Way We Progress

Turmoil and confusion are part of growth. It's the nature of the universe, just like the way the Earth formed with massive explosions, molten lava, and earthquakes galore! In life, you may be working on a goal and suddenly encounter a minefield of obstacles! Before you throw your shoe through the window, know that most "breakthroughs" can show up as quickly as the problems did.

We will make mistakes. It's okay. Just learn from them!

Anyone can make a mistake. Only a BIG FOOL makes it twice!

You might not like your progress right now, but don't take things too seriously. If you're doing the best that you can, what more can you ask of yourself?

Life is more like a baseball season, not a spelling bee!

Unlike a spelling bee, you get more than one chance. Even World Series winners lose one-third or more of their games in the long baseball season.

> *If you are facing in the right direction, all*
> *you need to do is keep on walking.*
> **-BUDDHIST PROVERB-**

As you realize the power of focusing on what you really want, beware of the flip side! Avoid repeated thoughts on what you don't want, or that will manifest, too! "I **don't** want a pimple the night of the prom," I thought over and over again, and sure enough, zit city arrived in full force! Essentially, we attract what we think about. Our outer lives are the mirror image of our inner lives. The best time to get specific about what we really want is right here, right now. Are you ready, or will you put it off?

The Champion Procrastinator

Last year's Procrastinator's Unanimous meeting was postponed again this year. It will possibly be held eventually.
-UNANIMOUSLY ANONYMOUS-

Before you step forward to accept the Champion Procrastinator's Award, ask yourself:

- Why are you procrastinating?
- Is the goal unpleasant or too difficult? Are you afraid of the goal or feel unworthy of doing it?
- Does your procrastination mean you really have something more important to do?
- Should your goal be put off or maybe never done at all?
- Is what you're doing the most important thing you should do today?
- Notice your procrastination. Either "just do it" or eliminate your need to do it!

During the final summer months of my doctoral dissertation, I was an accomplished procrastinator. I would make gourmet coffee, cook lavish meals that would take a couple of hours, look for just the right music to play, talk on the phone, check e-mails, burn incense, and even take frequent bathroom breaks. It's a miracle I ever got it done!

One key to happiness is the feeling that our physical, mental, social, and spiritual self is evolving in some way. We often get "stuck" in one or more areas, and motivation can dwindle. Society loves to label such people as "lazy," but I respectfully disagree. A closer look at those who seem to lack motivation reveals one or more of the following:

- a lack of meaningful and motivational activities.
- a fear of failure and self-doubt.
- a fear of success and the responsibility that goes with it.

To stay with long-term goals, some of us need daily reinforcement, while others make an instant decision to do something and just stick to it. I'm one who needs the daily support, but my dad, a heavy smoker for thirty years, decided to quit instantly and never smoked another cigarette again. He lived a good, long life as a result of it. Take the initiative, and do what works for you.

> *Do not go where the path may lead, go instead where there is no path and leave a trail.*
> **-RALPH WALDO EMERSON-**

Put another way....

> *If you ain't the lead dog, the scenery never changes.*
> **-LEWIS GRIZZARD-**

As leader of your own destiny, you have a lot of say in determining if your highest visions turn into dust or into gold.

Happiness Step Fourteen
The Truth Is...

If you had **unlimited** time and resources, what would you really like to be doing? Imagine there is a magic genie ready to grant you five incredible wishes with **no restrictions**! It's your life we're talking about, so don't wish for a new phone or a steak dinner! Go for it—be imaginative, and remember, you have to **ask** for something in order to get it.

Take lovemaking—if you never tell your partner what you want, you leave him or her guessing. In the same way, don't leave the entire universe guessing what you really want! If you believe God or whomever you pray to loves you, then you know that your higher purposes can be fulfilled if you persist. It may not be easy, but trust that opportunities will arise, especially if you are open to them.

Good things don't just "happen" to people. Good fortune comes to those who are ready for it!

- Jot down your top five wishes for your life. Be precise. No vague wishes!

Are you through? Great!

- Next, declare your wish for these things right now, preferably out loud. Ask God, the Universe, or whatever positive being(s) you pray to for these wishes to come true.

It's critical to admit you **want** these wishes to come true. Did you admit you want your wishes? I knew you would! Once you've done that, say to yourself (and this is a big one!):

- *I now allow the circumstances to be created for what I really want to manifest! I deserve these wishes. I am ready for them to come true.*

This step changed my life.

Now, say to yourself:

- *I believe my wishes will come true. I will never let go of them, and I will do all I can to enable these wishes!*

In your next quiet time, picture in your mind your wishes coming true. Take your time with the visions, and let them settle in clearly. Believe it. You can do **anything** you want to when it's in line with your higher purposes!

Transforming the "Fairy Tale"

So, you've taken the time to make some "wishes." Great, but let's turn off the Disney channel and get real. If you asked for these wishes sincerely, the **last** thing you want to do is leave them behind to blow away like Tinker Bell dust. Will your life be like the song "Boulevard of Broken Dreams," or are you ready to see what's behind door number one? You have every opportunity to empower yourself, starting now.

When that mega-shot of inspiration comes in, it's natural to want to podcast, email, Facebook, Instagram, and "tweety-tweet" it to all creatures in the known universe. While you're making your highest intentions known, beware of the flip side. There are people who will scoff at whatever you do or say that doesn't meet their approval or triggers their own fears and doubts. Many well-meaning parents steer their children away from the ideal job the kids want toward safe, secure, **boring** jobs, or jobs of status that make the parents happy but are **not** the destiny of their son or daughter!

As a musician, people would ask me: "So, what's your day job?" I happily answered, "Uh, this **is** my day job!" If you decide to share your future goals with people close to you, you may have to cope with a barrage of discouraging comments. Sometimes, it's best to share your highest dreams with others only on an as-needed basis. Whatever you decide, focus on your vision and don't give up. Remember, anything considered unrealistic to achieve was only that way until someone did it!

Reread your top five wishes. Do they give you a surge of energy? Or maybe you're doubtful right now. Make sure you really want your goal and that the goal is **yours,** not someone else's. Don't base your goals on the accomplishment itself. For instance, "I want to be the first in my family to get a degree" or "because my [parents/spouse/friends] will be proud of me." You have to want what you want because you need it for your higher purpose. Don't ask for what everyone else wants for you because everyone else isn't living your life!

We don't always know how things will work out, but they will the way they're supposed to. Trust that whatever is part of your higher purpose will come to fruition, but the process may be slow or uneven. Put your wishes out there, and vow to manifest them, but let go of the need to have total control. If you'll do your part, the "when" and "how" will come about in a way that's best for your development.

Many of us have trouble realizing how abundant the universe is, especially because of the poverty and crime that exists. When gifts and opportunities actually come, we don't know how to accept them. Everyone makes mistakes, but that doesn't mean we don't deserve good things to happen to us. Think of your good fortunes and talents as part of your higher self. When you have success, accept it with grace, and don't get too "puffed up" because anyone's success requires a lot of help!

After spending a week in the presence of His Holiness the Dalai Lama at a Kalachakra Ceremony for World Peace in Bloomington, Indiana, it became clear he is one of the happiest beings I've ever witnessed. He is full of joy, mainly because he is fulfilling his higher purpose every minute. His Holiness customarily receives many gifts, and he blesses them as Buddhist monks do. He only keeps the most essential articles (a robe, shoes, a bowl, a spoon, etc.) for himself, and he immediately hands the gifts to be dispersed wherever they will do the most good.

The countless gifts we receive in this lifetime are not for us to keep. We are to use them only as long as we need them and then give them wherever they're needed. With that understanding, you can upgrade your sense of what you deserve. Babies aren't afraid to ask for what they want and need. Why should you be?

> *We fear our highest possibilities... We are generally afraid to become that which we glimpse in our most perfect moments, under the most perfect conditions, under the conditions of greatest courage. We enjoy and even thrill to godlike possibilities we see in ourselves in such peak moments. And yet we simultaneously shiver with weakness, awe, and fear before these very same possibilities.*
> **-ABRAHAM MASLOW-**

If it helps you feel more deserving, offer your most important goals up to God. If you get these wishes, will you have "enough"? Are you asking for more than what you need? Do you feel good about your goals?

Happiness Step Fifteen
Prioritizing...

It's time to prioritize your top five wishes you've made. Imagine your genie can only grant four wishes. Which would you delete? Keep imagining the wishes disappearing until you identify your **one** most important wish! It doesn't mean all five wishes can't come true for you, but it's always best to spend the most time on your number one wish!

Here's another approach. If you were to lose everything (such as in 9/11, a major hurricane, other natural disasters, or wars), what would be the **one** thing you would want back? Granted this method is less fun, but it gets you to the root of what's most important.

The order of your priorities will be challenged often. Here are some examples:

Priority #1	Family unit
Challenge:	Your family completely disapproves of your new fiancé.
Decision:	Your family's wishes versus your love life.
Priority #1	Love life
Challenge:	You gradually realize your romantic interest is simply not the one you want to continue your life with.
Decision:	Your personal happiness versus the need to be with someone.

Priority #1	Religious beliefs/Spirituality
Challenge:	Your friends pressure you to do something you know is wrong.
Decision:	Following your moral values versus having the approval of friends.

Priority #1	Career
Challenge:	You just got a huge promotion out of state, which means all your family will be 2,000 miles away.
Decision:	Taking the job versus being close to family.

Priority #1	Social life
Challenge:	You have trouble spending enough time with your friends because you're working a job while working on a master's degree.
Decision:	Education/career versus your social life.

Without looking at your previous goals, list your wishes in reverse order, so your #1 priority (the last wish you would give up) is given last. After all, it's how you feel TODAY that counts.

5. _____

4. _____

3. _____

2. _____

1. _____

Below, affirm your wishes as if you already have them. No "ifs" or "I will." Say "I am" or "I have." For example, if you wrote that you wanted a good relationship with your loved one, you write: "I have a warm, dynamic, loving, fruitful relationship with..." Use your powerful words to make your goals come to life!

Affirmations

5. _____

4. _____

3. _____

2. _____

1. _____

It's good to repeat this happiness step to practice establishing the priorities of your top five goals often!

What If?

You wonder: "What if what I really want never happens?" Achieving a goal sometimes seems to take longer than waiting for spring to come to Minnesota. If huge roadblocks keep getting in the way of your important goal, what are the reasons? Sometimes what we think we want at some point may not be what we really need to evolve as a human being. Sometimes you'll be granted what you want just so the universe can teach you a lesson! It isn't just about "me" in this world. It helps to think that God, the universe, or some higher power is to be ultimately trusted!

Life isn't about getting everything we want (except for maybe chocolate). Using creative visualization (when you picture in your mind repeatedly what you want) works wonderfully—only if what you want is meant to happen.

> More tears are shed over answered prayers
> than unanswered prayers.
> **-ST. TERESA OF AVILA-**

Perhaps an unfulfilled goal will be answered later in another way. Sometimes people don't achieve a goal because they aren't actually willing to receive what they ask for. It's a paradox, but you may not be ready or feel deserving of your wishes. If you're meant to have it and you're persistent, you'll get it.

> Ultimately it isn't about getting what you
> want—you get what you _are_.
> **-NEVILLE GODDARD-**

Are you ready for the next set of breakthroughs in your life, including some that far surpass anything you expected? When you truly begin to believe in yourself, these breakthroughs will begin as soon as you allow them!

If you find yourself wanting to change the priority of your "top five" at any point, it's not a cardinal sin! Write your top five goals in short keywords and put them on a card or small piece of paper in your purse, wallet, or briefcase. Or you can tear off the next page. Read them each day or as often as you need to.

For Your Wallet or Purse

Tear off here or simply photocopy/scan/print this page or make your own handwritten page!

Top five goals

1. _____

2. _____

3. _____

4. _____

5. _____

Fold here.

Affirmations for my top five goals

1. _____

2. _____

3. _____

4. _____

5. _____

CHAPTER TEN
YOU CAN GET THERE FROM HERE
(SOONER THAN YOU MIGHT THINK)

Shortcuts to Your Goals

You've decided to work on that all-important goal and then determined that it will take forever and a day to do it! That makes the twelfth of never a good time to start! Before chucking it in your wastebasket of woes, imagine completing that same goal sooner than you ever believed possible! In many cases, you can realize some or part of your goals sooner. If I want to run five miles, I've got to do it one step at a time, but if I just need to get five miles down the road, I could hitch a ride! The willingness to seek shortcuts and to be open to new possibilities can keep you in the game:

Maya had just moved to a new area and wanted to make new friends. It was difficult at first, but she remained open to possibilities to meet new people. Unexpectedly, she met a nice woman at a bookstore that happened to know several others interested in the same book she bought. Soon she had a circle of new acquaintances, including one who loved to ride bicycles, something Maya liked as well. Through that friend, she joined a group of riders, and in that group, she met the man she would later marry!

Had Maya shut off the idea of making a friend at a bookstore, her life would have been different and lonelier. In another case:

Carl, an aspiring artist who wanted to study at the San Francisco Art Institute, was far short of the tuition he needed. As a high school senior, he continued to paint and look for ways to generate tuition money. By making his needs public, his high school awarded him a scholarship. Carl moved to San Francisco, even though he didn't have close to the tuition money he needed. There, he got an idea to cater prepared lunches to local businesses, and he began to generate good income. After saving for a few months, his aunt called, saying that because he had worked so hard toward his tuition, she would cover the balance!

These are not fairy tales. "Lucky" breaks happen for people who are persistent in pursuing their highest goals and are open-minded enough to look for shortcuts! The universe is a highly intelligent entity with infinite organizing power, and when you align yourself with it by not struggling against your higher purpose, amazing things will happen. Consider this: What if Carl had given up on his dream of being a successful artist?

The universe is always providing us with clues as to how to manifest our higher goals, but it often requires us to think in a different way as opposed to following our old habitual thinking.

A long time ago, in a faraway land, three brilliant men—a doctor, a lawyer, and an engineer—faced the guillotine for their political beliefs. The doctor was put on the chopping block first, but as the blade came crashing down, it stopped short, leaving the doctor unharmed. According to the rules, it was "divine intervention," so the doctor was set free.

Next, the lawyer was placed before the guillotine, and down came the blade full force, but it stopped short of its destination once more. The lawyer too was spared!

Now it was the engineer's turn. The blade comes down with rapid speed, and for a third time, it stopped short, sparing the engineer's life. The executioner prepares to untie his prisoner. As the engineer lay there, looking up at the apparatus, he suddenly said, "Wait! I think I see what the problem is!"

The willingness to abandon our old ways of thinking to approach a goal with a different perspective might just be a lifesaver!

Some goals take a certain amount of time, no matter what. I've always coached my university students to become the professionals they want to be in their minds years before they begin employment. To keep from getting discouraged or impatient, take key aspects of your long-term goals and bring them into your life **right now.**

Nicole wants to be a veterinarian and knows that it will take some years of training. For now, she works at the zoo twenty hours a week, helps train horses on a ranch, and is a part-time nanny. These activities are perfect preparation for her because she's close to animals and gets paid to care for others.

Like the strange but wise wizard Merlin, who lived his life backward, you project your goal into the future as if you already have it and then use your "now" to gravitate toward a positive future. With my students, one of two things happened: they either became what they wanted to be, or they discovered they didn't really want what they thought they wanted and changed directions.

It isn't always about what you have now; it's about what you are becoming.

Say you want to lose thirty pounds, but you can't do that in one day (although I've tried!). Begin to do the kinds of things that lighter people do, whether it's playing sports, dancing, walking, or eating healthy. Do you want a better place to live? Clean up your house and make it as nice as possible, and with constant positive thoughts and actions around getting that new home, you'll begin to move toward that future. Doing activities related to your long-term goals is a great morale-booster because they help hold you over until you finally achieve your goals.

If a goal you once had is no longer possible, you can still bring some of it into your life. I loved baseball as a kid, so I tried out for our championship high school team and did very well, except in hitting, fielding, and throwing. My career went elsewhere, but I'd watch a game when I could. Years later, while running, I found a perfect hardball on the side of the road in the middle of nowhere! I kept it by my computer to remind me of the great feeling I had when I would play ball as a kid. Funny thing, after a couple of years of looking at that ball on my desk, I joined a softball league for seven years, and was one of their best players—for the teams I played **against!** But, I had a blast!

Happiness Step Sixteen
Shortcuts! Getting There Sooner...

Pick one or more of your most compelling goals from Happiness Steps Thirteen (what I really want) or Fourteen (my top five wishes). Brainstorm how you can bring what you desire into your life much sooner. Jot down your ideas!

Affirmation time!

- *This week, I will do the following toward making one or more of my goals happen sooner, and bring more of that dream into my life **right now**:*

_____

Are there any dreams you've let go of that you'd like to reintroduce into your life in a new way? Pick at least one.

Old dream
_____

I will bring it back in a new way by
_____

Got more?

Additional Goal Time-Savers

Articulate Your Goals Specifically

If you really want it to happen, avoid vague goals.

Kinda Fuzzy…	I would like to make better grades.
I Can See Clearly Now!	I envision getting As in English and Speech, and will settle for Bs in Biology and Algebra.
Just a Start…	I want to be an artist.
Off and Runnin'!	I will make a living in art through part-time work by teaching art and working as a gallery director while continuing to paint. I will sell and exhibit my work locally and then nationally.

Want Your Goals

If you don't ask, you won't receive! Just like this puppy, you deserve a treat! You really **want** this goal, don't you? Make this goal your personal daily affirmation or prayer.

Kinda Sorta I want to be a spiritual person.
Doin' it! I will be a living example of my spirituality.

Believe in Your Goals

Visualize in your mind achieving your goal. You deserve it despite any imperfections you may think you have.

A Tad Doubtful I can have good relationships with people.
Feelin' It Now! My relationships are improving because I treat everyone with respect, including myself. I am my higher self as much as possible and recognize those characteristics in others.

Have a Strategy and Organize it

You want and believe in your goals, so develop specific ideas about how to achieve them. As you do, more solutions will manifest.

Wishful Thinking	I will study hard to be a doctor.
Mo' Betta Plan!	As I work to achieve As in my medical classes and Bs in the other classes, I will read magazines, books, and journals related to my field for a minimum of forty minutes a day. I'm applying for an entry-level job at the local hospital, and I've begun some volunteer work at the local senior citizen center.

The more organized your plan is and the more time you spend manifesting it, the more likely it is you will achieve it!

Git R Dun!

Accomplish something meaningful toward your goal every day. Make a self-contract to keep plugging away.

Blandly Generic	I will work hard each day to make the volleyball team.
Now We're Cookin'!	On Monday, Wednesday, and Friday, I'll do aerobics followed by practicing my serves. On Tuesday, Thursday, and Saturday, I'll lift weights and practice volleyball with three of my high school friends. Sunday? Collapse!

Have a Time Frame in Mind

When will you expect to achieve your goal? Some goals are long-term, and others can be achieved nearly instantly. For the long-term goals, set up a calendar of short-term achievements to keep you motivated. When you achieve a goal, take a bow!

Evaluate Weekly

It saves time to evaluate your progress at least weekly, so you can pat yourself on the back, make minor changes, or reassess your direction. Don't beat yourself up when you have a bad day; we all do. Besides, bandages are expensive!

Know Your Challenges

Every meaningful goal has challenges. What are they? How far are you prepared to go to make this goal a reality? Some goals may come with a cost. For instance, a successful, high-powered career will take some time to achieve and could make family or romantic relationships difficult. Can you live with that?

You're Not an Island

No goal can be brought about without the help of a lot of people. When the going gets tough, you get **help!**

> *The only thing hiding your problems will accomplish is making sure no one helps you with them.*
> **–DAVID NIVEN-**

Build human connections. Dedicate yourself to deepening your bonds with the people around you. You're here to enrich the world. Get help from good people when you need it. By achieving your goals, you'll inspire others to achieve their dreams too.

Happiness Step Seventeen
Follow Through With Your Goals!

Apply this to a minimum of three goals that you really want to achieve!

#1 Very important goal _____

To be completed by (date) _____

To achieve this goal, I will…

- jot down general strategies.
- seek assistance, support, and cooperation from the following people…
- anticipate challenges I will likely run into and plan how I'll overcome them.
- list and achieve short-term steps toward this goal within a month…
- describe my goal as if I already have it.

Contract with myself: Each day, I plan to do the following things to bring this goal into reality. Be sure to enter these into your daily planner!

Day 1
_____

Day 2
_____

Day 3
_____

Day 4
_____

Day 5
_____

Day 6
_____

Day 7
_____

Weekly Assessment

What I did well
_____

What needs improvement
_____

Solutions or changes
_____

Repeat these for any other important goal!

SECTION THREE
Put Time on <u>Your</u> Side!

CHAPTER ELEVEN
TIME PASSES AND TIME'S PAST

The Nature of Time

I used to think I didn't have time for all this happiness stuff. After reaching the depths of frustration, I asked myself: "What **do** I have time for?" Since I'd done a great job devoting my time to toward old, useless habits and activities that were the agenda of others, why not plan for my own happiness? I realized how I spent my time was absolutely critical to my well-being!

Let's look at the nature of time itself. Time is the continuous progress of existence according to our perception of what we think reality is. We gauge our concept of time according to known astronomical phenomena: the revolution of the Earth, sun, stars, etc.

Time passes at an even rate, yet it seems to pass quite differently for us if we're relaxing with friends versus passing a kidney stone! If we stare at the second hand of our watch for a while, time passes slowly, but if we're asleep, time goes by quickly. One teacher had this sign posted by her classroom wall clock to motivate her less-than-dedicated student clock-gazers:

TIME PASSES. WILL YOU?

The continuous passing of time can be divided into moments. If we say, "Wait a moment," we're implying that there's a beginning and end to each moment, but how short is a moment? Time can be dissected into **infinitely** small moments! For example, Buddhists identify the smallest unit of energy as a *kalapa* (a sequence of moments—each with a birth and death). There are **one trillion** *kalapas* in the single blink of an eye. While I may have grabbed a doughnut in one *kalapa*, it gets worse. Buddhists also describe a sequence of seventeen "mind moments" **per kalapa**. That's 17 trillion "events" per blink of an eye—each with stages of arising, duration, and dying! Not only does that knock around a few brain cells, but what happens between those moments? At least, we know what we **don't** know about time…

- We can't "freeze" it (video technology doesn't count!).
- We can't comprehend the shortest "moment" or the longest possible time.
- We don't know exactly how or when time began, let alone if it will ever end.

To keep our minds from imploding into dark matter, let's divide time into the past, present, and future. The past represents the sum total of what we recall, and to be honest, that isn't much! The present is between the past and the future, but where is it exactly? Well, isn't the present "now"? Of course, but as soon as you thought the word "now," it's in the past! So the present becomes the past verrrry quickly, doesn't it? But, the past is over, and the future has yet to occur, so **now** is the only thing we can do anything about. That makes **the present** our greatest gift!

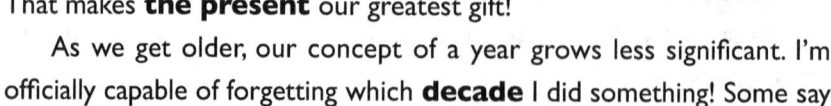

As we get older, our concept of a year grows less significant. I'm officially capable of forgetting which **decade** I did something! Some say time seems to be speeding up, but that's likely because of our fast-paced lives. Crosswalk signals barely allow even fast walkers enough time to get across a busy intersection. Restaurant servers ask you for your beverage choice before you even sit down. We hurry everywhere we go, and then hurry when we get there to move on to the next thing. Everyone's in a hurry to get somewhere other than where they are right now.

I think one of our greatest obstacles is to not live in the "here and now" of our lives. We spend far too much time regretting the dead past or worrying about the future. The **now** is where our spirituality lies. When we free ourselves from the burden of our past, then our present actions will be more effective for the creation of a good future. Refuse to allow anything to rob the quality of your **now** moments. Remember, what you focus on, you create!

Happiness Step Eighteen
Time-Saving or Squandering?

Pick a day this week and ask yourself throughout the day: "Is this the best way that I can possibly be spending my valuable time?" Notice throughout the day how you feel about what you do.

- Think of an instance when time seemed to pass by quickly. Is this something you can do more of?
- Think of an instance when time seemed to pass by slowly. Is this something you can do less of?
- Think of two instances when you felt pretty good about how you were spending your time. Plug these into your schedule!
- Think of two instances when you didn't feel very good about how you were spending your time. Reduce or eliminate them!

Daily affirmation:

- *Today, I will spend my time in the most meaningful way possible, and in so doing, time will pass by quickly and happily.*

Each day, reevaluate how you did, and keep at it!

Freeing Ourselves from the Past

The past can mislead us. We really don't remember it very well, and the further we go back, the less we recall. How much do you remember of your life when you were two? How about at age twelve? I can't remember much of anything from my freshman year in college. (There could be several reasons for that!) You won't remember what you had for lunch Tuesday a week ago unless it was particularly delicious or you got the trots! We only retain information that's either quite memorable to us or something we'll actually **use.** Anything else goes to hide in the cobwebs of our brain! Most of us remember less than **one-tenth of one percent** of our lives. And, if you're Keith Richards...

Besides what we don't remember, the past gets foggier still, because it is subject to our very biased interpretation of what we believed was our experience, which is often heavily influenced by our current frame of mind. If you're at a party, you might recall a past event differently than if you're doing your taxes! (Hmm...maybe that party **was** a business expense!) The way others interpret the past varies, too. History itself is an interpretation. The further back we go in history, the more we are dependent upon limited and biased evidence of anyone who took the time to write about an event. Historical interpretations also change as new ways of looking at the past come into play. For example, the way history is presented about past treatment of Native Americans is radically different today than sixty years ago.

Turn the clock back thousands of years, and the fog really rolls in! We have very few names of anyone, let alone interpretations on how he or she lived and thought. How will anyone be remembered 3,000 years from now? Today, with so many videos and recordings, who knows if our names or one single thing we did will be

known? While we learn valuable lessons from the past, we can't put too much emphasis on it or let it have any power over us because we cannot change it. The past is best used only as a reference point to help us have a quality present.

In the prologue, I mentioned my wife's accident and her traumatic brain injury. Toni remembers a few things from her childhood but very little since. She's relearned information about most of her family and select friends, but **that's it**. Ironically, she can't remember the names of her two previous husbands, but she knows her hairdresser's name! With no past baggage or regrets, **Toni is one of the happiest beings I know anywhere.** She laughs at the least little thing, and you can't help but laugh with her. Any time I'm singing the blues about something, hearing her laugh blows my funky mood right out the window!

Toni is living proof you don't need your past to be happy! Did you have hard times? Of course you did! Have you "failed" at something? Ditto! But difficult experiences bring us gifts in disguise. If there is any kind of organized intelligence in the universe whatsoever, then the chances are that our birth, our parents, and certain key events occurred to enable our growth, so it's best to let go of any resentment we have about our childhood or past.

The past is only a memory—a phantom of the mind. We bear memories, but **we are not the memories themselves.** Letting the past go doesn't mean denying it, but it does mean softening your heart about any of the past that you resent. Apply Happiness Step Four by releasing the weight of your past for your present's sake. Any perceived enemies from the past are souls undergoing their own suffering and ignorance. Forgiveness and reconciliations release huge amounts of time-wasting negative energy, so forgive daily!

We often cling to unhappy memories. Why? It's usually caused by guilt. Author Caroline Myss refers to this as "Wound-ology"—defining yourself by your old wounds. Bad memories stand out because human nature is good, and unhappy or traumatic events are exceptional to our higher nature. With practice, you can control how often you think of an unhappy moment. The bad memory does you no good except to bring you down. One virtue about the passing of time is that it softens the hurt of past suffering. If we lost someone close to us twenty years ago, the emotional power of that sad event may still be there, but it isn't as overwhelming as the grief we suffered then.

Alan Cohen invites us to have a radical "past-ectomy," which means getting rid of anything that ties you to the negative or useless past. For example, go through your clothes and remove anything you've not worn in a year. Do the same for cards, letters, books, photos, gifts, and anything that does not empower you in the present moment. Take an object and hold it. Ask yourself: "Does this empower or deplete my present?" Note your relationships, too. Do they draw you to an old negative way of life? If you have bad memories, use them to think of a way you can be more loving and compassionate in the future.

> *You can't drive your car forward if you're*
> *always looking in the rear view mirror.*
> **-PAT MESITI-**

Love who you were and who you are now, no matter what. Repeating negative memories will accomplish only two things:

- They will make you feel bad.
- They will prevent you from moving on to a positive future.

How often do you think of the good things you've accomplished? That almost seems egotistical in today's age of "bad news sells." Look at an old newspaper from a hundred years ago. They reported mainly good news and family events. That's one example of how we can definitely learn from the past!

Have you made a mistake in your past? Will you make one in the future? No? Ah, then you are a "perfect being"!

Perfect Being:	I have never made a mistake.
Human:	Not even **one?**
Perfect Being:	Well, I did make a mistake **ONCE.**
Human:	O, perfect one, how ever did that happen?
Perfect Being:	It was when I thought I'd made a mistake, but it turned out I hadn't.

Think of the past as a wise teacher who needed to give you lessons in order to get you to where you are today. In order to have a quality "present"...

- Think of your past.
- Realize how much you've learned from it.
- Love your past, no matter how painful it has been.
- Now leave it in the dust!

The past can cause us to wax overly nostalgic too. It's easy to be duped by memories of our highest experiences. Have you ever tried to recreate a remarkable experience exactly? It's impossible. There's nothing wrong with wanting to repeat that special moonlight dinner date, but if you try to repeat it exactly, you lose the enjoyment of the new moment. Keep the same spontaneity in your present moments that you had with your memorable past event. I'm reminded of this daily when I take Toni out somewhere. By the time we settle back home, she has forgotten where we went or what we did. Still, all moments have a richness of their own, so enjoy them as they come and go!

WELL I'LL BE A BLUE-NOSED GOPHER

Fears and doubts arise from our denial of the present. We're brooding over the past or inventing a worrisome future. Every moment of our lives, we can choose love or fear. Fear cuts us off from our connection to the phenomenal power we have now and, however unintentional, keeps us separate from God.

Cross out your "what-ifs" and send positive thoughts backward and forward in time. In the grand scheme of things:

> Time is merely the number of steps you need to take for something positive to occur.

The past can teach us valuable lessons, but we simply cannot stay there. It's time to move on.

Happiness Step Nineteen
Movin' On

We all have past baggage, but it's time to move on! Are you allowing anything from your past to negatively affect how you think and what you do? What is it? How is it affecting you? Say out loud or think:

- Whenever I feel negative emotions from the past, I will erase these feelings by doing the following...

Enter your activities into your weekly planner, either as an activity or as a reminder. Repeat as needed, and continue this until you've wiped the slate clean!

CHAPTER TWELVE
IS THE PRESENT "NOW" OR IS NOW THE "PRESENT"?

"Well I'll Be a Blue-Nosed Gopher!"

At the very beginning of the book I explained how Toni began to use this saying all through the day a few months after her accident and traumatic brain injury. Toni's delightful personality, along with her frequent blue-nosed gopher proclamations, has taught me in no uncertain terms how to enjoy the present moment. Toni's short-term memory lasts about forty-five seconds before she "forgets" what she said or did. It takes hundreds of repetitions before she can retain information. On the other hand, Toni lives totally in the "now." If you tell her some exciting news, she "discovers" it for the first time every time you tell her! If we're going on a trip in a month, she gets equally excited every time I tell her because in her mind, she's hearing it for the first time. By being a "blue-nosed gopher,"

Toni shows us that each new moment is precious because it is fresh. With no past judgments to impose on the moment, every moment for her is special. So it can be for all of us.

Choosing Now

The next question is: "How can I manage my time and **stay** happy?" Before you read every article, book, and manual about time management in the galaxy, read this:

> There is no better time saver than actively following your higher purpose!

What's tricky is that there's always something that has to be done. The dishes have to be done—eventually! If your boss is coming over for dinner, should you tidy up? For me, an army of cleaning experts possessing superpowers is my only hope! Another time you might need to let your house go sloppy. The happiness meter goes down when something we think we have to do shoves aside something that's really more important. We all have laundry, dishes, yard work, etc., but there are times when something else is more urgent.

If you're not in the mood to do something, you feel separate from it, and it means that there's something more important to do, even if it doesn't feel "logical." Maybe you need some rest! When you force yourself to do something, your mind wanders, time crawls, and the job is usually not done as well. If you can't ever get in the mood to do something, ask yourself why it's  important and why you think it "must" be done. When you're ready to do something, you'll save time by being fully focused in the present moment.

Does your higher purpose fit in with things you've done today, this week, or this month? Ask that question daily, and you'll begin to notice less important things you can put off or eliminate altogether.

At work, I would dutifully clean up my desk at the end of every day. I filed items and neatly stacked piles so I knew where everything was. Suddenly, one day, a little gremlin jumped out of my desk drawer and smacked me in the face! "Idiot! Your stupid regimen is taking **too much time!** How about exercising or cuddling with your wife instead?" My little gremlin wasn't insanity, but instead it saved me from it. My desk got messier, but I was happier. When it began to look like an F5 tornado went through, I cleaned it up and put  items in a "file it later or never" pile. Some things didn't get done for days, weeks, and even months because there were other things **more important to do.**

I had to pat my workaholic self on the back, look in the mirror, and say, "There, there! It's okay. Johnny Hero can go home now…"

> *There is nothing so useless as doing efficiently that which should not be done at all.*
> **-PETER DRUCKER-**

Of course, if something important just screams to get done, do it! Procrastinating on something urgent is like a firefighting crew not answering a five-alarm fire! Clinging to a rigid agenda without being flexible is something we resort to when we're under the sway of egocentric thinking. Are you doing the most important things in your life right now?

> *It is characteristic of the ego that it takes all that is unimportant*
> *as important and all that is important as unimportant.*
> **–MEHER BABA-**

Ego hides the present with obsession over the past and worry about the future. The **now** is all you have, really. Perhaps your **now** resembles any one of the nine versions of *A Nightmare on Elm Street*. If so, remove yourself from the situation, and if you can't yet, then accept it for now, but work on changing it. If you feel scarcity now, you'll feel the same way even after good fortune. The challenges are something set before you that you need to overcome. Get rid of your "should-haves" and "what-ifs." My biggest complaint is about those who complain about a situation and do nothing about it!

As our attitude toward each moment improves, our future will improve. Focus on the abundance that exists now.

> *If you live totally in the now, no problems can exist.*
> *If not now, when?*
> **-ZEN-**

Emergencies force us into the now. When was the last time you had a scare? You were certainly "in the moment" then! Fortunately, we can make most of our present moments worthwhile and positive. Allow what you do to have joy, ease, and light. Don't brood over the past you cannot have back and the future you can never fully control. Living without awareness of the present is like being a zombie!

Here is poor <u>(don't let this be you!)</u>, whose mind is currently vacant, because _____'s present moments are currently obscured. The body appears to be doing "things," but the mind is forever stuck elsewhere; it's preoccupied with years past and/or the future. ____ cannot enjoy this moment or any other. Worry is a constant com-

panion, no matter what. _____ is too busy suffering and worrying to enjoy quality time, have decent relationships, or to follow God (who resides in the present moment). May he/she R.I.P. (rest in the present) sooooon!

The conditions for happiness you want are already here! Allow your present moments to be enough. A French Song by Paul Misraki (the title song to the movie *Le Divorce*) is called *"Qu'est-ce qu'on attend pour être heureux,"* which means: "What are you waiting for to be happy?"

> *Happiness is always on the other side of the door.*
> **-YOUR CAT OR DOG-**

Do you always seem to want to be some place **other** than where you are? Breathe in and out slowly, and tell yourself "I am home." You don't have to run anywhere. God, the universe, is everywhere and nowhere (now-here) simultaneously. We all are where we need to be at this moment. There is an old joke about a musician who passes away and arrives at the pearly gates, but he wants to search elsewhere.

"Oh, yes, Mr. Smith, come right in. We've been expecting you."

"Uh, just a minute," the musician demands. "What kind of music do you have here? I'm picky about my music."

"Of course, we have the traditional heavenly harp music. After all, this **is** heaven."

"**Boring**. Don't you have any other kind of music?"

"Well, you can follow the man in the black suit over there. He'll take you to where there is 'other' music. But if you decide to stay there, you can never come back…"

"Sounds like a plan! Can I bring my guitar?"

The heavenly figure nods, so the musician follows the man in the black suit into an elevator, and they go down, down, down to the -4,000,666th floor. They enter a very swanky nightclub that is fully equipped with a bar, waitresses, customers, and a stage where a band is about to play.

"Oh man, this is it! Perfect! This is where I want to stay!"

"Are you sure?" The man in the black suit smiles. "You'll be here for all of eternity."

"You know it! Forget that heavenly scene!"

The man in the black suit leaves. The musician turns to the bartender, orders his favorite drink, and asks, "Isn't it about time for the band to start, and can I sit in?"

"They're starting, and you can sit in if you want." The bartender lets out a huge sigh as the band begins to play...

To complete this joke, take the first ten seconds or so of the most **obnoxious song you can possibly think of** and sing it, but don't finish it; instead, repeat the obnoxious part over again and again without stopping!

Don't create a living hell for yourself by leaving your paradise of the moment. Refuse to allow obstacles to dissipate your most cherished gift: the **now.**

Enjoy Your "Present"

*If you want to understand your present, look at your past.
If you want to know your future, look at your present.*
-WISE SAYING-

Planning for the future is advisable; worry is not. Enjoying the present with all of its challenges will help us become lighthearted, carefree, and happy. How many times have our present moments been diminished considerably because of worrying about something else? Become one with the "here and now."

Wendy was taking a difficult essay exam in her senior philosophy class. She had studied hard for it, but just before the test, she had a major argument with her boyfriend. She was quite upset, and she couldn't stop thinking about the argument as she began the exam. She then realized her writing was far below her standard, and she began to worry about how badly her grade would be affected. She finished her exam with tears in her eyes, knowing she'd done poorly.

The challenge for Wendy was a big one. Let's look at two scenarios that illustrate being "in the present."

Scenario One: Wendy realizes there is nothing she can do for the next hour to improve the relationship with her boyfriend, so she blocks out all thoughts about the argument with the resolve that as soon as the exam is over, she will follow up on the situation and try to make everything better. The exam is the urgent task at the moment, and the dispute can be addressed further after the exam.

Hmm…possible for gurus, wizards, and guests who've been on Oprah.

Scenario Two: Wendy, knowing she cannot concentrate on the test, gets up and asks the professor to be allowed to send one text regarding a family emergency that she will not answer until after the exam. Most reasonable professors would allow that; she can even leave her phone in silent mode in a corner of the room. She texts something kind, even if she believes he was at fault, and then finishes the exam. At least that might provide some temporary relief to allow Wendy to continue.

So, you've got a pressing problem that worries you:

If you can do something about it, stop worrying and do it. If you cannot do anything about it, stop worrying! Worrying about a past or potential future event accomplishes two things:

- It depletes your energy.
- It diminishes or destroys the quality of your present moment.

Unless you act immediately on your problem, worry has zero benefit. It blows the door wide open to stress-related illnesses and potentially addictive behavior.

> *The fast pace of our lives makes it difficult for us to find grace in the present moment, and when the simple gifts at our fingertips cease to nourish us, we have a tendency to crave the sensational.*
> **-MACRINA WIEDERKEHR-**

WELL I'LL BE A BLUE-NOSED GOPHER

Avoid the non-stop suffering of "destination addiction," where happiness is always in the future or somewhere else! A person living in the "here and now" simply **does.**

Here we are. Here and now. That's all there is.
-RAM DASS-

Happiness Step Twenty
Your "Now" Moments

Think of three recent instances when you felt you were truly in the "now" moment.

Pick three recent instances when you felt you were **not** in the "now" moment, but you were somewhere else. In each case, what would you rather have been doing?

List three things in your life you are willing to CHANGE in order to have more NOW moments.

CHANGE _____

Don't neglect to **delete** something less important so you don't overload yourself!

DELETE _____

Repeat this for the other two instances you thought, "Come on. You can do it!" NO CHANGE, NO GAIN!

Indian Time

An eye-opening time management concept is "Indian time," which is a term I heard often in traditional Native American communities as they proudly describe an aspect of their traditional lifestyle with a dash of humor! In traditional Native American teachings, speech is slow and careful, and the greatest respect is paid to those who are speaking. Interruptions aren't tolerated, and there is no hurry because teachings are considered important. Indian time is about doing what **really** needs to be accomplished. Scheduled tasks are "preempted" when something more important comes up. Here's one example:

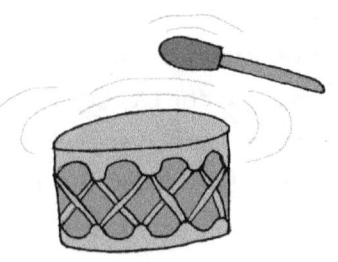

My wife and I were involved in organizing the "Mounds Pow Wow" in Whitewater, Wisconsin for five years. Our first year was a learning experience. The first "Grand Entry" (the main event where all dancers come out in full regalia) was scheduled at 1:00 p.m. on Saturday. It was a nice day, and a good crowd had gathered. As 1:00 approached, we noticed many of the dancers hadn't put on their outfits yet, and the head dancers were nowhere to be found. We had four or five drum groups there, but only one was anywhere near the grand entry area. At 1:00, people were looking at their watches, wondering when the "show" was going to start. The event started thirty minutes "late." What happened?

I learned about priorities that day. It turned out that at 1:00 p.m., some of the dancers, elders, and leaders of the event were simply "not ready" from a mental and spiritual standpoint. They could have run around, thrown on their outfits, and made a hasty dash to the dancing circle for the event to start "on time." Instead, it was more important to make sure all the necessary preparations were completed: saying prayers, purifying with traditional herbs (sage, sweetgrass, cedar), offering tobacco to God (the Great Spirit), and carefully putting on their outfits, of which every article had a special significance. Many of the elders had just arrived after leaving their homes at 4:00 a.m., and they needed a brief time to collect themselves mentally before beginning an entire afternoon (and evening) of dancing. Because the leaders waited to begin when everyone was "ready," the entire afternoon had a good feeling to it.

The best description of Indian time I know is:

You start when you're ready, and you finish when you're done.

You don't have to be Native American to use this principle. You'll never get **everything** done anyway, so delay some of those less important tasks, or don't do them at all! When you do what you love and prioritize properly, there will be no force or haste to your activities. Being happy involves valuing yourself and the important things you are doing and monitoring how you spend your time.

My wife, Toni, and I learned another lesson about being "ready" to do something in our fourth year as officers of the Whitewater, Wisconsin "Mounds Pow Wow."

> For ten months, the committee had been organizing this major community event. Two nights before the Pow Wow, our spiritual leader that year had the entire Pow Wow committee, head dancers, and head drum group gather for an outdoor feast. He brought with him a highly respected elder and medicine man. We soon realized this was more than a picnic. The real purpose of the feast was for this elder to ask "permission" from the creator (God) to have the event. We had been working on this for nearly a year! "Could the Pow Wow be cancelled just two days before the event?" we asked. The answer was: "Absolutely. If it doesn't feel right, we all go home."

"Have other Pow Wows like this been cancelled just before the event?" The reply was exactly the same. So, we all offered prayers for a good Pow Wow and visited. We honestly didn't know how this was going to go. Then a potential disaster occurred.

As the meal was served, my wife was asked to prepare the plate of food called the "spirit plate," which is offered to give thanks to the spirits (equivalent to angels in the Christian religion) for the food. A **small** (symbolic) portion of each food item is put on the plate, placed out by a tree, and left there overnight. Toni prepared the spirit plate and gave it to the man who had asked for it. To our horror, the man wasn't looking at the plate, mistook the spirit plate for a regular meal, and handed it to our distinguished guest as his dinner! The portions were tiny, and the food was all mixed up into an unrecognizable goulash! It was too late to correct the situation. The elder took the food and ate it with no visible reaction to his strange "dinner." He finished his plate, and suddenly a big grin appeared on his face. He started telling jokes, one after another, until the whole group was in stitches. Then he got up and said, "Let's sing some songs!" We all went to the drum and sang. That was the sure sign we were "ready" to do the Pow Wow!

While I've heard lots of good-natured jokes about "Indian time" from Native Americans at Pow Wows, it really teaches us not to do something unless it has a purpose and a good feel to it. This applies for everything we do. Since her brain injury, every time Toni gets off of the couch, bed, or chair, she announces, "I'm getting up now." Then she counts out loud: "One, two, and three!" If she doesn't quite make it up the first time, she'll have a good laugh and count off again until she actually does get up. She never gets up without that little count off, which tells us she's "ready," and it's undoubtedly kept her from falling!

Cats typically never do anything until they're ready. When they want to go outside, they do a yoga stretch, feline-style. That tells us they're prepared to venture into the great outdoors. If you think about it, you know when you're ready to do something.

Observe your thoughts about time. Do you catch yourself saying, "Hurry, hurry!" or "I'm too busy (to do what's important)"? Your thoughts create your reality. If you feel you don't have enough time, then your time management isn't accomplishing your higher purpose. Each day, tell yourself:

- I have all of the time I need.
- I do things in a relaxed, focused way.
- I have time each day to accomplish my higher purpose.

Have you ever known people who looked at their watch or the clock all of the time? I was one of those people.

Some years back, my wife gave me a colorful glass plaque of a Hopi Katcina dancer etched in sandstone. We hung it in the kitchen where the clock used to be and moved the clock to another room. For the next couple of months, I caught myself repeatedly glancing at where the clock used to be, but instead of seeing the time, I saw this Katcina figure looking at me as if to say, "Why do you want to know the time so often?" That little guy taught me about "Indian time" and helped me to look at the clock less often and focus on the moment. After enjoying the plaque for a couple of years, I gave it to a friend of mine who had had a heart attack, mainly due to stress. He was a compulsive clock-watcher too, and I told him to put it in place of a prominent clock in his home. He did, and soon the little Katcina had helped another poor obsessed clock-watcher!

Quality Time

Is it "quality time" yet? Unfortunately, that phrase is really a disguise for "not enough time." Industrial society's long-term obsession with obtaining money and power at all costs makes "quality time" (precious moments with family, kids, or any soul-nourishing activity) in danger of extinction. The implication is we should live a life of mostly "non-quality" moments (doing **what**?) and reserve only a few moments for quality time. Let's call it what it is: **time slavery!**

"Little Johnny" (yes, that was me!) was a very obedient **time slave,** receiving praise for always being in the office late at night working. Time slaves believe seventy-hour workweeks are good, and forty-hour workweeks are only for lazy slobs. Excessive careerism is a societal "should" that elevates the workplace above all human activities: child-care, marriage, personal time, community service, and cultural enrichment. If you suddenly passed away tomorrow, could you say you had enough "quality time"? End your time slavery **now.** Make **every** moment quality time!

Some quality moments can be uncomfortable and uncertain.

> *I am exactly where I need to be at this moment. All I need*
> *to do is figure out where the hell I am at this moment.*
> **–MARCIA MENTER–**

The dance of life is to make each moment as meaningful as possible. This does wonders for improving our outlook on life, our behavior, and our relationships. Each moment is uniquely different, and it will not come again. Each moment is a precious gem, which is why I always say, "Have a meaningful day."

CHAPTER THIRTEEN
THE UNCERTAIN FUTURE

Whose Agenda are We Following, Anyway?

The future **is** uncertain. How do we not let the storm clouds of an unknown future batter our sunny day? I once thought getting everything done would help my future, so I would dutifully start a to-do list, but then I felt like a total loser when I didn't complete it. So, I'd run around like a madman and get everything done, but instead of celebrating like I'd won Wimbledon, I felt less useful than my ten-year-old bottle of liquid paper. Why? (Here comes that bolt of lightning!) What I'd "accomplished" wasn't my higher purpose!

Make sure your "now" moments satisfy **your** soul and not someone else's vision for what your life ought to be. Otherwise, you're like an expert roofer that spends all summer roofing the wrong house! The question is: Are you planning **your** future?

Dr. Wayne Dyer's *Wisdom of the Ages* uses an untitled poem by E.E. Cummings to point out how easily we can follow someone else's agenda through misuse of these seemingly innocent words in our thoughts and speech:

- may,
- might,
- should,
- could,
- would, and
- must.

Let's see how these words can derail our personal agenda and sabotage our time management!

May, Might

It's no problem to ask: "May I have some red pepper for my pizza?" But before you sneeze, it's the other uses of these two words that put the completion of a deed in serious doubt! "May" and "might" imply we don't really trust ourselves with what we're going to do and leave the option of canceling our actions wide open. "I may/might do something" opens up the possibility of failure or non-achievement in our own minds and leaves a gaping **space** for something to get in the way! These words reveal doubt and weaken intention, leaving your mind easily open to the possibility of not manifesting your goal. How often do you say, "I may…" or "I might…"?

Examples:

"I **may** go to the university next semester."

Let's have a **plan.** Try this:

"I **will** go to the university next semester. Even if my financial aid falls through, I've got enough money for two courses. I'll work part-time to earn enough for two more classes the following semester."

Kudos! Another one:

"I **might** get my taxes done this weekend."

This is a special invitation to procrastination! How about:

I **am** getting up at 7:00 a.m. on Saturday morning to make some bacon, eggs, tortillas, and salsa, plus hair-raisingly strong coffee. I'll hit those taxes and work until 11:00 a.m. If I'm not done, I'll finish them from 4:00 p.m. to 6:00 p.m. on either Saturday or Sunday and put them in the mail by Sunday night!

Any questions?

The next three words are related to each other like bad cousins, and you can put them in any order!

Should

"Should" implies looking into the past and lamenting over how something "should have been done" or "should have turned out." If we think we should have done something, who is it that thinks this? Regardless of whether the "should" comes from us or others, we can't change what we did, so move on! The time we spent fussing over what should have happened ought to be spent on **making** something happen!

This applies to our current and future actions, too!

"I **should** own a home…"

Who is it that drives this "should"? Is this **your** agenda, or is your best friend a realtor? If it's your agenda, then act on it with a distinct plan.

"Since it makes financial sense for me to buy now, I **will** look into some properties and see what my options are. I'll soon be a homeowner."

But if you think you should own a home because you're not a homeowner and others your age are, then you're trying to follow the agenda of people you **don't even know!** Try this:

"While my parents, friends, and financial advisors tell me it's a good idea, I would rather keep my options open for travel, so I'm **not** a homeowner right now. The fact that I plan to relocate out of state in a year or two also figures into this decision."

Whatever the options, there are no "shoulds."

Could, Would

"Could" and "would" also allow doubt to block something we desire. As Dr. Dyer stated in his discussion, using these terms are "indications a vacancy sign is displayed because the brain's owner is unavailable." How many times do people exclaim, "I would do it, if only I could!" These words (or escapes from reality) will keep us from what we "would" or "could" do. How many "woulds" and "coulds" do you use and in what context? When we lived in East Texas, we heard people say "might-could," as in, "I might-could ask my boss for a raise." Regardless of the word combinations, are you allowing doubt to sneak into your life?

"We **could** go to Bermuda for a vacation."

You could also stay home and paint the bathroom. What is it you **really** want?

"We're **going** to Bermuda. I just bought the tickets for March first."

I'm cheering! Here's another one.

"I **would** sing for a living because I really love it, but…"

But **what**? Two possible ways out of this one…

"I **choose** not to sing for a living because my family is more important to me, and I want a stable, steady income without travel. I enjoy my current job enough to keep doing it, and I'm happy just singing occasionally."

Bravo! Or…

"I'm **going** to be a singer as my main profession. I love it more than anything else, and I'm prepared for the hard work, travel, and sacrifices I need to make to have the privilege to perform for a living."

Bravo again!

Must

The most criminal verbal violation of all is "must." When we "must" do something, we spend countless wasted hours doing things we think we "have to do" that are really the demands of our ego or of other people. Dr. Dyer called this "musterbating," which occurs when we continually think: "I must do this" or "I must do that" because we are **unable**  **to direct our own lives!** We "must" not do anything. It's too rigid of a word to apply except in dire or life-threatening circumstances. Following our higher purpose requires more flexibility than the word "must" can ever give us.

"I **must** do the laundry and clean up the kitchen."

Let's clarify this:

"I'll **do** the laundry and clean up the kitchen today. It's my top priority because we have company tonight."

Or…

"While things are a mess, I've got a project due tomorrow, so I'll just use paper plates and wear my old jeans and T-shirt today. I'll do the kitchen tomorrow night and the wash the next day."

Make today **your** day. Will you have the strength to be **very** selective with your "must dos," or will your identity be as lost as a "404 not found" web page? How many times do you think, say, or write the words "may," "might," "should," "could," "would," or "must" in a day? Notice also what others have you do without your consent, no matter how well-intended it seems.

Do, Actually

The words "do" and "actually" can also reveal doubt with our intentions.

"I **do** want to spend more time with my family and work fewer hours!"

A "reality check" translation: "I (actually) **do** want to spend more time with my family and work fewer hours, but some people, including myself, doubt I'll do this now or **ever.**"

This goal needs **commitment.**

"I'm spending more time with my family and working fewer hours, starting next week. No more overtime!"

Here's a way the word "actually" is often used with a negative spin:

"You **actually** cleaned your room!"

This really means: "What? You cleaned your room? I can't believe it 'cuz it's always a stinkin' mess!" There's not only sarcastic surprise about the good deed, but it flings past wrongdoings toward the "room cleaner" and tarnishes the merit of the activity. Even if the room was cleaned with good intentions, this is a **slam,** not a compliment.

A more considerate alternative:

"Your room looks great!"

The words "do" and "actually" can also imply disbelief about one's self or from others.

"I **do** talk to my teachers." (I know you don't believe me, but I do!)

"I **do** want to be an artist." (I haven't been sure, but I think I do!)

Next time you use "do" and "actually" in this way, ask yourself: "Where is all this doubt coming from?"

Pay careful attention to your thoughts and words to make sure you are managing **your** time, not someone else's! The choices about how you spend your time are yours, so carry them out with your special touch!

Happiness Step Twenty-One
Good Riddance to Weak Verbiage!

Which of these words (may, might, could, should, would, must, do, actually) **most often** weakens your resolve to do something? _____
Think of an example where you've used that word in a way that implies doubt or following someone else's agenda. Now rephrase that sentence to remove all doubt!

_____

_____

_____

_____

Any others? Repeat this as often as it does you some good! Enter these in your daily planner as an affirmation of what you **will** do because it's **your** agenda!

Uncertainty Shouldn't Be Uncomfortable

Everyone wonders what the future will be like at one time or another. There has been a huge demand for psychic hotlines with "experts" predicting the future and telling people what they may, might, should, could, would, and must do with their lives. People relinquish their judgment and control to a stranger for a few costly minutes. Would you put your life savings in a bag, walk into a busy city street, and give the bag to a stranger to watch over it?

With the influx of psychics, anyone with a genuine gift has one-half of a snowball's chance in hell of having credibility. There are people out there with genuine psychic gifts, and many of them do **not** go into business for profit. Strong intuitive abilities exist in all of us, and whether we develop them or not depends on if we're willing to work on them and how strongly we've been programmed to fear or ignore them.

A vision or description of a future event is a "possible reality." If someone predicts you are destined to become a great leader, and two minutes later you step out into the street and get hit by a speeding truck, then that is that. If someone tells you to watch out before crossing the street, and you're extra careful, do you live a long life because of the warning you were given?

A prediction can come to fruition, but only if the event sensed in the prediction continues to evolve over time and develop into the possible reality. Predictions can be inaccurate if something we do in the present alters that future.

WELL I'LL BE A BLUE-NOSED GOPHER

Nothing splendid has ever been achieved except by those who dared believe that something inside of them was superior to circumstance.
-BRUCE BARTON-

Barton challenges the belief that the universe is nothing but a random series of chaotic events (although my jazz band rehearsals resembled that sometimes!). Art, musical compositions, and theatre productions are examples of predictability versus randomness and tension versus release. Live performances have a special spontaneous quality, which is far more rewarding than watching a video. In the same way, the future is always a battleground of control versus chaos.

If you could know the exact future, would you really want to? Maybe I **don't** want to know in advance that the Cubs are going to blow it in the ninth inning. I had to be coerced into seeing *Titanic* because I knew the ship was going down! The best stories have twists and unexpected turns. Our future will be the same. Changing circumstances will lead us to new horizons we never expected. The best we can do is to keep a clear picture of what we want our future to be like, be open to all possibilities, and use the present to empower a bright future.

Uncertainty of the future can make us afraid, but the future can be better than we ever imagined! Every choice you make, no matter how small, has enormous potential. Remain alert to opportunities through your realization of the uncertain future. "Lucky breaks" really don't come about by accident.

Breakthroughs happen when your prepared goals connect with opportunity.

Some people are hesitant to follow through with a goal because it will take a long time to accomplish:

Anita was a very successful accountant. One day, she confided to her best friend: "You know what? I hate my job! I've always wanted to be a doctor."

Her friend asked, "Then why don't you become a doctor? You're brilliant. I know you'd be a great doctor!"

Anita complained, "But it will take me ten years to be a doctor, and I'm thirty-five already! I'd be forty-five before I become one!"

Her friend then asked, "Anita, how old will you be in ten years if you're **not** a doctor?"

Anita can have what she wants if she's willing to be persistent with her career change. Once you have an intention to do something, there will be new choices to make that require flexibility and openness to new possibilities when they arrive. Sometimes opportunities happen suddenly, but if you've kept sight of your highest ideals, you'll be ready for them, and you will be less likely to settle for outdated solutions.

It's what you do with your time **right now** that helps your happiness. Obsession over the future is an attempt to escape from an unsatisfying present. Are you a "waiter"—always waiting for a future that never happens the way you want it? Bring your future into the present by living tomorrow's dream today!

 ## Happiness Step Twenty-Two
A Happier Future

- Am I dedicating enough time to my most important higher purpose? YES NO
- Are my goals realistic and challenging? YES NO
- Am I happy with the balance in my life between work and pleasure? YES NO
- Have I simplified my life? YES NO
- Am I taking enough time for personal development? YES NO

When you can answer "yes" to all five questions, your sense of happiness and well-being will soar like an eagle!

- In your quiet time, imagine several of your favorite possible futures, and while you do this, notice when you get a really joyful feeling. When that happens, hang onto that vision and do everything you can to bring it to fruition!
- What is one choice you could make that would significantly improve your chances at having a positive future?

What are you waiting for? Begin working toward that choice right now! Enter some actions you will do into your schedule, and each day, congratulate yourself when you do something toward fulfilling that happier future!

SECTION FOUR
Embracing Endless Energy

CHAPTER FOURTEEN
ENERGY—GOT SOME?

The Energy around Us

Don't you want to feel enthusiastic, effortless, inspired, creative, and charged with energy? I can get that feeling until my double espresso wears off! How do we keep a high enough energy level to accomplish ambitious goals? Before ordering another espresso, let's notice how energy works in terms of matter, light, sound, thought, and spirit.

According to laws of physics, energy cannot be created or destroyed; it can only be transformed. Material objects, light, and sound all emit energy. However, when it comes to studying energy related to our thoughts and our spiritual energy, we're about as advanced as the Flintstones.

Energy not only surrounds people and/or objects, but it can remain in an area for some time. An old house or building, for example, can retain residual energy from its past inhabitants. Some people are sensitive to the energy from emotional impressions left behind. This is strange to those who only recognize what can be seen with the naked eye, but just because we can't see something doesn't mean it doesn't exist. You can't see wind, but you can sure feel it! Sound waves, TV signals, and magnetic fields are examples of invisible energy. Whatever energy is left from traumatic past events can't be analyzed very well with our current technology, but it clearly exists, and it can be felt by those sensitive to it. For instance, I speculate that most people would not want to sleep in the same bed where someone had been brutally murdered, even if the bed were cleaned up. I believe developing an awareness of the energy surrounding us is a valuable skill to develop.

We sense physical objects (matter) according to how close they are to us. Every object has its own unique energy, as does every individual person. For example, if someone is within a few inches of you, you will sense his or her physical energy in your personal space.

Next, we sense energy through sight and sound from our most frequented immediate surroundings: our home, workplace, or any area we can see and hear. This energy has much to do with influencing our overall emotional state. That's why it's vital to make your immediate environment as healthy and pleasant as possible (see Happiness Step Six). You can also take steps to block outside negative emotions that may be circulating in your immediate area. If the environment you frequent resembles Alcatraz, then take whatever measures necessary to change it or evacuate! Until you can change it or leave, send love toward whatever trouble there is. Imagine bathing negative thoughts and energies in white light. Negative energy only feeds off of more negative energy. If you think about it, it's hard to hate something forever that only sends you love!

The next type of energy we sense is thought energy, which extends out indefinitely and is subtler than the others. It's easy to pretend our thoughts don't matter to our external environment. While we can't see thoughts, we can certainly witness their results! For instance, we haven't yet scientifically proven what love energy looks like, but the power of it is undeniable. Love alone has the power to bring humanity together. When enough people realize the power of thought energy, the impact will create a paradigm shift in human consciousness that will rival the invention of the internet!

Last, but very important, is your spiritual energy—that unrestricted part of who you are. Since the universe (or God, if you will) is naturally unrestricted, your higher nature is in your spiritual energy field already. Negative emotions and evil emit a frequency that is separate from the divine light. Negative energy is empowered only if you pay attention to it or allow it in. Keep your energy fields clean and uncontaminated!

Every thought you have can either strengthen or weaken you. To have higher energy, you have to strengthen your thoughts. Higher-frequency thoughts help you to…

- move in motion with your higher self,
- water the seeds of imagination and creativity,
- do what you love,
- give kindness without expectation,
- remember to forgive, and
- surround yourself with spiritual role models.

Expand your reality. Give your problems up to spiritual guidance, meditate, and/or pray. Know that, in its own unique way, the universe will answer back!

How's Your Energy Level?

All of us have energy highs and lows. I can bounce around like a three-week-old puppy in the morning, but by mid-afternoon, I'm dragging like a giant sloth. Our bodies cannot go full throttle 100 percent of the time any more than a runner can run a marathon at a full sprint. Yet we try to force ourselves to work when we're tired, manipulating our energy with energy bars, sugary foods, or my old standby—anything with caffeine! Daily energy peaks and valleys are related to diet, sleep, and emotional balance, but it is also related to how much of your life is related to your higher purposes.

It makes sense to do our most important activities when we have the highest energy, but that's not always possible. However, consciously matching your most important work with your higher daily energy can really make a difference! For example, you might prefer an early morning workout if you come home at night physically exhausted from work. If you have a sedentary job, you might want to work out over the noon hour or right after work. If you catch your co-workers autographing the permanent imprints of your butt on your office chair, take the hint!

Unless you're fully bionic or on a steady diet of kryptonite, you'll need to pace yourself. Expending energy too quickly can create exhaustion and burnout, while starting too slowly can force us into a frenzied catch-up mode. Know when to hold 'em and when to fold 'em. Don't gamble your energy away on wasted time.

So, you want a higher energy level in your life? ("Yes!" I would yell. Then I'd look at my to-do list and crawl back in bed.) The principle is this:

> To have more energy, you must first allow the **time and space** for more energy to come in! This means making room for the activities in your life that bring you good energy.

WELL I'LL BE A BLUE-NOSED GOPHER

Happiness Step Twenty-Three
Energy Check!

Take a moment to note when your energy peaks and valleys are. Draw a line from left to right, and place the vertical height of your line above the corresponding hours of time as it represents your energy levels over twenty-four hours during a typical **day where you went to your job or workplace.**

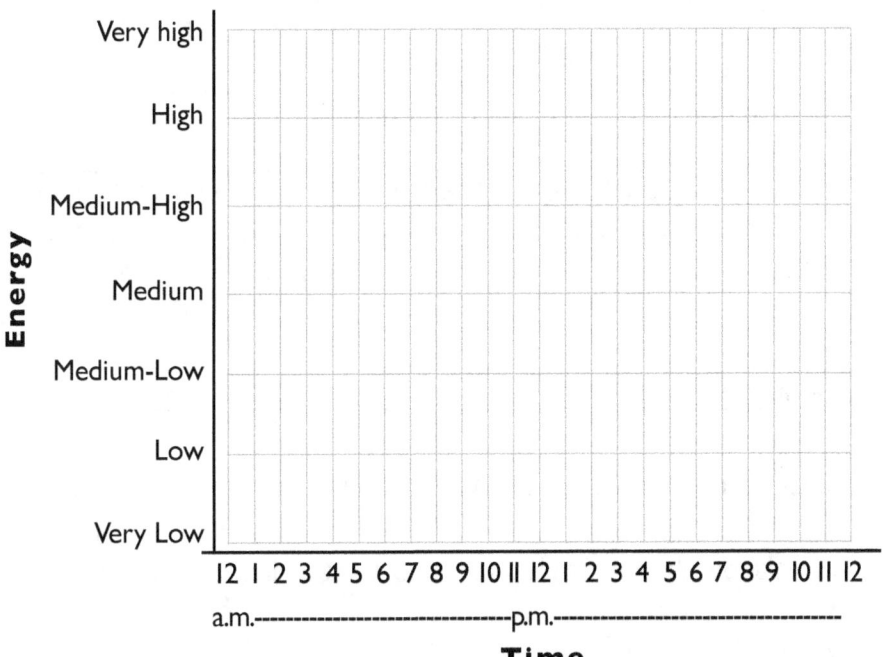

Next, draw a line from left to right, and place the vertical height of your line above the corresponding hours of time as it represents your energy levels over twenty-four hours during a typical leisure day **where you did not work at your job.**

List one meaningful activity you do that would be more effective if scheduled at a time of higher energy:

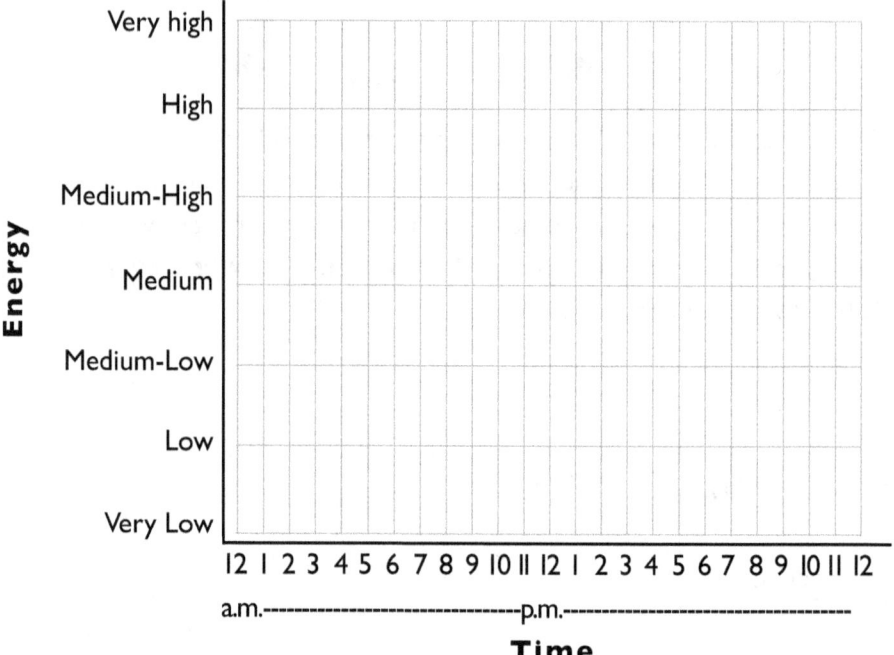

Activity _____

Current time _____ Improved Time _____

To make the above possible, I will move this activity _____

to this time _____

If you've got others, there's no time like the present to change your energy patterns! Schedule these changes into your daily planners!

Directing and Exchanging Energy

We absolutely can use energy to direct ourselves toward a positive future. Dr. Depak Chopra's *Law of Intention and Desire* shows us that we can create a conscious change in our lives through the qualities of attention and intention. What we pay attention to will grow stronger, while intention gives us the ability to keep our goal in sight. Your attention to your goals now, added to your intention for your future goals, will manifest positive results—as long as they are in line with your higher purposes (referred to by Dr. Chopra as the spiritual laws of success).

Have you ever experienced a time where everything just seemed to go your way and fall into place? This was no fluke, but it came about because the energy of your body and mind was in flow with the universe. The organizing potential of our attention/intention is exactly why thought energy can bring about a meaningful life.

If you've felt like a mere bug on the windshield of life, there's good news! You're **not** an insignificant blob drifting in outer space without a pilot! **All** thoughts and actions (good and not-so-good) generate energy that goes out and ultimately comes back to us. Every single thought and action **matters**.

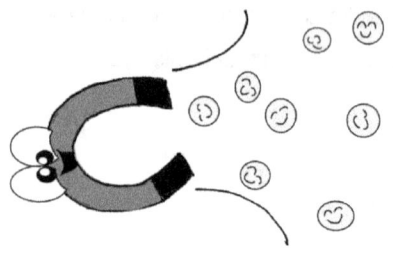

The energy you create through positive thoughts and actions will attract the circumstances you need for growth. In a magnetic field, when a critical mass of one type of molecules is present within an area, they attract other molecules to them. The same thing happens with our thoughts.

If your intentions and what you pay attention to are aligned with your higher purpose, than that thought energy, if sustained over time, will bring powerful, positive results!

For good energy, keep the goals you want foremost in your mind daily, free of fears and doubts. Let your intuition guide you about when to do what's important, and how to pace your energy throughout the day. When you keep your batteries charged by loving what you do and working on something meaningful, there is no limit to what you can create!

Unless you're dining at a five-star restaurant in Paris, nothing is handed to you on a silver platter. Don't throw in the towel when you don't get the results you were expecting. Allow yourself one good yell or a short cry, and then pick yourself up and realize each difficulty you encounter enables you to fine-tune your direction. Any mortal who ever accomplished something significant encountered trials and tribulations along the way. If there's apprehension, a sense of dread, or an energy drain regarding your goal, it's a sure bet you need to reassess why those feelings are taking place.

Energy is more than about **me, myself, and I.** The universe is designed for constant energy exchanges—to give freely and receive graciously. No matter how many problems you may be coping with, if you stop and think of the many gifts you've been given (yes, even that two-year-old fruitcake you've stashed), then the significance of being generous is a no-brainer. The question is how to best to do this in a way that works for you.

Give to others the same kinds of energy you want to receive—a smile, positive thoughts, and love, without the intention to get it back. Ironically, these come back to us in even greater amounts! "Rewards" often pop up unexpectedly, and then we wonder why we deserved such good fortunes!

Make giving part of your nature. The sun distributes its energy everywhere without discrimination (although northern winters made me wonder!). When we give, we're not giving what's "ours" to anyone. We don't really "own" anything; we're just using it for a while and then redistributing it to those who need what we have to offer.

An altruistic attitude elevates our energy field and reduces personal suffering. If you lose a kidney due to illness, you suffer, but if you volunteer one of your kidneys to save a loved one's life, the suffering is less because of the willingness to make a sacrifice. The most meaningful things we do are activities intended to benefit others. If you're a pet owner, you have to be altruistic (our cats remind us of that daily!). You buy them food, give them unconditional love, and they become valuable members of the family. That's altruism in action.

People who give genuinely are the happiest beings on Earth. They unselfishly help others and don't discriminate who they help. Realistically, if it weren't for the hard work, dedication, and kindness of people we don't even know, we wouldn't accomplish anything! That's why it makes little sense to be discriminating about who we help, particularly if someone has a need for what we can offer.

Ultimately, love is the reason why we help others. Pick a way to contribute that's meaningful and within your time and budget. Offer help because there's nothing else you'd rather be doing. Jesus constantly demonstrated that acts of service to others are the highest work you can do on Earth. To sacrifice resources and time for a worthy cause is part of everyone's sacred higher purpose.

Sometimes we just get too wrapped up in our problems to think of helping others, or we feel what we offer won't matter. We're culturally ingrained to think that people in poverty, hospitals, prisons, nursing homes, or homeless shelters are like a bottomless pit that we can't help. Organizations requesting charitable gifts overflow our mailbox. Yet, if a gift you give helps but **one** person, it does make a difference! Poverty and suffering can be overcome—one person at a time. We've all endured suffering, so why turn away from others who suffer?

In order to give effectively, we also have to know how to receive! We usually get in life what we wish others to have. Feeling satisfied with what we have is vital because most of us have an abundance of things to be thankful for. "I don't have enough" tends to continue scarcity! If you send loving thoughts toward others, love will eventually come back to you. When you see the good in others, you'll see the good in yourself.

Many have trouble accepting good fortune or praise because they feel unworthy. Sometimes gifts come when we're at a low point in our lives, making it a challenge to believe the good fortune "should" happen!

A tropical storm was blowing full force with flooding of epic proportions. A preacher had decided to stay behind to watch over his church building. As the waters seeped in, a man in a rowboat offered him a ride.

The preacher waved. "No, thank you. God will take care of me." So the man in the rowboat left.

The waters now raged into the church, forcing the preacher up to the second floor window. A fisherman in a canoe came by and offered to take him to safety.

The preacher again responded, "No, thank you. God will take care of me." The man in the canoe left.

Now the waters rose into furious waves, forcing the preacher to the rooftop. A huge barge sounded its horn, and the people on it offered to rescue him. "No, thank you. God will take care of me."

As the barge left, a huge wave toppled the preacher off of the roof.

Soon the preacher arrived at the pearly gates of heaven, and a booming voice said, "Why are you here? It's not your time yet…"

"Gee, Lord, I thought you were going to take care of me, so I waited!"

"I sent you a rowboat, a canoe, and a huge barge! What were you expecting—a cruise ship?"

If you've ever given something to someone that they didn't accept or appreciate, you know that awkward feeling. I would rather fart in church than go through that! When I remember someone who sincerely loved what I gave them, I felt like I was giving away the grand prize on *Jeopardy!* So say thanks. Accept gifts, good fortune, love, and even compliments graciously! When you are open to the gifts the universe has to offer, abundance will  arrive. That's why learning how to receive is just as important as learning how to give!

When you've found inner peace with yourself, you'll have endless energy. Each day, put your attention and intention toward what's important. Add to that your intuitive power plus generosity, and you gain the ability to direct your energy toward a magnificent future.

CHAPTER FIFTEEN
OVERCOMING ENERGY BLOCKERS AND DRAINERS

Meteor Showers and Black Holes

Using energy wisely works wonders until our Starship Enterprise is ripped apart by huge meteors, and we crash-land on Planet Klingon! I call these meteors "energy blockers and drainers." An "energy blocker" is anything that interferes with our valuable personal energy. Some are mere nuisances, like pebbles to our starship, but others are more like asteroids, enough to block or even demolish the energy we need to complete an important goal. An "energy drainer" is like a fuel leak to your "ship" that happens when the energy you put out is being flushed down the cosmic toilet or sucked out of you like a giant black hole! Let's look at six common energy offenders.

Obvious Energy Blockers and Drainers

- Unnecessary activities
- Poor pacing or timing of your energy
- Poor health

Subtle Energy Blockers and Drainers

- Fear and doubt
- Attachments
- The Energy Void

Unnecessary Activities

There may be a few indolent hedonists who take relaxation and recreation to excess, but a much more common energy blocker is compulsive "busyness" in activities that aren't the most important ones. This often goes unnoticed because while there is lots of activity, it isn't what really needs to be done. What an energy-zapper!

> Bob has been really busy and is behind on a major report due to his boss at 8:00 a.m. the next morning. At 7:00 p.m., he begins the report, which will take him about five hours. Then "stuff" happens:
>
> - A friend drops in to visit. (Thirty minutes)
> - Bob gets four calls on his cell phone, and he answers all of them. (Twenty minutes)
> - He stops to cook some dinner, and he realizes he's out of some ingredients he needs and drives to the store. He returns, cooks, eats, and does the dishes. (Ninety minutes)
> - Taking out the trash, Bob stops to say hello to a neighbor. (Fifteen minutes)

- There's a good ball game on TV so Bob has it on in the background. It's an exciting and close game, too. (Thirty minutes)
- Bob decides to do a load of laundry. (Thirty minutes)
- He converses with twelve different people through texts and answers four emails. (Forty minutes)
- After the ball game, Bob can't decide what music to play. After considerable browsing, he finds something. (Fifteen minutes)

It's after midnight, and Bob has only done minimal work on his report. He's beginning to get very tired. He makes coffee, and he works furiously on the report. Despite the coffee, he falls asleep at the computer, wakes up at 5:00 a.m., and writes the report in a near panic. He arrives to work tired, disheveled, stressed, and unprepared.

-THE ABOVE PERSON'S NAME HAS BEEN CHANGED TO PROTECT THE GUILTY-

Do the math: he wasted **four and a half hours**, yet Bob was very "busy." It's easy to come up with suggestions to reduce his non-essential activities. He could have excused himself politely from the friend, saved the laundry until the next night, not answered the phone, fixed something quick for dinner, recorded the ball game, and resisted checking and answering e-mails. He would have had a higher quality report done by midnight, minus the stress and energy loss Bob suffered that evening and the next morning.

There was nothing wrong with any of Bob's activities; he just did them **at the wrong time.** The following evening, the same activities would have been fine. Procrastination, combined with being "busy" with lesser priorities, will have a devastating effect if continued over time.

There are likely deeper reasons for Bob's **ir**responsibility. Maybe he hates doing reports and is better suited for another line of work! If you continually place **other** activities in front of what you're supposed to be doing, take a hard look at what you're supposed to be doing. Does it match what you really want?

Poor Pacing or Timing of Your Energy

Unless you're Robocop or the Bionic Woman, you have a finite supply of daily energy. Poor pacing or timing of your energy will bring results from the den of mediocrity. How? One common fault is overworking when tired. What you do is less creative, more stressful, and is either rushed or stagnates due to fatigue. To avoid long-term consequences, take a step back, look in the mirror, and ask yourself why you believe you "must" work under these conditions! Reevaluate your life **before** health problems begin.

Another energy blocker is failure to use available time for something important when we **have** the energy. Procrastination in moments of good energy can be costly because we don't always have it. We might lead ourselves to believe energy can be "banked" somehow, which is about as reliable as public Wi-Fi. Too many attempts to bank or manipulate your energy ultimately create later energy loss or even illness.

The timing of what we do has everything to do with energy effectiveness. Tune into your personal energy by noticing it often. If it feels right to do something right now, then do it. If doing that "something" never feels good, then reassess why you're doing it and if it's worth doing.

Here's to Your Health

The greatest energy blocker of all (often taken for granted) is poor health. If you become seriously ill, priorities change in a hurry. Medical professionals agree that good mental and spiritual health directly influence physical health, which is a pretty compelling reason for research on happiness!

How often we become ill largely depends on our immune system, which can ward off nearly any attack when the elements of air, fire (energy), earth (solid matter), water, and space are balanced in our bodies. Stress and emotional disturbances create imbalance, which lower our resistance to invaders. Physical difficulties are often the result of spiritual difficulties. Our individual physiology is heavily influenced by our thoughts as well as our health habits. We blame germs and viruses for the cause of illnesses, but unless the plague of the century arrives, illnesses happen when our bodies allow the **possibility** for the immune system or an organ to break down, which is usually created via negative emotions, prolonged stress, or poor health habits. If a tree is rotten on the inside, it will topple. Peace and tranquility are not only critical for our health but for our very existence!

Getting sick is more than coincidence—it's a sign you need to love or care for yourself more. With illness, the body creates a mandatory "slow down and take care of yourself" period. If not heeded, you could become seriously ill. When necessary, our higher selves literally allow an illness to provide our body an opportunity to release old energies, rest, and re-energize. Illness challenges us to open our hearts and bring the mental and physical system together in more harmony.

Ask yourself: "If I caught a cold, what nurturing thing would I do for myself?" Take a day **soon** to do those exact things. When you love and

honor yourself more, you raise your vibration and the course of any illness changes. "Miracle" cures occur when people make a drastic attitude change toward life!

An unforeseen blessing from my wife's memory loss is that she has "forgotten" about illness! It's simply not on her radar. Once, while she was still in the hospital, she got pneumonia, and we were quite worried, but whenever we asked her how she felt, she would smile and say, "I'm fine. I'll be all right." Then she'd laugh her little laugh. When she was hit by a car that fateful night, she told the woman who ran to help her, "I'll be all right." Despite the trauma, Toni **knew** she would be all right. Toni's had just two colds in the last ten years. After dental work, she takes a nap when we get home, and when she wakes up, she's forgotten she was ever there and never needs even aspirin! It's no coincidence that her happiness, daily laughter, and a supportive environment keep her illness-free.

Good diet, regular exercise, clean air, and enough rest are keys to living a balanced life. Each day, nurture your mind, body, and spirit.

I was particularly impressed when I visited the Maharishi University of Management in Fairfield Iowa. In the 1950s, His Holiness, Maharishi Mahesh Yogi, brought the ancient Vedic practice of Transcendental Meditation to the modern world. At the university, students meditated daily for two hours in the morning and two hours in the evening. Rather than elicit the "do whatever it takes to learn this material or else…" mentality, the faculty emphasized good exercise, a healthy diet, and proper rest to enable meaningful learning. During my three visits there, I was amazed at how engaged the university students were in the learning process, regardless of the subject. The meditation and the emphasis on health was a major factor in the success of their students.

Ask your body what it needs to be healthy. If you pay attention, your body will usually signal you when you need a certain kind of food, if you're restless due to lack of exercise, or if you're tired.

With the expense of medical insurance and side effects of prescription drugs today, my recommendation is the DGS insurance plan: **Don't Get Sick!** If only insurance companies would cover preventative programs instead of waiting until something's broken. I envision a world where we pay medical professionals to keep us healthy on a regular basis, and if someone becomes ill, then there's no charge to anyone.

I'm not the perfect embodiment of health by any means. As a teenager, I should have been the poster boy for Clearasil and, later in life, a model example of weight loss products that **didn't** work! I'm no expert, but I try to follow these principles (okay, with occasional cheats) in order to be able to practice happiness with the best possible health:

Drink plenty of good drinking water (not tap water!).

Go organic as much as you can afford: fruits, vegetables, meats, spices, and cleaning supplies. Otherwise, you ingest harmful chemicals and toxins.

Reduce or eliminate foods with white flour, white sugar, table salt, or pork.

Avoid fast foods because of poor nutrition and "hidden" addicting chemicals! Why do you think the triple-bacon cheeseburger exists and **sells?**

Be very picky about restaurants. Notice the food quality but also take in the "vibes." Thoughts are energy, and they definitely influence food quality. The mood and temperament of cooks and servers affect the food you consume. Follow this ancient Vedic principle followed by millions of people worldwide: never eat or prepare food if angry.

Reduce or eliminate all artificial sweeteners and products that contain aspartame, sucrulose, splenda, dextrose, sucrose, fructose, artificial flavors, and artificial colors in foods. Eliminate or drastically reduce sodas and diet sodas.

Eliminate or drastically reduce high fructose corn syrup, monosodium glutamate (MSG), hydrogenated oil or partially hydrogenated oil, palm oil, and trans fats.

Do not buy food products filled with ingredients you cannot pronounce. Many of these are labeled "all-natural" ingredients.

Do not put anything toxic on your body that you couldn't eat without calling poison control; use natural cosmetics and skin products.

Get proper rest. It's always been said that early to bed and early to rise is best. (I confess: I'm typing this at 12:20 a.m.!) Some of us have a different biological clock, so at least observe the first sentence!

Exercise daily. Do what works for you, and be persistent. Exercise is also a great way to help your body to rid itself of toxins!

Reduce or eliminate smoking!

Avoid the stress of having to continually drive in heavy traffic to the best of your ability. Do not use a handheld cell phone while driving.

Be grateful. Laugh often. Give love and hugs. Take breaks from work.

Enjoy nature, get outside, and get sunlight whenever possible!

Enjoy your pets. Enjoy your plants. Enjoy your relationships with people and this beautiful planet Earth. Love life while you have it!

Setting meaningful goals, self-discovery, and having good energy are nearly impossible if your health is poor. I believe poor health can be inextricably linked to lack of self-discovery because our mental, spiritual, and physical selves are all connected. Knowing your higher self and having good health are all connected. Here's to your health!

CHAPTER SIXTEEN
SUBTLE ENERGY-ZAPPERS

Fear and Doubt (Again!)

We've looked at the obvious energy blockers and drainers in the last chapter, but the subtle ones can also zap our energy like a leaking tire. The first perpetrators are the perennial partners of fear and doubt, which bring an avalanche of anxiety about the past, present, and future. Timothy Gallwey wrote a number of books about how to overcome stress as it affects performance, and in *The Inner Game of Music*, co-authored with Barry Green, the mindset of "relaxed concentration" is delved into. Whether working, giving an important presentation, or playing a tennis match, you simply focus on what you're doing, not allowing worry about the result to affect performance.

When you get a surge of energy to do something major in your life, fear and doubt may show up, or comments from others can rain on your parade, even if the remarks are well intended.

Rose is very excited about her plans to own her own bookstore/coffee shop. Let's look at what her friends tell her.

- "It's really hard to start your own business these days. Statistics show that most first-time businesses fail."
- "You have to know exactly what people want, and tastes change with the wind."
- "You know coffee prices are going up constantly. You'll lose profit on food, and the health department will always be checking up on you."
- "You'll be competing against corporate stores that can get everything cheap. How will you make it?"
- "It's hard to find good employees. You'll have a lot of turnover."
- "Your customers will stay in your store for hours reading for free and buying only the occasional cup of coffee."
- "You'll have really long hours; you'll never get away, and you'll have to keep perfect financial records."
- "Rent for your building will be high; everything costs more than you think it will. Oh, those utilities!"
- "Like the world needs another bookstore and coffeehouse! Get real!"

After this, Rose might only have energy for a long nap! She'll need a lot of courage, resolve, and commitment to override the crushing weight of these comments. We can't bury our heads in the sand regarding our endeavors, yet, the truth is that we admire fearless people. There are countless success stories about courageous people who didn't hesitate to fulfill their own dream despite condemnation from others. Rather than be envious of those living their dreams, wouldn't you rather live yours?

Energy is always in motion throughout the universe; it never dies. With spiritual energy, our problems and potential solutions have a constant vibration of energy as well. Higher thought-energy frequencies (toward evolving) aid in problem-solving. Lower thought-energy frequencies (toward stagnation) perpetuate problems. Override your fears, and you'll render negative thought-energy harmless.

Think back to when you last conquered a fear. You were most likely energized with a sense of accomplishment. Fears are cleverly disguised as doubts, which focus on what **can't** be done versus what **can** be done. The "yeah, but…" kind of thinking rules out options before they've been explored and empowers someone else's negative thinking. If you suspect a doubt might be correct, dig deeper for the reason behind the doubt. If you've thought this dream through and really want it, you'll find solutions!

No matter what we do, we'll encounter naysayers for practically **everything** we do in our lives. Here are some personal examples:

For starters, my mom had a tubal ligation two years before I was born, so there was no way she was going to birth another child, right?

Surpriiiise! I have no clue how I snuck in to this world nor did the doctor. I wasn't found in a basket on our front porch or delivered by a UFO. Thankfully, my parents never treated me as a "mistake."

I was dismissed from the fourth grade band because I "didn't have the talent" for music.

*I'd wanted to be the next Al Hirt on trumpet, but my parents got me a flute. I could only get a feeble whooshing sound out of the flute, and besides, it was a girlie instrument. My band teacher sent me home with a sealed note suggesting any activity **other** than band. He hadn't encountered my mom yet. By the time she got through with him, he was sending his daughter over to give me private lessons, and that saved my musical career. Thanks, Mom!*

I was repeatedly bullied in my early teens, and made fun of for being a "band nerd."

The bullying motivated me to get in shape, and I learned the value of teamwork and strong leadership from my band director extraordinaire, Mr. Don Gunderson.

As a sophomore in college, I announced my plans to major in music. I can still hear the deafening silence when I told my parents. The response from them and others was: "But how will you make a living?"

Impractical me couldn't answer that question initially, but I kept working on getting better and doing what I loved to do. I didn't worry about it. Since that announcement, I've never worked outside of the music field, and my parents did support me after the initial shock!

As a full-time professional musician, I was fired from one band, joined a new show band, and then turned down a lucrative offer for a worldwide tour with Dick Dale so I could stay with the show band, but they fired me after only six weeks!

I was kicking myself for not going on the worldwide tour, but that ego-deflating experience taught me that jobs are about fitting in as much as ability and talent. I soon found another band that brought me steady work, higher pay, and one more little perk: I met my future wife on the first stop of our road trip!

When I got my master's degree, I was told: "There aren't any jobs out there."

I only had to get **one job.** *Despite many rejections, I got the "one job."*

I was advised not to go straight from my bachelor's degree to my master's without getting public school teaching experience. As soon as I finished student teaching, I was offered a job as an assistant band director.

Flattering as that offer was, I just couldn't get into it. I loved teaching, but I dreaded doing what I had to do to get middle and high school kids to behave. I would rather flip burgers! I never did apply for a job teaching public schools, and McDonald's was spared from my services.

When I was appointed department chair at UW-Whitewater, **everyone** warned me about the stress I was in for. I was even offered "condolences"!

The job became a major impetus for my research on happiness. The *job had stresses, but I resolved not to allow others to define how the job would be **for me.***

I was warned against retiring early, but I did anyway.

I cannot begin to tell you how rewarding it is to see my wife happy at home and have more time to follow my writing passion, play jazz, etc.!

I had a strong vision to get my wife and family back to Ventura County, California for some time, but in 2016, I got the urge to do it right then and not wait any longer. I heard every comment imaginable from friends and family about how California is too expensive, and why we shouldn't move there.

It wasn't easy, but a year later, we were moving into an affordable home in beautiful Camarillo, CA. Had I waited, house-hunting would have been extremely difficult due to the fires and flooding that occurred that fall, displacing many from their homes.

Challenges can make our shadows of doubt grow. I remember being disappointed about three different jobs in academia I didn't get, but each time something more suitable came along to make me thankful I didn't get those other jobs! The same can be said for breakups. You can't marry everybody! Believing everything is for your common good renders negative energy harmless. Here's someone who overcame some adversity:

In 1831, he suffered a business failure.

In 1832, he was defeated in a bid for the state legislature.

In 1833, he underwent a second business failure.

In 1835, his fiancée died.

In 1836, he experienced a mental breakdown.

In 1838, he was defeated for speaker of the state legislature.

In 1840, he was defeated for the office of elector.

In 1843, he was defeated for land officer.

In 1846, he won an election to Congress but was defeated in his 1848 reelection bid.

In 1855, he was defeated in a run for the Senate.

In 1856, he was defeated in his bid for vice president.

In 1858, he lost again in another attempt at the Senate.

In 1860, he was elected president of the United States.

Abraham Lincoln led the nation through some of its darkest hours. The adversity he went through in his pre-presidency days undoubtedly prepared him for the challenges he faced as president.

> *The falls of our life provide us with the energy to propel ourselves to a higher level.*
> -DR. WAYNE DYER-

How Attachments Rob Energy

Attachments can take away our energy, inspiration, and happiness and hold them hostage for a lifetime. Attachments are feelings that one **has** to have some "thing" or event to occur in order to be happy. We become inflexible, and when things don't go our way, negative emotions make themselves at home. When we withhold our happiness "until" or "unless" this or that happens for us, we literally give **outside** conditions control over our well-being. Our energy depletes, and we become mired in the lower thought energy frequencies of security, sensation, and power. Letting go of what you think you must have to be happy frees up your energy and allows you to discover what serves your higher good and what doesn't. Then you can save your energy for what's truly important.

The Energy Void

Another subtle but potentially deadly energy drain happens when our surroundings lack the inspiration or energy we need to make our goals happen, much like an electric cord without a place to plug in. We suffer from an "energy void" when our immediate surroundings are not conducive to realizing our higher goals due to our physical location or the people around us.

Alyssa is graduating from high school and has always wanted to be a professional basketball player. She lives in a small South Carolina community with a population of 3,100. Alyssa is by far the best basketball player in the area and has gotten an outstanding scholarship offer out of state. Her ultimate dream is to play in the WNBA. All of her family and friends are in South Carolina, and her parents think her goals are unrealistic. They want her to manage the family's dry cleaning store, especially because Alyssa is intelligent, capable, and already understands the business through helping her family.

Alyssa has to consider how close she is to her family along with her ability and desire to play basketball. If she accepts the scholarship, her parents don't have any other family member to manage the store. If she stays and abandons her WNBA dreams, she'll help her parents and stay close to her friends, but she will never know if she were cut out for professional women's basketball.

There's no easy answer, but if Alyssa has a long-standing vision to play basketball, she ought to go after it. In which case, she needs to be around other high-caliber players. If she pursues the pros and doesn't make it, at least she can return to the dry-cleaning business knowing she gave it her best shot. There's nothing wrong with being an athlete or running a business. The problem arises if we **never know** what would have happened if we had followed the dreams that tug at us.

Following your dreams can make travel and relocation a necessity. If you really want to be a doctor, you're going to have to go to medical school. If you want to run a ranch, raise horses, or grow crops, you'll need to leave if you live in New York City. If you live in North Dakota but want to work on Wall Street or sing in a dinner theater, welcome to New York!

Surround yourself with "doers" who demonstrate their commitment to a high ideal like you do. Going to the University of North Texas with its outstanding reputation in jazz studies gave me the privilege of being around truly dedicated peers.

> I would go into the practice room area, get my two hours in, congratulate myself, and leave. Of course, there were many other musicians practicing too. I began to notice that the same musicians were practicing before I got there and were still practicing after I left. Funny coincidence, these were the best players that others were usually jealous of. Wake up call! Two hours a day doesn't cut it for Mr. Wannabe. Thanks to that unspoken inspiration, I was soon practicing four hours a day and simply reduced my credit load to accommodate what was important to me: honing my music skills.

Seek to be around stimulating, positive people in places that enable you to have the energy to live the life you love. Anyone with a success story has a list of people, places, and situations that inspired them.

Avoid putting yourself in situations where your strongest interests are not appreciated. Notice what kind of energy you're picking up from others. Remove yourself from "energy vampires"—whiners, complainers, or chronic time-wasters that suck your energy dry whether they realize what they're doing or not. Be wary of those who discourage you from being who you are, however well-intentioned they may seem. Keep your immediate energy field free of depletion from constant doubting, ridicule, or time-wasting situations.

If you're around positive energy, welcome it into your space. If you happen to be around negative people, you **do not** have to accept their energy field! If someone offers you a gift of doggy doo-doo, you don't have to take it, even if it's gift-wrapped! You have the ability to transform the lower, denser thought energy of others into a higher frequency through your positive thoughts, words, and actions. If that doesn't work, then send them love and leave the situation ASAP to avoid your own energy drain.

To escape the energy void, Cheryl Richardson, author and life-coach, recommends going on a treasure hunt to find passion in your life. Look for symbols of your passion in your home through the things you love. Expand that to the books, movies, and people that inspire you. Keep track of these clues, write them down, and follow them to make those all-important energy connections.

Don't be a plug without a place to plug in. Make energy connections, and you'll see a big difference in how quickly you move toward your goals.

Happiness Step Twenty-Four
Unclogging the Drain!

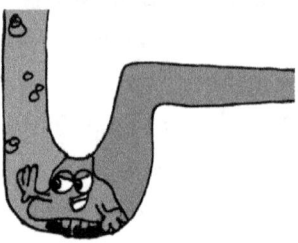

What blocks your energy and drains you the most? Rank each item below from 1 to 6, with number one being your biggest energy drain.

___Unnecessary activities
___Poor pacing or timing of your energy
___Poor health
___Fear and doubt
___Attachments
___The energy void

According to the numbers you put above, think or write something that will unclog your energy drain in that area. For example, "Today I will overcome my unnecessary-activities drain by finishing my report before I answer any emails or check my cell phone."

1. _____
2. _____
3. _____
4. _____
5. _____
6. _____

WELL I'LL BE A BLUE-NOSED GOPHER

You can unclog a different drain each day or seriously work on one blocker/drainer for a while—whatever does the job! Don't forget to enter your plans directly into your calendar of activities and put them into **action!**

CHAPTER SEVENTEEN
ARE WE HAVING "FUN" YET?

Relearning How to Have Fun

All too often, the workaholic's mantra is: "I don't have time for fun." Not only is that the ultimate energy drain, but do you honestly want to be around someone like that (assuming it's not you, of course!)? Do you want more energy?

- Do more activities that are energizing!
- Do more activities that are relaxing!

Is that simple enough for you? What is energizing and relaxing to you is related to aspects of your life's purpose. I hear someone protesting, "But I have a **life…**"(implying a life of all work). It may be a life…just not a good one. Let's add this:

Change or get rid of whatever interferes with your energizing and relaxing activities!

If your life is vacant of energizing activities and

relaxation, major changes are needed. We're on this planet to be productive, but that doesn't mean we must suffer interminably!

Notice youngsters and their boundless energy. It's more than youth that keeps kids romping around. Kids know how to have fun, and unless they've suffered trauma, they haven't yet "learned" how to have their energy blocked!

> *Grown men may learn much from little children, for the hearts of little children are pure, and therefore, the Great Spirit may show them many things which older people miss.*
> **-BLACK ELK-**

Fun is a shot of pure energy at any age. University students may be exhausted at midnight studying for a difficult exam, but what are the chances the same students would be too tired to "party hearty" the next night? Hmm…It's human nature to want to have fun.

Humans need to laugh more often! Our bodies release enzymes during laughter that induce healing. Tears of laughter have a different chemical composition than tears of sadness. Since her brain injury, my wife, Toni, often laughs and cries at the same time! Have you ever laughed so hard you cried? There are few things more catching than Toni's laugh. I call it the million-dollar laugh because our hospital bill was over a million dollars (thank God for good insurance) and because I feel like a millionaire every time I hear that laugh.

Laugh at work, too. Only Dr. Doom-'n'-Gloom wouldn't want good humor at work!

> When I was department chair, the music faculty scheduled a meeting with the chancellor of the university to discuss major grievances, and the meeting had the potential of being quite stressful. Desperate for a unique approach, I opened the meeting with: "We've all been under a little stress lately…" I handed the

chancellor a talking pillow in the likeness of Dr. Sigmund Freud, and I asked him to squeeze it so it would talk. With a very thick Freudian accent, the little pillow's speaker began…

"Why don't you lie down on the couch? Relaaaaxxxx. Tell me about your childhood. A-haaa! (Pause) That will be 300 dollars, please."

Suddenly the chancellor broke into laughter and couldn't stop laughing, and so did we. It broke the ice, and the meeting went about as well as it could have.

Humor works even in "serious" occasions:

The first time I participated in a Native American sweat lodge, I was nervous. The two-three hour ceremony offers heartfelt prayers, but the heat is very physically demanding. I was surprised by how much humor there was! As soon as the flap door is closed, it's so dark you can't see an inch in front of you. The elder in charge began, "Okay! If it's your first time in a sweat lodge, raise your hand." (No one could see their own hand, let alone anyone else's!) We all broke out laughing.

Humor Yourself!

Humor helps us put more passion and energy into what we do and keeps us from getting too serious. We operate better with happiness and balance as opposed to anxiety. Delight in the fun of it all. Laugh often, long, and loud. Laugh until you gasp for breath! When you go to bed, recall your day, and if you haven't had some laughter, get up and **do something fun!**

> *Time spent laughing is time spent with the Gods.*
> **-JAPANESE PROVERB-**

Another thing to learn from young kids is that they rarely hold grudges for long. They may quarrel, but once it's over, that's that. Adults, on the other hand, can be masters at disguising and repressing their true thoughts and feelings, and anger kicks in! Before blowing up a small island, repeat Happiness Step Four. If we forgive and let go of our grudges, we'll be more apt to want fun in our lives.

> For nearly a year, I played six nights a week at the Goldfinger Greek restaurant in Dallas, Texas. In the Greek band, I learned that if something was wrong, it was addressed immediately in no uncertain terms! They would argue to the point where I thought fists would fly! Then, suddenly, the dispute would end, and in no time, the guys were slapping each other on the back, laughing, and joking like nothing had happened! Other times they would address me in a stern tone about playing Greek music properly, and then they would bring me a plate of delicious *mousaka* from the kitchen!

What a learning experience that was! I was challenged by being around people who were open, expressive, and immediately forgiving. By getting things off their chests, they left "room" in their hearts to have fun. Why should I harbor a single grudge about some ridiculous argument or because someone wasn't "nice" to me?

Our fun and sense of humor can only be ruined if **we** allow it. Our "fun balloon" starts losing air with the pressures of adolescence, which is followed by college/career pressures. By middle age (I hear more air escaping), we join the "deadpan club" because grownups are supposed to be serious, right? If we're lucky, we'll see old age, but our balloon could be out of air with cumulative worries about health and anything else we can imagine. My dad used to say, "Old age? I don't recommend it!" Then he would quip: "But it sure beats the alternative!" He lived to be eighty-seven and would joke about whether he should go back to Illinois to attend his high school class reunion when he was the only surviving member!

No Time for Fun? R.I.P.

As we get older and accumulate more responsibilities, having fun requires planning, so I implore you to **make time for it!** Rethink thoughts that say "I'm tired," "I don't feel well," or "I'm getting a cold." We don't need to **prove** how hard we work to ourselves. Take time for new interests, and let the fun begin!

The pressures of my doctoral dissertation, earning tenure, and administrative work at first created a life where I didn't do **anything** that wasn't work-related! I decided to change that and scheduled in some recreation. I received these exact comments from three different academic colleagues:

- "You went to a **movie**? I haven't gone to a movie since I started here."

    *Insinuation: And you **shouldn't either**. Don't you have more productive ways to spend your time?*

- "You went to a **ballgame**? I wish I had time for that."

    *Insinuation: **My** job doesn't allow for it. How do **you** manage to get your research done?*

- "You went to **lunch?** I haven't had time to eat lunch for ten years."

   *Insinuation: And **you** could stand to lose a few pounds…*

Well, far be it for me to go to a theatre or a ballgame. I should be doing my research every freaking second. And lunch? Forgive me for eating!

Wait a minute! It's **my** life—not somebody else's! I abandoned the "work 'til you drop" mindset that anyone who takes time for fun is a lazy "slobovitch" (my new word!). Before we adopt a lifetime membership in the "doom-and-gloom society," consider the consequences of not having fun: a drab, boring, unbalanced life with burnout and poor health. R.I.P!

> *Drop the idea that you are Atlas carrying the world on your shoulders. The world would go on even without you. Don't take yourself so seriously.*
> **-NORMAN VINCENT PEALE-**

Fun is planning and sharing activities with people we enjoy being with. If you enjoy your work, leisure activities will feel better too! You'll rarely seem tired. Include some recreation that includes things you love to do, whether it be sports, movies, games, socializing, or something with comedy in it.

Sometimes we have to be the first to initiate cheerfulness and be resistant to the bad moods of others. The better we get at this, the less we'll allow our own tough times to affect our well-being. This doesn't mean we don't care when others are sad, angry, or when bad things happen. It's just that if we become adversely affected, it's harder to help others.

QUESTION: How can I be happy or have fun when there is so much suffering, ignorance, illness, crime, and negativity in the world?

ANSWER: You can never be sad enough, angry enough, or unhappy enough to bear the suffering of **all** the world's problems. We have *to rise above suffering so we can function and help others. When you need guidance, do you look for someone in a terrible mood and overwhelmed with negativity? Of course not! Be the strong one— that someone to turn to when times are tough.*

Taking everything too seriously bogs down what we want to accomplish. By lightening up, we lessen any overblown self-importance. One of the foundations for comedy is learning to laugh at ourselves. Have you ever laughed later at a situation that didn't seem funny at the time? Instead of watching the depressing nightly news, I started watching late-night talk shows, and I'd hear about the same events with a humorous spin. What determines how much fun you have in life? You do!

A woman was discussing a trip to Rome with her hairdresser, who responded, "Rome? Why would anyone want to go there? It's crowded, dirty, and the food is disappointing! You're crazy to go to Rome!"

"We got a great rate with a new airline—Breeze Easy!"

"Breeze Easy?" exclaimed the hairdresser. "They're terrible! Their planes are scrap, their flight attendants are rude, and they're always behind schedule. Where are you staying?"

"We'll be at this exclusive little place over on Rome's left side called Teste..."

"Stop right there. I know that place. It's a dump; it's the worst hotel ever! The rooms are small, the service is non-existent, and they're way overpriced."

"Well, we're going to go the Vatican to see the Pope."

"You and a million other people," laughed the hairdresser. "He'll look like he is the size of an ant. Well, good luck on this trip of yours. You'll need it."

A month later, the same woman came back in for her hair appointment. The hairdresser asked her about her trip, and the woman responded, "It was absolutely wonderful! Not only did we arrive on time in a brand new jet, but it was overbooked, so they bumped us up to first class. The food and wine were fantastic, and I had a nice steward who waited on me hand and foot. And the hotel was a jewel! They'd just completed a major remodeling. They were overbooked, so they gave us their owner's suite at no extra charge!"

"Well," muttered the hairdresser. "I know you didn't get to see the Pope."

"Actually, we **did!** We were touring the Vatican, and a guard tapped me on the shoulder, saying that the Pope likes to personally meet some of the visitors, and if I'd be so kind as to step into his private chambers, the Pope would personally greet me. Five minutes later, the Holy Father himself walked through the door! I knelt down, and he spoke a few words to me."

"Really?" asked the hairdresser. "What'd he say?"

"He said, 'Where did you get that lousy hairdo?'"

It's all about attitude. Rather than thinking of your glass as "half empty or half full," think of it overflowing with abundance because that's what it is. You have all you need to have more fun in your life—right now!

Happiness Step Twenty-Five
Lightin' the Fire or Chillin' Out?

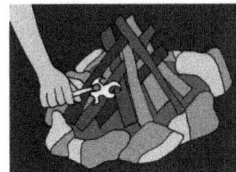 

Think of three activities that would give you a spark of energy. Plug them into your calendar this week, including the exact day and hour.

Now, think of three activities that you look forward to when you truly want to relax. What is keeping you from doing these activities as often as you'd like? For your health and a happier life, it's time to make a ─────

Plug three relaxing activities into your calendar now!

Is there anything at all that was "fun" that you did as a kid that you would like to bring back into your life? Don't be afraid. Pick a day and do the activity in some way.

Finally, what is one thing you could do this week to make your life incredibly fun? Go do it or at least get started with it! Plug it into your schedule!

SECTION FIVE
Ego Check!

CHAPTER EIGHTEEN
I'M <u>NOT</u> AN EGOMANIAC!
(NOW GET OUT OF MY WAY!)

Seeing Ego for What It Really Is

If you've got the time and energy for a meaningful life, and you're ready and rarin' to go, then why isn't this book **over?** It's because we need to consider a very deceptive foe: our **ego**, which can make happiness disappear faster than a drop of water in Death Valley.

What is "ego" anyway? Dr. Sigmund Freud believed that the ego referees the endless battles between our most basic desires (id) and our conscience (superego). While his ideas were advanced for his time, they underestimated our ability to go beyond security, sensation, and power. The concept of higher self didn't mix with Freudian ego theories. In the Tibetan language, ego is called *dakdzin*, which translates to "grasping to a self," which is the

root of all suffering. In plain English: self-centeredness! Walt Kelly made the following saying famous in his politically-based *Pogo* comic strip; "We have met the enemy, and he is us." To realize that our own mind is our biggest lifelong challenge allows us to overcome self-sabotage and make the changes we need to move forward.

Don't confuse ego with self-confidence, which we all need lots of. *Au contraire,* the ego wants the universe to revolve around **me**. Ego would have us believe: "I am what I have, what I do, and what others think of me." That's it—nothing more. The ego wants you to ride the roller-coaster of desires for comfort and convenience, demands of the mind, and outbursts of emotions  while it fears your divine, higher self that is unaffected by external events.

When Jesus said, "The kingdom of God is within you," he wasn't referring to your big screen TV or your new job. If you allow ego's "needs" to substitute for that divine part of you, then you become mentally and spiritually malnourished, like a branch cut off from the vine. Your higher self is not separate from your mind and body. Everything about you, including your birth, was brought about by past causes and conditions dependent on many people and circumstances. We are irreversibly linked to all humanity, but your ego wants you to think you're somehow separate from everyone else. You are never separate from God or the universe, but your ego will try to convince you otherwise!

~~I think, therefore I am.~~
–DESCARTES–

Rather than the above statement, which subscribes to ego, try this:

I am (inseparable from the universe), therefore I think.

Dr. Ron Roth equated: **E-G-O = Easing God Out** (and everybody else too!). Ego wants the world to be only about **me.** It isn't. Unfortunately, this attitude is too common. Drive in any city, and you'll find plenty of egocentric drivers with little regard for the lives of others. Where **they** are going and how fast they get there is all that matters.

The ego's self-centered nature is a most formidable enemy; it's cunning and knows your weakest points. Happiness will never be if you seek permanence with ego-based needs where no permanence can be found. Yet we repeatedly give in to ego's demands like a cocaine addict, and after a brief high, we'll be left empty of any lasting happiness. Instead, allow your higher self to direct your body, mind, and emotions.

Fear of Losing Control

Ego is fueled by a need for control and plays brilliantly on our fear of not having it. Sometimes we'll get what we think we want (control) and sometimes we won't (out of control!). The universe is the same way: organized solar systems and galaxies are contrasted by utter chaos. Anyone expecting total control of everything might as well jump into a volcano. But don't jump yet! Would you **really** want total control? An old *Twilight Zone* TV episode comes to mind:

> Mr. Valentine, a criminal, robs a pawnshop, kills two people, and is shot dead in a shootout with police. He wakes up in a luxurious apartment and is greeted by a pleasant man in a suit who essentially offers him everything he wants. The robber is skeptical at first, so he orders everything—money, gourmet food, wine,

women, and fancy cars, and all are delivered promptly. The man soon realizes he **is** dead, but he is getting everything he wants. He gambles and wins the jackpot every time. Everyone loves him and accommodates his every single wish. Soon, Mr. Valentine becomes bored out of his mind. He gets irritable and starts begging for some things to be **out of his control!** At the end of the show, he screams, "If I stay one more day, I'm going to go nuts! I don't belong in heaven, see? I want to go to the other place!"

The man in the suit replies, "Heaven, Mr. Valentine? Whatever gave you the idea that you were in heaven? This **is** the other place!"

We can't grow if everything we want is given to us. When we leave the prison yard of having to have control, true freedom begins. Our greatest accomplishments often arise out of the world of uncertainty. There is power in knowing that "you never know."

There was a farmer in a village with a horse he treasured. One day, the horse ran away, and the farmer's neighbor came to his house to offer his condolences. "You never know," the farmer replied.

The very next day, the horse came back, leading a beautiful wild mare alongside him. The neighbor saw them and exclaimed, "That's wonderful! What a stroke of good luck!"

The farmer replied, "You never know."

A few days later, the farmer's son was trying to break the wild horse in, was thrown to the ground, and broke his leg. Of course, the neighbor came over to say how sorry he was that things had gone badly. The farmer replied, "You never know."

A short time later, a war began, and the army came through the village in search of young men to fight, but since the farmer's son's leg was broken, he was allowed to stay at home. "You are a fortunate man!" the neighbor said when he heard the news. You already know what the farmer replied!

-RAM DASS-

Let go of your resistance to what you can't change. While you're the "pilot of your plane," other circumstances may determine when and where you fly! Ego (the mind) wants control over your intuition (the heart). A need for control is really a sign we need to change something about ourselves.

We must be the change we wish to see in the world.
– MAHATMA GANDHI-

When you become free of demanding control and fear-based thoughts, how can you not succeed?

Did I "Win" or "Lose"?

Another way ego can block goal fulfillment like a 6'10" bouncer at a nightclub is through fear of poor results. "What will everyone think if I fail"? "How do I rate?" These questions reveal external success indicators are all that matter. Instead of searching outside of ourselves for approval we'll never get from everyone, look within. By doing the best we can without obsessing over the opinions of others, our results will often exceed expectations.

Rafael was one of the top sales managers at a highly successful marketing firm, and he knew that the vice-president of the company was about to retire. He'd been working hard toward getting the promotion, but when someone else was selected, Rafael was very disappointed. Rather than being "sour grapes" about it, he continued to work hard and got along well with his co-workers. Later that year, one of his accounts became quite lucrative, and Rafael was hired by a new company with a salary increase and promotion to vice-president after a year. Two years later, Rafael became CEO of the new company. By not letting a disappointing result get the better of him, he was able to take his career to a new level.

Ego plays on fear of future loss or disappointment. It's easy to forget that anything gained will eventually be lost anyway. Losses and gains are illusions. Ironically, losses create an opportunity for new growth. Through Native American teachings, I am reminded that we don't really "own" anything nor do we "lose" anything. Our enjoyment of the people we know and things we have is temporary. What always remains is the higher self.

Do something for the sake of doing it, not for a result. Most actors would love to win an Academy Award, but are those who did not win a failure? Extremely few who do what they love would change their lives based on a result. "Failure" is a term imposed by the opinions of others. Don't kick the wall over a result. Besides, they don't make walls like they used to! The dance of life means much more than any outcome can ever give us.

> Why should we be in such desperate haste to succeed, and in such desperate enterprises? If a man does not keep pace with his companions, perhaps it is because he hears a different drummer. Let him step to the music which he hears, however measured or far away.
> **-HENRY DAVID THOREAU-**

WELL I'LL BE A BLUE-NOSED GOPHER

A real danger of "results-oriented" thinking occurs when we need to be excellent at every **single** thing we do without understanding the time commitment involved.

> Amber was miserable. Her parents had wanted her to be a business major despite her desire to major in sculpture. With her business courses, she was disappointed with only obtaining a "B" average for fifteen credits of college. Her thirty-hour-a-week job was overwhelming, the relationship with her long-distance boyfriend was spiraling downward, and she was angry that she didn't make the starting squad on the university basketball team.

The depressed overachiever goes into overdrive: "Why **didn't** you get better grades? What's **wrong** with your job? Why **isn't** your relationship with your boyfriend better? Why **can't** you make the team? What's **wrong** with you?" Amber needs a big hug, not this browbeating!

But shouldn't we strive for excellence? Of course, but only where it matters the most! Decide where you want your excellence to be. You may have to settle for "pretty good," "good," or even "fair" at other things. To keep your sanity, some of your skills will have to be "second fiddle"! No mortal excels at every human task because to be excellent at something takes a lot of **time!**

Perfectionism can be paralyzing. It can keep you from being who you really are because you are hiding under the security blanket of being a workaholic. Instead of spending your time trying to become "somebody" to appease the image of yourself the ego wants, try becoming "nobody"! Being "nobody" means you're a vehicle for your **higher** self, which ignores the labels of ego. Once you realize that attempting to be "somebody" to appease your ego is a dead-end road, you appreciate the importance of being "nobody." Only then will you **really** be "somebody"!

In school, many chase only the symbols of success, so learning is placed as a distant second priority to getting "A" grades and degrees. We measure everything by outside criteria at the expense of satisfying our soul's need for nourishment. Learning can be stressful because it involves doing what hasn't been done before. Emphasizing grades alone generates only short-term learning. The "knowledge" quickly fades unless students can personally internalize and use the information. Our greatest learning occurs when **we** see its value.

We often turn to past results or statistics to measure how we're doing now. Yet, if we consider only past criteria, then new, creative ideas become highly unlikely. The march to a higher order lies in the experience of uncertainty, which challenges us to be more flexible in our definition of what "successful results" really are.

> My wife Toni got her B.F.A. in art. She was a fine potter; she could paint, draw, and do 3-D art pieces. Since her traumatic accident, she has no memory of what she once could do. When she sees her paintings, pottery, the tile table, and statue she built from scratch, she looks with wonderment. "I did **that?**" She'll say, "Wow!" Then she'll resume whatever she's doing.
>
> Today, she still loves to draw with her one good arm. Her drawing is nowhere near what it once was, but she has no lamentations over her new "results." She loves to draw now just like before. How important are her past "results" in her enjoyment of art? Zilch. Nada. If she became sad over her past accomplishments, what good would that do? If Toni draws a picture of a kitty today, is she a failure because she isn't able to do what she once could?

WELL I'LL BE A BLUE-NOSED GOPHER

HALF EMPTY

HALF FULL

Some of Toni's friends shake their heads at what she **can't** do compared to her pre-accident days, while others marvel at what she **can** do now. Toni is happy **every** day, delights in whatever she tries to do, and laughs when she messes up. I learn from my beautiful wife every day about happiness. Her glass is full of abundance. She is my hero.

There will always be someone who will intentionally or unintentionally try to impose his or her criteria on you and explain how and why you should live up to whatever expectation he or she has. As you become more successful, there will be more people that won't like you. Everyone loves cute little kids showing off their talents, but as soon as they get a little older, they're subjected to a world of jealousy. **It's your life.** You can never fulfill everyone else's agenda for you, so you might as well fulfill your own.

Lay your success and failure at God's feet.
-MAHATMA GANDHI-

When you look at sunsets, each one is unique. No one would say "there ought to be more red clouds to the south and more golden clouds to the north." (If they did, I'd root for the clouds to dump some hail on their head!) Our lives are like the sky: an ever-changing masterpiece. Some days, like sunsets, are more appealing than others. If we're doing our best to fulfill what we're here to do, we'll be less preoccupied with "results." Results only matter to your ego. If you get good results, enjoy them. When you don't, just move on and keep doing what you love to do.

How much do results matter? Here's a baseball box score I found online:

On June 20, 1947, the Cleveland Indians defeated the Boston Red Sox 3-2. Ted Williams, one of the greatest players in baseball history, went 0-4. Neither the Red Sox nor the Indians won the World Series that year. None of the players or umpires from that game are alive anymore. There were 34,167 fans in attendance that day in Boston, and most were probably disappointed with the result.

Why this foray into the past? Think of the "results" in your life and compare them to a season's worth of box scores from 1947. Wins and losses. What matters? There were great people who loved to play, and fans who loved the game. Anyone can have a bad day, just like Ted Williams did on that day. A result you get or don't get should just be a speed bump as you go through life's journey. By the way, the New York Yankees beat the Brooklyn Dodgers in seven games to win the World Series that year.

Results vary. Following the path of your passion keeps your priorities in perspective. But, for extra credit, give yourself permission to have one royal, grandiose screwup to keep your ego at bay. In his song, "The Times They Are A Changin'," Bob Dylan states prophetically:

For the loser now will be later to win…

The slow one now
Will later be fast…

And the first one now will later be last*

---

* Copyright © 1963, 1964 by Warner Bros. Inc.; renewed 1991, 1992 by Special Rider Music. All rights reserved. International copyright secured. Reprinted by permission.

WELL I'LL BE A BLUE-NOSED GOPHER

The headlines of yesterday are gone today. The applause dies. Awards tarnish. Achievements are forgotten. Accolades and certificates are buried with their owners. You're more likely to remember…

- teachers who aided your journey through school,
- friends who helped you through a difficult time,
- people who taught you something worthwhile,
- people who made you feel appreciated and special,
- people whom you enjoyed spending time with,
- heroes whose stories have inspired you, and
- the ones who **cared.**

CHAPTER NINETEEN
MORE EGO TRICKS

The Know-It-All

The ego has more tricks up its sleeve! It loves to dupe us into thinking we know more than we actually do. Introducing the KNOW-IT-ALL!

Know-it-alls…

- have to show everyone how smart they are; after all, there's an image to protect!

- act like they know everything, and if they don't know something, they fake it!
- know **everything** about **everybody** and **every** situation at all times!
- have **no** idea how badly they come across to others!

Do you know a know-it-all? There isn't much you can tell them, is there?

> *The intelligent man who is proud of his intelligence is like the condemned man who is proud of his large cell.*
> **–SIMONE WEIL-**

Know-it-alls have an inherent need to be right and to have **control.** They waste so much energy convincing people they know everything that they have no time to actually **do** something! A greater virtue is to relinquish the need to convince others that our point of view is right. Many intelligent people in this world know many things. How often they feel they have to prove it is another thing.

Nan-in, a Japanese Zen master, welcomed a university professor who came to inquire about Zen. The professor began to expound all he knew about Zen to the master. After a few minutes, Nan-in interrupted to ask the professor if he would like a cup of tea, and the professor accepted. The professor continued to talk, and Nan-in kept pouring the tea into the cup, letting it overflow considerably. The professor said, "Stop! It is overfull. No more will go in!"

"Like this cup," Nan-in said, "you are full of your own opinions and speculations. How can I show you Zen unless you first allow room in your cup?"

-ZEN-

As a teenager, I was a know-it-all saxophonist.

I already played flute, and the fingerings were similar, so I found a few reeds and soon I was honkin' away like nobody's business. I was first chair tenor sax in the high school band (the **only** tenor sax player). I hadn't had any lessons, but I was a cool sax player!

After a while, I realized I wasn't as good as I thought. The more I practiced, the more I found out how far I had to go. Now, after many years as a pro, I have more to learn than ever. Looking back at that fourteen-year-old sax player, I realize **that** guy knew only enough to fool himself.

When conflicting information is presented, the know-it-all hides in ego's shadow. Not being completely right would require (oh horrors!) a **change** in thinking and actions. If you find out you're wrong, admit it!

Mahatma Gandhi once led a protest march and halted it midstream when he realized it wasn't the right thing to do at the time. He said, "My commitment is to truth as I see it each day, not to consistency."

And now, the **know-it-all manifesto**:

With my knowledge and expertise, I **know** with **certainty** that I am **right.** People who think like me are the good guys, and those who don't are the bad guys. I will correct those who are **wrong** and refuse to listen to anything they say because my side is **right** about **everything!**

Before you bow down, aren't wars and terrorism fueled by people with egos so huge that they will do **anything** to enforce their "right" views? A further irony is that individuals who think like this have been idolized! Hitler, Bin-Laden, Genghis Khan, and others didn't get a position of power by being stupid. Some intelligence, ego "gone wild," and support from others created a catastrophe and the deaths of thousands of innocent people.

A wise groundskeeper at a bed and breakfast in New Orleans introduced the following proverb to me. It took me a few repetitions to understand it, so read each line slowly, pausing at the dashes to visualize each line's valuable lesson.

He who knows not—and knows not that he knows not—is a fool; shun him.
He who knows not—and knows that he knows not—is a child; teach him.
He who knows—but knows not that he knows—is asleep; wake him.
He who knows—and knows that he knows—is wise; follow him.

If we think we know a lot, we're usually delusional and self-righteous. When we become aware of how much we don't know, learning can begin. The irony is that when we finally do gain true knowledge, we'll probably be accused of being self-righteous by those jealous of our knowledge!

Keep a beginner's mind—in the expert's
mind the possibilities are few.
–SUZUKI-

Pity

When we don't get what we want, our ego hosts a "pity party." "Oh, woe is me! Poor ME!" Did your car not start? Did you skip breakfast? Did a friend let you down? First, be thankful you have a car, food, and friends to complain about! If you're in a tough predicament right now, you're not alone! Lamenting only makes it worse because here we are again, focusing on **ourselves** instead of others. If we're sick, broke, lonely, etc., it really helps to give to **others** the essence of what we lack in our own lives. Do you feel sick? Nurture yourself and others. Are you broke? Be generous to others with your love and time. Feeling lonely? Go to someone else who's lonely and be nice to him or her, even if it's someone you don't know.

Whenever I start feeling sorry for myself, the universe finds a way of showing me things aren't really that bad:

> During my doctoral residency at the University of Northern Colorado, I was particularly down and out and feeling overwhelmed with problems. My car was in the repair shop, and I was walking back to my apartment on a windy 25° day, carrying two grocery bags, immersed in self-pity. I saw a young man trudging very slowly toward me, barely able to walk. As he approached, the man smiled at me and said, "Hello," but it was clearly difficult for him to talk, let alone walk. He obviously had suffered a serious misfortune, and it was going to take him a very long time to get to his destination on that frigid day in Colorado. Yet he was able to smile and say hello to "poor" **me!**

No matter how bad things are, there's always someone less fortunate than you. Go help someone worse off than you. You'll feel better! Say this as often as you like:

DR. JOHN C. WEBB

I am abundant.
I have all I need.
I have enough.
I am enough.
-MARCIA MENTER-

Our Image vs. Who We Really Are

Our ego would like us to think that creating and protecting our **image** is more important than being who we really are.

A man who is wrapped up in himself
makes a pretty small package.
-JOHN RUSKIN-

I often think that if the size of everyone's head matched the size of their ego, a lot of people wouldn't fit through the doorway!

George Harrison addressed the ego's blown-up importance of self in his song "I Me Mine," performed on the Beatles *Let it Be* album. In 1980, Harrison commented about this constant blabber of "I, me, and mine":

> "I Me Mine" is the ego problem. I looked around, and everything I could see was relative to my ego. You know, like "that's my piece of paper," and "that's my flannel," "give it to me," or "I am." It drove me crackers—I hated everything about my ego—it was a flash of everything false and impermanent which I disliked. But later I learned from it—to realize that there is somebody else in here apart from old blabbermouth. "Who am I" became the order of the day. Anyway, that's what came out of it: "I Me Mine"—is about the ego, the eternal problem.

Your ego would have you living more like a movie character than your true self. If you're pretending to be somebody you're not, why? Be careful, for ego "gone wild" will do practically anything to protect status. It's up to us to realize being who we are counts far more than an "image."

I'd attended a few Pow Wows, but I had never danced in the circle because I thought I might not do the right steps. At one Pow Wow, as I was admiring the dancers in the circle, a man came up to me and asked when I was going to dance. As I mumbled some poor excuse, he pointed to the arbor in the center of the circle where the drum groups played. "You see those four posts around the arbor? You just take your ego and hang it up on one of those hooks there. Then you can dance and not worry about anything."

Well **that** worked! If we'll just hang our ego up somewhere whenever we get too full of it, we'll be a lot happier!

In the ego's world, status, appearance, money, and power are all that matters. There's nothing wrong with these things when they are accomplished through following a higher purpose and helping others. The quest for status for its own sake creates a need for approval or kudos, and if we don't get them, anger and insecurity arrive like the plague. It's time to trade in that old clunker of a negative self-image for a new set of wheels!

Too often, people resort to any means necessary to affirm the image of what others think it "should" be, including lying. Why? We all want people to think we're well-off, intelligent, and surrounded by adoring loved ones, even when we're not!   The fact is:

The truth may hurt sometimes, but at least it's the truth!

If we live according to our true nature, what is there to worry or fear?

The "Need" for Praise

Another way the ego can dupe us is through the "sugarcoated" effect. Sincere praise is great when warranted. Then again, praise from others can have ulterior motives related to the quest for status and power:

"You're the best boss I've **ever** had!"
"You're my BFF" (for now!).

If your status and power were to be removed, would you end up singing the song blues singer, Bessie Smith, made famous? "Nobody Knows You When You're Down and Out" is about what happens to a millionaire gone completely broke.

If you climb up the status ladder and become well-known, you will receive unjust praise **and** unfair criticism, so remember:

- accept whatever praise and criticism you get graciously, and
- any ego that is easily inflated is also easily deflated.

We naturally have an affinity toward those who are nice to us, but that's not a pass to disrespect someone because they dislike or think differently than we do. At the same time, don't be drawn to seeking kudos like a bug to a light bulb!

Imagine **everyone** praising you no matter what you do; no matter how poorly you did something. Even when you do something completely wrong, everybody praises you, and this continues forever!

This is Mr. Valentine in *The Twilight Zone* all over again! Under these conditions, we'll soon **beg** to be criticized! Then we might actually learn something.

Regardless of status, everyone deserves to be treated well, regardless of appearance, title, or economic means.

In the 1970s, I wore a longer hairstyle, drove a van with California plates in Texas, was a college student, and had the occupation of "musician." These things brought out a lot of instant judgments about me, including from the police! Later, when I first began university teaching, I was subjected to similar attitudes around town until they realized I was a professor, and suddenly out came the red carpet!

I was the same person. Why the different treatment? It was all about appearance or status. Looking back, I realized my ego was guilty of needing niceties because I needed to be **somebody!** Our egos make it so easy to be "full of it"!

> *I am not concerned that a man does not know of me; I am concerned that I do not know of him.*
> **-CONFUCIUS-**

The world doesn't revolve around us anymore than the universe revolves around the Earth. If we can get out of ourselves long enough, we might be able to learn what the universe has to teach us.

There's more to it than what meets the "I."

Taming the Beast

Now that ego is recognized as a formidable enemy, how do you deal with it? You can't "kill" your ego because it's part of your identity. Just don't allow it to lead you away from your higher purpose. The ego only becomes powerful if you allow it. Keep the gorilla in the cage! If you prefer cats, will it be a little kitty or a mountain lion? That depends on you.

Like taming a wild horse, taming your ego will take time. Surrender your ego to that higher part of you. Think of your ego as a room where you can be free to come and go. You know the room is there, but you don't have to live in it! Simply tell your ego it has no control over you today. In his book, *I Can See Clearly Now*, Dr. Wayne Dyer mentioned a small frame he kept on his desk that read:

> Good morning.
> This is God.
> I will be handling all of your problems today.
> I will not need your help.
> So have a miraculous day.

Happiness Step Twenty-Six
Ego Check!

Circle the letter of the choice that applies best to you and then go through the affirmations. Be honest with yourself. Keep your answers private, but you'll know deep inside if you're fudging.

- How much am I bothered when I don't get what I want?
- a) a lot b) more often than I'd like c) sometimes d) only occasionally e) rarely

- Affirmation: *I release my need to control everything in my life. I have preferences, but I will not allow my happiness to disappear when I don't get what I want.*

- I am self-centered:
- a) a lot b) more often than I'd like c) sometimes d) only occasionally e) rarely

- Affirmation: *I acknowledge that I am here to offer my time to help others in a positive way.*

- I get angry:
- a) a lot b) more often than I'd like c) sometimes d) only occasionally e) rarely

- Affirmation: *When my anger is triggered, I will not allow it to get the best of me.*

- How much am I bothered by uncertainties in my future?
- a) a lot b) more often than I'd like c) sometimes d) only occasionally e) rarely

- Affirmation: *I trust that everything will work out for my higher good.*

- When in a disagreement, I feel the need to prove myself "right"
- a) a lot b) most of the time c) sometimes d) only occasionally e) rarely

- Affirmation: *I release my need to be "right" when I'm in disagreement with others. I will learn and be open to how others came to a different conclusion than mine*

- How important is gaining approval from others to me?
- a) very important b) pretty important c) important sometimes d) not very important e) not important at all

- Affirmation: *I follow my higher self, and let go of the need to gain approval from others.*

- I feel sorry for myself
- a) a lot b) more often than I'd like c) sometimes d) only occasionally e) rarely

- Affirmation: *I avoid complaining or feeling sorry for myself. I am grateful for what I have and work toward improving any situation that bothers me.*

- How important is receiving praise and accolades to me?
- a) very important b) pretty important c) important sometimes d) not very important e) not important at all

- Affirmation: *I continue to do what is meaningful regardless of whether or not I receive accolades. I accept praise or criticism only in terms of how I can learn and will not involve my ego.*

- Circle the statement that's most accurate for you, then say the affirmation below the statements:
    a. I have to be better than everyone else at everything I do.
    b. I like to be really good at everything I do.
    c. I do the best I can at what's important. I'm willing to let a few things slide.
    d. I prefer to focus on one or two really important things at the expense of other aspects of my life.
    e. It doesn't really matter how good I am at something, it's the doing that counts.

- Affirmation: *I vow to do the best I can, enjoy the ride, and not obsess over results.*

Happiness Step Twenty-Seven
Happiness Weather Report

Before we go to the next chapter, let's take a moment to assess your overall happiness in your lifetime so far. Which category best reflects how you feel on a daily basis?

Category	Description
Guru	I'm very happy and at peace all of the time. Nothing gets me upset, and I'm nearly always at peace with myself and others.
Rainbow	I'm happy and at peace most of the time. I rarely get upset and out of balance, and when I do, I'm able to recover quickly.
Mostly Sunny	I'm usually happy and at peace. There are occasions when I'm upset, but I do recover. It takes me a bit longer to recover from major stresses.
Partly Cloudy	I'm happy a bit more often than not. I find myself getting upset sometimes when I shouldn't. A fair amount of the time, I'm not happy, but I ultimately get out of my funks.
Partly Sunny	I'm happy about half of the time, but I'm unhappy over one or more things. Sometimes I recover from my bad moods, and sometimes they linger.

 Mostly Cloudy — I'm unhappy more often than I'm happy. I'm upset a fair amount of time over something, and I can stay in a bad mood for a while.

 Cloudy — I'm usually unhappy. When I'm upset, I stay that way for quite a while. While I'm happy sometimes, I feel that it won't be long before something happens to upset me.

 Stormy — I'm unhappy a great deal of the time. I'm only occasionally happy, and my unhappiness is a predominate feeling daily.

 Hurricane — My life is one of continuous stress and unhappiness. I'm hardly ever happy or at peace with myself or others.

What's your weather report? What "weather" would you like to have? If you want a sunnier forecast, what does your gut tell you? Jot down what you're **really** willing to do to improve your forecast. Add this into your calendar **often** because you absolutely deserve to enjoy some sunshine!

CHAPTER TWENTY
RISING ABOVE THE MUCK

Chasing Happiness or Running From it?

The idea of a "road to happiness", walking down a shady lane in a peaceful valley is enchanting, but sometimes our pursuit of happiness seems like running around a revolving door!

Rather than pursue anything, or search down a road, know that "finding" happiness may not be necessary at all if you realize you already have what you need to be happy. That may be hard to believe if your life feels like you're driving the wrong way on the freeway! In that case, it's beneficial to look for more ways to rise above the mucky mess our ego can create!

Discovering "Enoughness"

To improve happiness, we desperately need to reverse society's trend toward preoccupation with the ego-driven part of ourselves above all else. In the 1940's, Psychologist Abraham Maslow created the concept of "self-actualization," which states that one can reach his or her own full potential by living a meaningful, creative life when focused on more than physiological needs. Ken Keyes Jr., in his *Handbook to Higher Consciousness*, discusses a number of ways to live for more than our physiological needs, and overcome ego's dominance. Our basic physiological needs can be summarized this way:

- **security** (food, shelter, survival, protection),
- **sensation** (all aspects related to our senses) and
- **power** (wealth, status, pride, and having control).

Meeting our basic physiological needs is important, but as Peggy Lee asks in one of her hit songs: "Is that all there is?"

If we spend all of our time worrying about survival, safety, money, power, or sensual gratification for our ego, we waste our energy seeking what we can never have enough of, which is why there is so much addiction in our society. Most that attain the pinnacle of wealth, status, or endless sensual gratification are still unhappy. Why? They lack a sense of "enoughness!"

Only he who knows what is enough will always have enough.
-LAO TZU-

So, how do we overcome any tendencies we might have to spend our lives merely to satisfy our physiological needs and our ego? I propose a deeper look into four qualities/concepts to develop in order to rise above ego's sway.

- Compassion
- Abundance
- Impartiality
- Unity

Compassion

When we practice compassion, we see all that we have in common with everyone, including the desire to be happy. We affirm the positive qualities of all humans, whether or not they demonstrate those qualities! We view others in a loving manner, not through negative emotions. We offer support and love for those who are suffering, which is a great way to avoid self-centeredness.

Given are four affirmations to help us be compassionate.
- *I am compassionate by being able to place myself in others' shoes.*
- *I am altruistic without a need for kudos or paybacks.*
- *I do life's work joyfully and unconditionally with a good sense of humor.*
- *I am peaceful, refraining from hostility unless absolutely necessary.*

<u>*I am compassionate by being able to place myself in others' shoes.*</u>

Unless your name is I.B. Snarly, it's a no-brainer that compassion and caring make the world a better place. Therefore, its development is something we should all practice. I'm serious when I say we need courses in our schools that cover how to be caring and compassionate. It does no good to develop intelligence unless we use it in a compassionate way.

In the first commandment, "Love thy neighbor as thyself" was decreed, but that didn't mean love only family or friends! **Of course** you love those close to you...Well, there's weird old Uncle Elmer, but he's family. When Jesus told us to love our enemies, what did he mean? That's a tall order, yet our adversaries challenge us in ways that enable spiritual growth. You don't have to hug your enemies and join them at the campfire, singing "Kumbaya," but you can extend your unconditional compassion and prayer to them.

When we think of others like we do ourselves, we create a caring attitude. Helping others is the beginning of the payback for the many gifts we've received. The welfare of many is more important than the welfare of one, so why should we only think of ourselves? Developing compassion to extend beyond those close to us is a noble accomplishment and will bring a deep, long-lasting happiness. Begin your practice of compassion with your loved ones, family (even Uncle Elmer!), and friends, but then move on to the challenge of extending compassion to everyone, yes, everyone! How else can the world progress?

<u>I am altruistic without a need for kudos or paybacks.</u>

In the chapter on personal energy, we looked at the value of altruism. When we extend our love outward without expectation of payback, it creates an atmosphere of openness and trust. The television show *Extreme Makeover: Home Edition* (and similar shows) demonstrates the joy many people get when they help others in need. If we don't practice giving, accepting, and sharing the love in our heart, we'll be missing one of life's greatest gifts. This anonymous epitaph exists on a tombstone in Royal Leamington Spa, a town in Warwickshire, England:

Here lies a miser who lived for himself
who cared for nothing but gathering wealth;
now where he is and how he fares,
nobody knows and nobody cares.

The value of community service is holding more weight in schools and in the workplace. Dr. Steven Krebbs, a former colleague of mine at UT Tyler, taught a course called "Doing Good," where students got involved with community projects, such as Habitat for Humanity and helping at an animal shelter. Bringing happiness and success to others with no strings attached is a real happiness boost!

WELL I'LL BE A BLUE-NOSED GOPHER

Wealth is an ugly beggar without the rich heart.
–RALPH WALDO EMERSON–

Helping others gets us out of our own "suffering mode."

The Sun Dance of the Native American Tribes of the plains and woodlands is one of the most intense and purifying ceremonies in existence. Only a select few are qualified to endure this grueling event, where, after a year or more of ceremonial preparation, dancers go through four days and three nights of dancing with no food or water and very little rest. On the third day, some tribes elect to include piercing of the skin through pegs that penetrate the chest, and those pegs are attached by rope to a sacred tree in the center of the  circle. Participants dance until the pegs rip through the flesh. The intense pain endured for this ceremony is for a very specific purpose, which varies for each dancer. The dancers willingly endure and absorb the suffering of others to help relieve their suffering. Sun dancers usually commit to at least one Sun Dance a year for four years, and many continue beyond that. Deaths or serious injuries as a result of this sacred dance are very rare.

Taking on suffering voluntarily for the sake of others is a noble cause, but that doesn't mean it's easy. The sun dancers I've met are greatly respected for their bravery and compassion. In the same way, the next time you perceive you're having hard times, think of someone else's suffering and pray to take on their suffering willingly for their sake. Offer positive thoughts or prayers to them. If you can't think of a specific person to help, offer your own personal suffering to God, Jesus, the Buddha, Allah, or others as a willing act of love and sacrifice instead of focusing on the suffering you are going through. Vow to overcome any self-centeredness, which only invites misery. That way, you will be happier, gain more friends, and have fewer regrets.

I do life's work joyfully and unconditionally with a good sense of humor.

If you're inclined to believe you'll never be happy, I urge you to reconsider. You really don't want to go there. If you're not happy, it means that some aspects of your thinking or actions haven't worked. Why would you spend another **minute** behaving and thinking in the same way that will continue your unhappiness? You **will** have happiness when you make it a priority and refuse to settle for anything else.

You choose your feelings at every moment. You are worthy and have a right to be happy, regardless of the past. If you're unhappy because you don't have something(s) you want, then your happiness is dependent on outside factors, which guarantee a roller-coaster ride. To think your life is hard makes your life harder. It wouldn't take long to find someone in a worse predicament, would it? Today is a beautiful day. Make today the most beautiful day of your life—until tomorrow!

Now for a profound concept...

Positive thoughts and actions bring happiness.

Negative thoughts and actions bring suffering.

Hot damn! It doesn't get any simpler than that! But to follow this idea takes some doing! It's like telling someone who needs to lose weight to "just eat less"! Except for the privileged few that can instantly decide to be happy or lose weight, the rest of us will require **practice!**  We'll need to go to war against our negative emotions and learn to overcome negative events that surround us or events over-emphasized in the media.

If we're in physical or mental pain, how much we suffer depends on our attitude and focus. If we bring misery to ourselves or to others through thoughts or deeds, there is no possible benefit. Any suffering we create for any living being creates suffering for ourselves, and we'll carry the burden of our misdeeds and/or deceptions like a constant, unwanted weight on our backs.

Have you ever been in such a bad mood that **nothing** can make you smile or laugh-not even a video of Grandma and Grandpa dancing to "Y.M.C.A."? Try this: Be grateful for all you have, and go cheer someone else up worse off than you are. You'll find yourself laughing and smiling more—not only at the wedding video, but even at simple things like little Daisy playing with her doggie toy. That's because you've been doing meaningful and altruistic things. Remember, humor is everywhere, so let's find some!

I am peaceful, refraining from hostility unless absolutely necessary.

One of the foremost characteristics of happiness is inner peace, which enables external problems to bounce off of us harmlessly like a stone thrown at a mountain. With inner peace, you can deal with troubles calmly and rationally. Offer more love, harmony, and peace, and those around you will become less negative. You'll experience less confrontation and have less desire for it. Having serenity about what you do will accomplish far more than obsessing over results, status, or material acquisitions.

The world can be a violent and not-so-nice place, but when given a choice as to what to focus on, choose peace. Practice being a peacemaker. Do you like being with complainers? Rather than complain, do something constructive about what bothers you. Create your own world of happiness because no one else can do it for you. Inner peace is achieved by our thoughts and actions, especially those stemming from compassion.

 ## *Happiness Step Twenty-Eight* ### Ego-Squelching Activities

Doing these will feel good! Put them in your weekly planner!

Compassion

- Do something loving and compassionate for a friend, family member, or loved one.
- Do something altruistic for someone you don't know or, if you're up to it, for someone who may even oppose you in some way.

The next time you're in a bad mood, first ask yourself why. Then, decide exactly how long you want your mood to last. When you're ready, replace your bad mood with...

- positive thoughts about something,
- doing a good deed or action that will bring benefit to another, and
- adding some humor or fun to your daily life.

Think of a current circumstance in your life where you need to be an example of inner peace. Say the following affirmation:

- *I will have the fortitude to be steady like a rock the next time ____ arises.*

Enter a couple of more things into your daily planner that will help squelch that tricky ego!

CHAPTER TWENTY-ONE
PERFECT LIFE— PERFECT PROBLEMS

Abundance

In the next two chapters, we'll look at the abundance we have in our lives, where we realize it is indeed a perfect world because all experiences (easy or difficult) help us grow and free us of our ego-driven demands. We see our attachments and addictions for what they are and the value of overcoming them. Reducing attachments enable the enjoyment of the here and now. Our attitudes toward events become more loving and accepting as we realize the universe continually gives us all we need for happiness and abundance.

We begin with two affirmations:

- *I realize that the universe is a perfect place. My problems are necessary for my growth.*
- *I am humble and respectful to all. I see life as abundant and the world as a series of miracles.*

I realize that the universe is a perfect place. My problems are necessary for my growth.

Hard times toughen us and teach us valuable lessons. Being broke, down and out, hungry, sick, lied to, or cheated on may be your story (or a heckuva good country tune!). When your life resembles a pile of compost, being around a happy person can be really irritating!

Q. What happens when you play a country tune backwards?

A. You get your spouse back, your house back, your car back, your money back, and maybe even your dog back!

Take solace in that nothing stays bad forever! It's best to learn how to roll with the punches and not interpret your life as good or bad. In other words:

Don't cut off your head just because you have a headache!

I've mentioned that happiness is a choice we make, but so is suffering to a good extent! Life is a spiritual journey, so challenges should be welcomed. For instance, you might endure a run, walk, or bike ride in 90° heat for its ultimate benefit (even if it's for the ice-cold beer waiting in your fridge).

Suffering is a part of the natural order of things and occurs to all life forms. Everything physical has growth and demise. Nothing grows forever, and dissolution is necessary in order for new growth to occur. There was suffering at our birth; we have illness and pain, and we move steadily toward old age (if we're lucky!). Suffering is unavoidable, but it doesn't do any good to concentrate on it!

I once popped a calf muscle running back to catch a fly ball. Ouch! I went down for the count! After a few choice words, I had to decide how much to lament over the injury. I could minimize it, learn from it (by definitely stretching my legs more!), or I could allow the injury to dominate everything in my life! When I decided to take control of my state of mind, the suffering lessened.

We also suffer when something that once brought us enjoyment no longer does.

Living in Southern California, nothing feels better than to jump into the cool waters of the Pacific Ocean on a warm day in summer. But even in the hottest part of summer, the water is only in the upper-sixties at best, and after about five or ten minutes of splashing around, you get cold **really** fast! Shivering and shaking, I would run out of the water with my skin a slight shade of blue. The beach towel on the warm sand, once seemingly too hot, felt great!

If we're hungry, we can enjoy a slice or two of pizza, but if we eat too many pieces, we're looking frantically in our medicine cabinet for some heartburn relief!

Something that doesn't bother us one day might bother us considerably on a different day.

Mylene is in a cheery mood driving home from work. She'd just received her year-end bonus; it's Friday, and she is excited for a party that night. As she walks into her condo, her roommate is playing music really loud. Mylene smiles and dances her way into her room to get ready for the party. All is well.

Fast forward...The party is a bust, and she is called in to work all weekend. On Monday, her boss yells at her over some mistake she'd made. Coming home, Mylene is in a foul mood; the traffic is terrible, and she has developed a sinus headache. As she enters her condo, her roommate is once again playing music really loud, but this time, Mylene complains, "Why do you always have to play that music so #*#$ loud?"

The loud music got two opposite reactions from the same person. The variables had changed Mylene's perception of the loud music. Variables aside, it's our own thoughts that ultimately create happiness or suffering. If we can change our **perception** of our circumstances (our boss, bad traffic, a headache), then our "suffering" will definitely diminish!

Let's review the nature of "suffering."

- Suffering exists.
- Suffering has cause.
- Suffering doesn't last forever. It will end.
- There are ways to overcome or greatly reduce suffering.

If you really **want** happiness, affirm this to yourself **often:**

<u>I believe happiness is possible for me. I believe I can overcome suffering.</u>

Sure, our suffering helps us mature, but we don't need to keep wallowing in the pig trough! If you're in a rut, what matters is if you believe you can get out of it! Don't live the role like an Academy Award winner! Some believe good things will never happen for them and will give you 1,234 reasons why they won't. Well, congratulations! Your non-belief in a good future gets you (drum roll, please…) **a crappy future!** A good future begins with the belief that it will happen **sooner** rather than later!

One thing suffering can teach us is how to be more compassionate to others who are in the same or worse predicament as we are. It's simply about attitude.

> *If there's a way to overcome the suffering, then there is no need to worry. If there is no way to overcome the suffering, then there is no use in worrying.*
> **-SHANTIDEVA-**

Practicing happiness is as much about improving our attitude toward suffering as it is about feeling good and trusting that "misfortunes" often benefit us in mysterious ways.

Once upon a time in a tropical land, there lived a king whose lieutenant was a positive thinker to the point where the king was annoyed by his constantly finding good in everything. One day, while in the jungle, the king was chopping a fresh coconut for breakfast, and his machete slipped, cutting off his toe. The aching monarch limped to show his misfortune to the lieutenant, who exclaimed, "That's wonderful!"

"What did you say?" asked the king, astonished.

"This is a real blessing!"

Hearing this response, the king became very angry.

"Take it from me," the lieutenant exhorted, "behind this accident there is some good we do not see."

"That does it!" the king exclaimed, hurling the lieutenant into a deep, dry well.

While limping back to the castle, the king was apprehended by headhunters who decided that he would be an excellent sacrifice to the volcano. The warriors took him to the tribal priest, but the holy man noticed that the king was missing a toe. "I'm sorry," the priest informed the king. "We can't use you. The volcano goddess accepts only full-bodied sacrifices; you are free to go."

Overjoyed, the king hobbled out of the tribal camp. Suddenly, it dawned on him that the lieutenant had been correct; there was indeed a hidden blessing behind this seeming misfortune!

As quickly as he could, the king found his way back to the well where he had left the lieutenant. To the ruler's delight, his companion was still sitting in the well, whistling happily. The king offered the lieutenant a rope and pulled him out of the well, apologizing profusely.

"I am terribly sorry I threw you in there!" the king confessed as he dusted his advisor's shoulders. "I was taken prisoner by some wild natives who were about to cast me into the volcano. But when they saw my toe was missing, they let me go. It was actually a miracle, which you foretold. I so thoughtlessly cast you into this pit! Can you ever forgive me?"

"No apology necessary," replied the lieutenant. "It was also a blessing that you left me in the well."

"Now how are you going to make something positive out of that?" queried the king.

"Because," the lieutenant explained, "if I were with you, they would have taken **me** for the sacrifice!"

-ALAN COHEN-

I am humble and respectful to all. I see life as abundant and the world as a series of miracles.

We all receive endless opportunities to practice humility in easy or tough times.

Every semester in my career, student evaluations of my teaching were required. As a jazz studies professor at Chadron State College, I did very well working with the students who loved jazz. But at UW-Whitewater, I was initially assigned to teach five classes consisting of ninety non-music majors per class, and my evaluation numbers took a beating worse than a piñata at a birthday party. That was humbling! Over time, evaluations improved in those big classes, but during the final semester of writing my dissertation, I was getting very little sleep. I told the class the stress I was going through, and I apologized to them when things went imperfectly due to the pressure I was under. My evaluations shot up like a rocket!

I had humbled myself, and through my vulnerability, they saw me as a human being going through trials and tribulations just like they were. They realized that I really wasn't that much different from them, just a little older! My humility brought out the best in me.

Humility requires us to treat all people with equal respect, especially ourselves. This includes loved ones, friends, and those who oppose us. Despite disagreements, we recognize people are seeking happiness just like we are. Over time, positive feelings toward others will grow to include all creatures and even inanimate objects!

Once during a rough patch, I felt ready to nominate myself for a Grammy in the "saddest and most pathetic song in the world" category. Luckily, I was reminded about the abundance the world offers us. If we spend time fretting over what we don't have, we're wasting our time by not using the abilities we do have. It's perfectly acceptable to want to get out of a miserable situation, but we can't be dependent on other people or events for our well-being.

We often tell people to "have a great day." I implore you to appreciate the beauty of each ordinary day with all of its gifts because they don't last forever. There will come a day when we will grieve and beg to see a "normal day" again.

> *Normal day, let me be aware of the treasure you are. Let me not pass you by in quest of some rare and perfect tomorrow. One day I shall dig my nails into the earth, or bury my face in my pillow or stretch myself taut or raise my hands to the sky and want, more than all the world, your return.*
> **-MARY JEAN IRION-**

It does no good to focus on any perceived scarcity in our lives. By cultivating peace of mind, we realize we already have what we need. Scarcity is always longing for something more, no matter what. You might own a nice Chevy, but you long for a Maserati, so you feel meager, but a Maserati owner may feel deficient while longing for a newer one! If you are lacking something you truly need, trust that your good intentions and deeds will amount to something, and that the organized universe will respond.

You don't have to be famous or rich to love life. If you enjoy life, you'll probably enjoy most of what you do. What are life's treasures? For me, it's the purring of one of our cats, my wife's head on my shoulder, the sound of thunder, the rustling of leaves on a windy day, and maybe a glass of fine wine. A deep sense of appreciation for all of life's "miracles" accelerates manifestation of yet more gifts. When something (like a house) appreciates in value, what happens? It goes up in price. In East Texas, a lot of folks would say, "I appreciate you," and that meaningful saying would always raise the value of conversations.

WELL I'LL BE A BLUE-NOSED GOPHER

It's better to lose count while naming your blessings than to lose your blessings while counting your troubles.
-MALTBIE O. BABCOCK-

Happiness Step Twenty-Nine
Facing Adversity

- In your quiet time, think of a major adversity you've faced in your life. How did that situation strengthen you?
- Think next of a current adverse situation in your life. How might this situation strengthen you?

Jot down how you will turn this difficult time into an opportunity for learning and growth, and follow through with your plan, including entering it in your calendar!

CHAPTER TWENTY-TWO
MORE GARBAGE TO THE DUMPSTER

Lightening the Load

Most of us believe that there's some sort of purpose or master plan to our existence. This helps keep us from blowing up like a hydrogen bomb when we don't get what we want. Trusting that things will ultimately work out as they should helps when things get rough. Let's look at two more ways to see the abundance in our lives, along with two affirmations.

- I am overcoming attachments and addictions to what I "need" to be happy.
- I am less fearful of adversity and uncertainty.

I am overcoming attachments and addictions to what I "need" to be happy.

To overcome having to have certain things or results in order to be happy enables us to rise above the roller-coaster of emotional ups and downs in favor of a consistently good frame of mind. We recognize the potential power attachments and addictions have over us, and it takes real resolve to eliminate them. That's because the **ego monster** growls: "I will decide what will be required to make me happy. When I get the new car and the new job and the spouse I want, maybe then I'll be happy." Stop right there! Like an unwanted virus on your computer, happiness dependent on outside conditions is an **attachment!**

It's fine to want success and to enjoy it when it comes, but if you think achievements alone will bring lasting happiness, then your suffering is guaranteed! We'll always add to the list of what we need for our happiness to **continue**, keeping it forever out of reach. Don't surrender your well-being to external circumstances.

Our ego hypnotizes us into believing we need more money, status, and things to attract the "right" friends, lovers, etc. into our life. We need a higher-paying job, regardless of the stress, right? We accumulate more things, more worries, and a greater need to protect what we've worked hard for, affording little time for happiness or relaxation. Ironically, having more material possessions brings about more potential suffering with fear of losing them. Like success, nothing in the physical world lasts forever. Jesus said, "One must truly die and be born again." It's our attachments that have to die so that our happiness can be born.

Quite simply:

Self-centeredness is the creator of our suffering; it increases our attachments, our desires, and our negative thinking.

Of course we need material things to survive. Most of us need a car to get around, but if you **must** have next year's Ferrari to keep from being utterly miserable, then you've got an attachment. Consumer culture preaches that happiness is gotten from obtaining material wealth. If that were true, then the more we owned, the more happiness we would have. There's nothing wrong with material things; it's the **emphasis** on them that creates suffering.

> *Thousands upon thousands of rivers flow into the sea,*
> *but the sea is never full—and if man could turn stone*
> *into gold, still would his heart never be contented.*
> **-CHINESE WISDOM-**

Inside the box below, write **all** the things you **must** have to be happy:

☐

I think you're getting the point. But here's a little ditty…

All I Need to be Happy is...

Get my bachelor's and master's and a doctorate or two
    with time for a girlfriend or more than a few!
A high paying job with no problems or stress
    located in Tahiti or Hawaii no less!
A bestselling book that's known the world 'round,
    and it sure wouldn't hurt to lose a few pounds!
For my friends to all love me with constant approval,
    and for a wizard to facilitate my debt removal!
For my relatives to adore me and all get along,
    and driving in my Jaguar, I can't go wrong!
A mansion, wine cellar, and Olympic-size pool
    plus six-pack abs would be totally cool!
A lucky lottery ticket to find my bliss,
    but deep down I know I'll add to the list.
To have all these things **and** live a life that's free?
    I think all this "happiness" just isn't for me!

Many have a difficult time handling affluence when they get it because they always want more. Engrossed in obtaining more wealth and protecting it, they lose the enjoyment of the here and now. Do you know of someone who is materially wealthy that complains about his or her "misfortune"?

> Since Toni's accident, her values changed. She doesn't care for fancy clothes, elegant food, or expensive jewelry. She's happy as a lark with spaghetti, a coke, and a colorful blouse, even if it's only $9.99. Other than her wedding ring, she really prefers not to wear jewelry (she's the **ideal** wife!). Toni has everything she needs to be happy every day.

Pets show us how to live life without attachments. They take good care of their bodies, adapt to change, and have fantastic survival skills.

They're content with the basics: food, water, and shelter, and their love for us is unconditional. They live in the here and now—no fretting over the past or worrying about the future. People who state, "I wish I were a cat/dog/horse/etc." are really longing for a **life without attachments** (which bring most of our stress).

The way to nullify attachments is to change them into preferences. It's one thing to **prefer** something and work toward getting it, but it's quite another to be dependent on it for your well-being! By all means, savor the great moments life brings, but to crave and "need" something in order to be happy brings suffering like an arctic cold front. Ram Dass likens an attachment to eating an ice cream cone. Read this out loud in one big breath:

> You start to eat it and you've got to keep eating 'cause it's going to melt and you can't keep that first rush of the ice cream cone forever because after a while you are going to have had enough and you know that when you take your first bite so even in the first bite is the suffering of the anticipation that it's going to be over.

We can't eat ice cream forever (though I've tried it with chocolate mint!). As soon as we're too full, we suffer. Yet we cling to things that we think give us happiness. There's nothing wrong with wanting things unless we throw a tantrum when we don't get the lollipop. If your favorite sports team loses (and I'm used to that), you realize you didn't have control over the situation, and while you're disappointed your team didn't win, allow yourself one big "aaarrrggghhh!" and move on.

Think of your attachments as "flawed happiness." I liken them to scratching a mosquito bite; the more you scratch it, the more it itches! Here's one example of an attachment:

"I have a strong libido, and I have a fit if it's not satisfied."

Let's try that again. Take a deep breath.

"Ok, I have a strong libido, but I won't have a catastrophic conniption when it's not satisfied. I'll deal with it."

It makes no sense to lose peace of mind.

> *Ask for what you want, but don't demand it.*
> **-KEN KEYES, JR.-**

Don't forget the "asking" part of this equation! If you have people guessing what you want, your chances of getting it are less than winning the Alabama state lottery (they don't have one!). The more specific you are, the better. If you think people won't give you what you want or that you don't deserve it, it's an invitation for more scarcity in your life rather than abundance.

The second part of this quote "....but don't demand it" is just as important. Have you spent a lot of time trying to manipulate the outside world to fit **your** agenda? I hear Dr. Phil saying, "And how's **that** workin' for ya?" Is everything and everyone else to blame for your problems and sufferings? Believe that, and you'll crash more often than bumper cars. Don't carry that B.S. bag of attachments and addictions anymore. Flex your muscles and hurl that bag into outer space!

Shedding attachments helps us rise above fear, doubt, dishonesty, jealousy, and excess. The manner in which we handle life's traumatic events will improve. We'll be free of our past conditioning that limits our future. Become willing to try new things, step into the unknown, and trust that whatever happens will be for your good somehow.

Now for the really tough one:

Avoid becoming <u>overly</u> attached to anything you will eventually lose.

This applies to **everything** we have. Yes, everything. Possessions are difficult enough to part with, but it's really hard when we lose those we love. Face it: Unless we pass on first, we lose everyone we know in the physical plane. Knowing that, we have to prepare to not allow the loss of loved ones to completely incapacitate our ability to move on. Being overly attached to anything brings utter despair when it's lost. Sure, there is a grieving period for everyone, but we have to learn to accept what we lose without judgment and carry on the best way we know how. Gain and loss are a big part of everyone's life, and none of us escape the lessons they bring at one time or another.

We can even be attached to being unhappy! Some find a curious solace in feeling misery, believing it's what we "should" and "ought to" have, likely arising from guilt or feeling unworthy. Take control of your happiness so you can make a positive difference in the lives of others.

Happiness Step Thirty
Morphing Attachments into Preferences

It's time to magically morph our attachments into preferences. Think of an obvious attachment of yours that erodes your happiness. You don't have to give up all of what you want—just your need for something beyond the basic essentials or for having to have things a certain way. Rethink your attachment into a preference so that you will no longer depend on it for your well-being. Write this affirmation:

- *To turn this attachment _____ into a preference, I'll do this:*

Voilà! Poof! Attachment gone! (For now…but it may come back and require a repeat of this action!)

- Now pick another tough one, and repeat! Got more? Feel free to write your affirmations wherever they will do you some good (sticky notes on the refrigerator, in your wallet or purse, etc.).

Work on these as long as you need to. After a week or so, ask yourself:

- In what ways did I keep this attachment from eroding my happiness?
- When did this attachment get the best of me?

- How can I do an even better job overcoming this attachment?

Another "attachment-freeing" exercise is to get rid of excess material things. When your stuff has outlived its usefulness, why keep it? Choose some things you have too much of. Tell yourself that while it's okay to want this, you do not "need" it for your well-being. Free yourself from excess. Make a list and follow through.

- I now release my need for the following items...
- I will discard these items...
- I will donate these items...

For an "A+" grade, find an item or two that means something to you but would be greatly appreciated by someone else, whether it is a friend, family member, someone you work with, or even a stranger. Make a list and follow through again:

- I will willingly, without any negative emotion, give the following item(s) to the following person(s).

After you've done all this, how do you feel? Hopefully great! Let's move on to the next affirmation.

<u>*I am less fearful of adversity and uncertainty.*</u>

Stuff happens. We wanted the Ace of Spades, and we're dealt a Two of Clubs. We're sailing along, and suddenly we're looking at Hurricane McSwirly. "Why me?" is the unanswered question. How do we deal with what life throws at us and not sink into the briny deep?

Expecting the world to treat you fairly because you are good is like expecting the bull not to charge because you are a vegetarian.
-DENNIS WHOLEY-

It's normal to have some trepidation in tough times, but ask yourself: "What has my fear, anger, worry, etc. done for me other than raise my blood pressure?" If you can improve a situation by all means do it—without boarding the emotional roller-coaster. Calm thoughts are much better for your health than stressful ones. When life throws tomatoes at you, make some salsa! If it's worse than tomatoes, remember this wise old saying:

You cannot polish a buffalo chip.

Unless you're in the fertilizer business, discard that "chip" and move on! We can't fix everything! Pick your battles, and realize sometimes you have to take a deep breath and simply walk away from a really negative situation. Take the risk of following your happiness! Even if you don't know what that happiness is, you already know what it isn't, don't you? The risks are much less than you might think. The real risk is being unhappy and remaining stuck. It's sad when people begin on a sincere path to better themselves, only to give up the minute an obstacle arises, and it will. We're here to overcome these kinds of things.

Uncertainty can be just as scary as adversity. One thing is certain: Nothing in the physical realm stays the same, so it pays to be ready for whatever life throws at us and to appreciate the good times.

> *Man cannot for a thousand days*
> *On end enjoy the good,*
> *Just as the flower cannot bloom*
> *A hundred days.*
> **-TSENG-KUANG-**

Every choice we make has a degree of uncertainty to it.

I attended a clinic given by Dr. Wyatt Webb (no known relation!), and the topic was facing our fears of uncertainty. One man in our group was a respected physician. He confided to the group he wanted to change careers, but he was fearful about leaving his practice and uncertain about beginning a new profession. After encouragement from many that day, he realized his fears had been holding him back and that he had to follow his heart and take the leap to a new career. It was a life-changing day for him!

Jesus asked his disciples: "Can anxious thoughts add a single day to your life?" The Buddha reminded us that the root of all suffering is craving. Ironically, our fears are generally about not getting what we want, are they not?

Fear knocked at the door. Faith answered. No one was there.
–PROVERB–

When uncertainty controls your life, it's like living in a mansion but only using one room. You never go into the other rooms, **and** you spend your life worrying about them! My wife taught me a lesson about uncertainty…

I took Toni on a cruise recently, and she would ask where we were many times each day due to her memory issues. She would quip, "I don't know where we're going, but that's okay!" When it comes to the uncertainties we face, I couldn't state it more perfectly than that!

Fearlessness is the first prerequisite of a spiritual life.
-MAHATMA GANDHI-

Nothing will undermine our spirituality when we trust that any situation offers us what we need in order to learn.

I recall my very first Native American sweat lodge. This sacred, purifying ceremony is an incredible experience, and it is open to any sincere person wishing to partake in prayers for people in need while enduring intense, prolonged heat. The lodges are conducted by one or more highly-esteemed pipe carriers who have earned the right to conduct sacred ceremonies, but as first-timers, my wife and I were understandably nervous. We looked at the large rocks being heated up to a glowing red in a bonfire outside. The rocks would be put inside the lodge, and we knew we were about to get really hot! Wondering just how hot, I asked one of the regulars how many "grandfathers" (rocks) would there be for our ceremony. He looked at me matter-of-factly and answered: "You'll get what you need—no more, no less."

I thought about this a long time afterward. Elders in charge of sweat lodges know how much heat to give everyone through the prayers, and every sweat lodge is different. In the same way, the Creator knows what we need. There's no need to fear.

If we never suffered, we would be denied our deepest and most permanent learning experiences.

When I was seven years old, I became very ill with a fever of 107°. It caused permanent hearing loss, and with that came a lot of frustration. Now I see how it helped me. I had to sit in the front row to hear the teacher, and I transformed from a bratzilla to a brainiac. It gave me at least a mild understanding of what people with a physical handicap go through. I now see the blessing behind the curse!

All adversity has lessons, and even manure has its use! You don't have to like it or carry it with you—just be at peace as you deal with problems, and let your negative feelings go. Don't dwell on them. Vow to turn your negative situations into a more powerful future.

If God brings you to it, he'll get you through it.
-WISE CHRISTIAN SAYING-

When adversity arrives, the eagle sets an example.

An eagle knows when a storm is approaching long before it breaks. The eagle will fly to some high spot and wait for the winds to come. When the storm hits, it sets its wings so that the wind will pick it up and lift it above the storm. While the storm rages below, the eagle is soaring above it. The eagle does not escape the storm. It simply uses the storm to lift it higher. It rises on the winds that bring the storm.
-AUTHOR UNKNOWN-

Remember, it isn't the burdens of life that weigh us down; it's how we handle them. Use the storms of your life to rise even higher. Suffering is a form of purification. Use your willpower and wisdom to overcome it and move on. Take your garbage of attachments and worries to the dumpster!

Happiness Step Thirty-One
Don't Worry!

What's worrying you? Is there something that concerns you right now? In your mind, invite one of your worries over for coffee, tea, or your favorite beverage. Tell your worry what you'll be doing to reduce and minimize it so you can move on with your life. Jot this down, and enter it in your daily planner with specific days, times, and activities.

_____

_____

_____

Include some activities you'll do to reduce your worry time for issues you cannot control.

_____

_____

_____

Now thank your "worry" for the beverage time, and tell it you're breaking up! You can't meet anymore. You'll be too busy "doing," and you won't have time for worry!

CHAPTER TWENTY-THREE
JUDGE NOT, WANT NOT

Impartiality

When we develop the ability to be impartial, we learn to observe our physical actions and thoughts with a newfound objectivity. We observe our social roles and life's experiences without fear and vulnerability. We avoid unnecessary judgments or comparisons and enjoy life's journey without having to have a certain result determine our happiness. Given are four affirmations:

- My impartial, higher self directs my actions and thoughts. I avoid judging others unless my only intention is to help them.
- I am autonomous and independently ethical regardless of my surroundings.
- I enjoy life as it is without my happiness depending on external events.
- I am creative, free of the fear of judgment from others, willing to learn, and aware of how little I know compared to how much there is to know.

<u>My impartial, higher self directs my actions and thoughts. I avoid judging others unless my only intention is to help them.</u>

> *When you have found inner peace, you have no more feeling of need to become—you are content to "be."*
> **-PEACE PILGRIM (A WOMAN WHO WALKED CONSTANTLY OVER TWENTY-EIGHT YEARS FOR PEACE)-**

To simply "be" means to go with the flow without judgment or behavior based on past actions and future worries. It means to enjoy life's blessings and challenges as they come. It's a high that isn't affected by outside events nor does it wear off. There are people in all walks of life who are living examples of "simply being."

I was privileged to see the Cannonball Adderley Quintet at *Concerts by the Sea* in Redondo Beach, California. The music was great, and there was an especially good vibe among the group. Cannonball Adderley, one of the finest alto saxophonists **ever,** was so gracious and hip, but I also noticed Walter Booker on the upright bass. From the first note to the last, he was in a state of bliss. He had his eyes closed and a big smile on his face the whole evening, yet he was intently listening and reacting to whatever was happening musically.

Sitar virtuoso Ravi Shankar was known for popularizing Indian classical music throughout the world. The concert we attended in Chicago featured his daughter Annoushka, also a sitar "superstar." There was a tabla (Indian drums) player, and two others played tamburas (drone instruments). To play Indian ragas requires considerable training and expertise, but the main purpose of the music is to bring positive energy to the audience. That night, the spellbinding chemistry between the musicians transferred joy to the audience. After the concert, nearly everyone had a smile on his or her face!

These musicians, loving their music and living in the moment, were untouched by judgment from others. If something imperfect occurred, it was met with laughter, but it did not affect the mood or the quality of the music. It's a privilege to witness great masters in any field going with the flow and giving their gift to us.

Why not bring impartiality into our lives on a daily basis? Impartiality frees us from having to compare everything in the entire solar system. Unless you've been hired to be a judge in the next hit reality show, criticizing everything or everyone focuses only on "what's wrong"—a ticket to scarcity thinking.

Let's not judge others and interpret their actions unless it's solely for their well-being or safety. If you've been hired in a profession that requires judging someone's ability to perform an action properly, then that purpose is served by helping the one being judged. Comparisons for their own sake are ego-driven, unnecessary, and divisive. Those who have to define someone else by their opinion only define **themselves** as someone needing to judge!

Impartiality applies to how we judge ourselves as well. Here's a powerful statement to incorporate anytime, anywhere:

> *I judge nothing that occurs today.*
> **–COURSE IN MIRACLES–**

We can choose any activity and do it without judgment.

DR. JOHN C. WEBB

"I Run"

I run.
I don't know where I'm going.
I don't know where I've come from.
But I've always been running.
    Not running from anything.
    Not running to anything.
Just running.
I run.
I don't know who I am.
I don't know who others are.
But I've always been running.
    I pass people by.
    Others pass me by.
Just running.

Simply "being" helps us to...

- simplify our lives,
- do what is good for us,
- be in a healthy environment, and
- know our true nature and purpose.

Why judge yourself as a "success" or "failure"? Just give it your best shot.

True nobility is not about being better than anyone else; it is about being better than you used to be.
-DR. WAYNE W. DYER-

Happiness Step Thirty-Two
Just Being

Recall a time when you felt blissful, in flow, and were "simply being" without worrying about judgments or labels. What could you do to capture that feeling once again?

_____

_____

_____

_____

_____

_____

Schedule it in as often as possible!

Next, think of a way you will simplify your life and have less clutter. Today, or very soon, do one thing toward that end. Then, you guessed it, do another! You can do it!

_____

_____

_____

_____

_____

_____

_____

_____

Let's continue to the next affirmation about impartiality:

<u>*I am autonomous and independently ethical regardless of my surroundings.*</u>

We'll all be faced with times when our ethical or moral principles are challenged. Should you drive after having a few drinks? Should you overlook a friend who shoplifted an expensive item? Should you encourage a customer to sign a contract knowing they  won't be able to afford the payments with his or her income? The possibilities are endless. When you develop a sincere desire to bring more happiness and peace to the world, the choices you make will be based on ethics rather than gaining approval or preset rules that may not always be the best solution for a particular situation. Ultimate gratification is found by doing what's right with honesty and integrity, even if it means you lose a friend or a job. Trust that you will be rewarded for your tough, but ethical, decisions.

I enjoy life as it is without my happiness depending on external events.

Free from depending on specific results for our happiness, we eliminate judging or defining our lives as good or bad. We gain the capacity to enjoy each moment, even when our lives are as chaotic as a cafeteria full of preschoolers. Allow your enjoyment of each moment to supersede the need for success and achievement. You do the best you can. Sometimes you'll get the results you want. Other times, not so much. We need to learn how to lose graciously at times.

> Ernie Banks, "Mr. Cub," a great baseball player and a Chicago Cub for his entire career, endured year after year of mediocre Cub teams and the fickle Chicago weather. On chilly, foreboding days in April, with weather more suitable for penguins, Ernie would proclaim, "Let's play two!" His love for the game was unsinkable. Why not play two games, despite the weather or the team's record?
>
> Adversity, distractions, and disappointments need not ruin your love of life. Keep following your higher self, and nothing will bring you down!

Happiness Step Thirty-Three
Erasing Disappointment

Think of a significant event when you didn't get something you wanted and your reaction was not satisfactory. Jot it down.

_____

_____

_____

How could you have better handled the situation?

_____

_____

_____

Let's make an affirmation.

- *The next time something not-so-good happens to me, I will handle it in such a way where I can at least feel good about my reaction.*

Jot down a couple of ideas. Remember, you want to be proud of the way you handled disappointments years after the event!

_____

_____

And now, to our last affirmation about impartiality:

I am creative, free of the fear of judgment from others, willing to learn, and aware of how little I know compared to how much there is to know.

No one (especially you!) needs to be a variety show judge, rating everything that happens in your life! Impartiality doesn't imply indifference; it means you'll care less about what everyone else thinks and move forward. When ego no longer ties you to needing approval, always having to win, protecting an image, or pretending you know everything, you'll create great ideas from the heart because you care about others. Our highest moments of creativity, profound inspiration, and knowledge will arrive when we transcend our fears and any ego-driven illusions.

CHAPTER TWENTY-FOUR
SEEING THE BIG PICTURE

Unity

When we apply the concept of unity in our lives, we learn to "get out of ourselves" and merge with the natural flow of the universe. To become one with universal love, peace, energy, beauty, wisdom, and clarity can be a tall order, but it can be achieved with an attitude change toward harmony over discord and open-mindedness over close-mindedness. Here are four affirmations:

- *I am a deep thinker, feeling a connection to the world and the people in it.*
- *I choose friends carefully and can be in solitude without being uncomfortable.*
- *I am grateful and appreciative of myself, others, and the simple things in life just the way they are.*
- *I am spontaneous and flexible, realizing and accepting what can and cannot be controlled on a daily basis.*

I am a deep thinker, feeling a connection to the world and the people in it.

By taking the time to think through problems and solutions according to our higher nature, we develop the capacity for deep thinking. Three of my favorite words, **"upon further investigation,"** help us avoid jumping to conclusions based on limited knowledge. We use our ability to be impartial, examining all sides of a situation before making a decision.

With the technology and social media available at our fingertips today, the possibility of connecting with people all over the world is endless. More than ever, our actions and thoughts can have a profound effect on others, and vice versa. Face it: We are **nothing** without the assistance of many, many people, and our survival is completely dependent on others. Were the happiest moments of your life possible without special people? Happiness cannot be bought, nor can it exist independently of others.

Let's get rid of the idea that we're somehow separate from everything. No one is separate; we are all part of a totality. Peace on Earth begins with the compassion and love we show toward everyone we encounter, regardless of how we're treated. There is no honor in only treating a few people well. Even the most evil people in history could do that! Love and compassion can grow throughout the world—if we just give it!

Happiness Step Thirty-Four
Showing Compassion and Love

The more we have a good heart, the better our overall disposition will be. Ask: "Will the next thing I do bring happiness to those around me?" If the answer is yes, by all means, do it, and if the answer is no, don't do it. Pretty simple, huh? What will you do today to bring happiness to others? Enter that activity into your calendar, and keep doing more of them every day!

Let's discuss the next unity affirmation:

<u>I choose friends carefully and can be in solitude without being uncomfortable.</u>

Imagine a world with no people or living things in it but you. Who would be around to see that fancy convertible or the Louis Vuitton clothing and accessories? There would be no one to admire us and feed our ego! Even cruel dictators require others for their own indulgence! We need people in our lives, and we exist to help others.

With a positive nature, you'll attract others who are positive. You'll carefully choose who you want to be close to by realizing who best fits your higher nature, regardless of their perceived status. You'll lose the fear of being alone, and use "alone time" for reflection and self-development. The wise choices you make will ultimately lead to more rewarding relationships.

When we let go of our ego, we attract more people to us. When we abandon our **need** to have certain people think favorably of us, others will begin to like us more! Until then, there will be resistance from others when we try too hard to "impress."

My very first road gig began with six nights a week for six weeks at the Holiday Inn in Ventura, California. Being twenty-one and single, I tried everything to meet ladies when the band took breaks. Being naturally a bit shy, it was not my normal personality to just go up to people and introduce myself, but I did. After five weeks of zero luck, I realized it was pointless to try to meet a woman that final week because I was really looking for more than a one-night stand. So I stopped trying so hard and just hung out, being myself. That **very** night, as we finished playing and I was ready to face the lonely hearts club once more, a beautiful woman approached the bandstand and asked me: "Are you guys through playing **already?**"

The rest was magic. I had just encountered Toni, my future wife and soul mate.

By leaving my ego behind and just being me, the universe opened up **immediately** (or maybe took pity on me!).

I am grateful and appreciative of myself, others, and the simple things in life just the way they are.

One thing that will always bring a better day is to stop for a moment and give genuine thanks for all that you have without focusing on what you don't have. Monks, sages, and prophets have been living in what we call poverty. They have no money, own nothing but the barest necessities, and give everything they have to others, yet they are the happiest, most enlightened beings on Earth!

Gratefulness helps us appreciate what can easily be taken for granted: fresh air, a friend, someone who does something for us, etc. You'll need less in order to be happy and avoid cluttering up your life with extraneous activities and preoccupations. Imagine for a moment that you had great material wealth, but you suffered from poor health, no friends, and no peace of mind. What kind of life would that be? Accept graciously the material wealth you receive, but keep in mind that its purpose is to help others. If misused, wealth can be the source of considerable suffering, or if it is used for good, it can bring great rewards.

Each day, you can choose to be grateful and appreciative—or not.

It's 6:30 a.m. William slaps at the alarm clock and nearly breaks it as he curses. He's got a headache again. He looks at his wife, thinking: "She looks old without her makeup. She has it made—she's retired with no stress, and she gets to sleep in." He sighs. He makes coffee, but then he spills some on the counter, uttering a few choice expletives. "There's a crappy week coming up," William thinks, hating his job. He curses as his shower takes forever to warm up. He can't find the shirt he wants, so he wakes up his wife to see if she knows where it is. He finds it, but it's wrinkled. Cursing, he begrudgingly irons it, but now he's late. He starts to leave, but it's cold and rainy outside. He thinks to himself: "Another **miserable** day!" He frantically looks for an umbrella, but he can't find it. Muttering, he leaves without even saying anything to his wife. "No time for breakfast," he sighs, "but even then I'll never lose weight." His neighbor gives him a cheerful hello, but he just walks quickly to the bus stop. Even though work is only a mile away, William never walks. As he goes to get on the bus, he realizes he's forgotten his wallet and has no money. After a creative stream of curses, William runs back home, gets in his car, and drives like a madman to get to work in time for a crucial meeting. As he changes lanes recklessly, he fails to see a car in his blind spot and brushes the side of a car. He has to pull over and file an accident report. By the time William gets to work, he is in a horrible mental state and is late to his meeting. He gets on the elevator, which stops at the second floor. The custodian gets on and gives him a cheerful "good morning." William glares at him in silence, tapping his foot impatiently, nearly in tears over his rotten morning. William gets off at his floor and storms past his coworkers, who dread having to work with him and deal with his foul moods.

Two miles away in the same city...

Tony wakes up at 6:00 a.m. like he does every morning. He turns to his sleeping wife and gives her a soft kiss, being careful not to wake her up. "She just looks more beautiful every day," he thinks to himself. "I'm so glad we agreed for her to quit her stressful job and retire early. It's harder on the pocketbook, but she's happy, and we're getting by." He makes a big pot of coffee so his wife can enjoy it later. Tony spills a little coffee and wipes it up. "I see we need paper towels," he notices and writes it down on the grocery list. He looks forward to his job because the physical labor keeps him in shape. He gets in the shower, and while waiting for the water to warm up, he lets the cool water hit him. The feeling is exhilarating at first, waking him up. Tony enjoys the shower and then looks for his shirt. He can't find it, so he looks around for another shirt. It's wrinkled, so he quietly irons it and puts on his clothes. "Still plenty of time." He smiles. He has a light breakfast and goes to leave. Seeing that it's raining, Tony grabs his umbrella and overcoat, thinking, "We sure need this rain; it'll green up all the lawns." He writes a quick note to his wife, adds a few terms of endearment to it, and goes for his walk to work. Tony stops and talks to the neighbor for a couple of minutes. Now Tony will have to step it up a bit, but he doesn't mind. He says hello and waves to several people walking by. Arriving at work, he's still ten minutes early, so he chats with the security guard on the second floor. He gets his janitorial equipment and gets on the elevator. On the elevator, he sees the executive vice president of the company, Mr. William Johnson. "Hello, Mr. Johnson," Tony says, smiling.

But William just glares at him, tapping his foot impatiently. "Poor guy," Tony thinks to himself. "He's always so unhappy. I wish there was something I could do."

William, the executive vice president, makes $260,000 a year at the same company where Tony, the custodian, makes $32,000. You get the picture. How we perceive each event in our lives has **everything** to do with how our day goes for us.

At the University of North Texas, I took two graduate courses from Dr. Forrest Rollins. One course, "Learning and Motivation," met at 8:00 a.m. (a joke in itself!). But Dr. Rollins was not at all like the other professors. He helped us each to discover what was relevant to our own learning on a personal basis. One of the memorable things Dr. Rollins always said was: "Every day is a beautiful day…no matter what." Back then I had a hard time with that statement, but now I see that every day, with its challenges, adversities, or even bad weather, is indeed perfect for us.

Nothing can ruin our day unless we **allow** it. Once I overslept and missed his class. I felt terrible, not for fear of my grade, but because I had genuinely missed something.

The message of being grateful and seeing the beauty the universe has to offer is not a message found often in higher education. Dr. Rollins reached thousands of students with this message and changed lives for the better. I owe a lot of my inspiration for this book to him.

Others have taught me to appreciate the simple things in life. My mom, who often suffered from poor health, would often sing to me:

> Oh what a beautiful mornin',
> Oh what a beautiful day.
> I've got a beautiful feelin'
> Everything's going my way.
> **-RODGERS AND HAMMERSTEIN** (*OKLAHOMA*)-

Think of someone you know who is full of appreciation for life. My father-in-law, Tony Jaramillo, comes to mind.

I always looked forward to his backyard barbeques, his lively company, his laughter, and his ability to make others laugh. He treasured the simplest things: a sunset, a bird taking a bath, or a Frank Sinatra tune. Tony sold shoes for many years and took pride in his job. He never made a lot of money, but he was a millionaire in my book because his enthusiasm for life proved to me beyond a shadow of a doubt that the value of enjoying life surpasses anything status or wealth can ever bring. I miss him dearly.

May we all appreciate the gift of life and make every moment as special as possible!

Happiness Step Thirty-Five
Saying Thanks

To bring yourself a better day, say this each morning:

> Today, despite any difficulties in my life, I recognize the many gifts I have been given. To realize the abundance in my life, I give thanks for…(think of **everything** you appreciate).

Make a list, and keep it handy!

And now to the last unity affirmation:

<u>I am spontaneous and flexible, realizing and accepting what can and cannot be controlled on a daily basis.</u>

Isn't it almost neurotic to want the world the way **we** want it and not the way it is? We can't change the entire world to suit our whims and desires! As this eighth century Indian poet Shantideva taught us:

Instead of trying to coat the entire Earth with leather, put on some sandals.

It's fine to want something. It's another thing to have a volcanic meltdown when you don't get it! Skip the "suffering" part and move on. **You** decide how you react to external events.

If your happiness depends on having control, you will suffer a lot and **often.**

Remember that not getting what you want is sometimes a wonderful stroke of luck.
-H.H. DALAI LAMA-

When you don't get what you want, be flexible. It may be time to go in a different direction and try something new. Let your old disappointments go. You'll be freer and happier.

Happiness Step Thirty-Six
A Little Self-Analysis

To rise above ego's imprisoning ways, we hope to do our best to use compassion, recognize our abundance, maintain impartiality, and strive for unity with the miraculous universe. Let's look at the affirmations given in the last section to see where we're doing well, and where we might improve. Write the appropriate letter to the left of each item.

a. Great! Perfecto Mundo! Fantastico!
b. A winning record! A few lapses but okay.
c. Fair to middlin' but I could use a little work.
d. Mediocre at best.
e. Helllllppppp!

Compassion:

_____You are compassionate by being able to place yourself in others' shoes.

_____You are altruistic without a need for kudos or paybacks.

_____You do life's work joyfully and unconditionally with a good sense of humor.

_____You are peaceful, refraining from hostility unless absolutely necessary.

Abundance:

_____You realize that the universe is a perfect place. Your problems are necessary for your growth.

_____You are humble and respectful to all, seeing life as abundant and the world as a series of miracles.

_____You are overcoming attachments and addictions to what you "need" to be happy.

_____You are less fearful of adversity and uncertainty.

Impartiality:

_____Your impartial, higher self directs your actions and thoughts. You avoid judging others unless your only intention is to help them.

_____ You are autonomous and independently ethical regardless of your surroundings.

_____You enjoy life as it is without your happiness depending on external events.

_____You are creative, free of the fear of judgment from others, willing to learn, and aware of how little you know compared to how much there is to know.

Unity:

_____You are a deep thinker, feeling a connection to the world and the people in it.

_____You choose friends carefully and can be in solitude without being uncomfortable.

_____You are grateful and appreciative of yourself, others, and the simple things in life just the way they are.

WELL I'LL BE A BLUE-NOSED GOPHER

_____You are spontaneous and flexible, realizing and accepting what can and cannot be controlled on a daily basis.

Choose one item you feel compelled to work on the most, and begin! It's best to focus on one issue at a time. Decide exactly what you plan to do to improve, and plug it into your schedule at key times. Keep it in the forefront of your mind often!

When you feel ready, pick another one. Doesn't it feel good to make positive changes in your life? Even "failed attempts" are better than not trying at all! Work on these as long as you need to, depending on how badly you want to subdue that tricky ego!

SECTION SIX
Casting Off the Chains of Negativity

CHAPTER TWENTY-FIVE
POTENTIAL WRECKAGE

Battling the Negative Emotions

As we work on ourselves and our happiness, the biggest challenge is dealing with negative emotions that knock on the door when "life" happens! Emotions represent the body's reaction to how our mind interprets events. Negative emotions are a form of non-acceptance or resistance to what is, has been, or might be. Confronting attachments and negative emotions requires perseverance and courage, so let's prepare for battle.

A Cherokee elder was teaching his grandchildren about life. He said to them, "A fight is going on inside me. It is a terrible fight between two wolves. One wolf represents fear, anger, envy, sorrow, regret, greed, arrogance, self-pity, guilt, resentment, inferiority, lies, false pride, superiority, and ego. The other stands for joy, peace, love,

hope, sharing, serenity, humility, kindness, benevolence, friendship, empathy, generosity, truth, compassion, and faith. This same fight is going on inside everyone."

They thought about it for a minute, and then one child asked his grandfather: "Which wolf will win?"

The elder simply replied, "The one you feed."

-NATIVE AMERICAN TEACHING-

Are negative emotions ever "good" for us? I've stated that challenges can be good for us, but negative emotions only work if they are kept in check, and the energy from them is **immediately** channeled to do something good. In most cases, as a byproduct of "ego gone wild," negative emotions will lead us to do things we will regret.

I can be hurt by nothing but my thoughts.
–A COURSE IN MIRACLES-

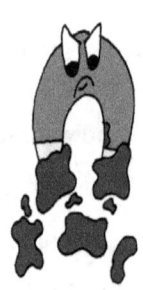

We might not grow halos or angel wings, but when we see the destructive potential of negative emotions, we'll be more apt to work on reducing them. The danger of staying in a negative frame of mind is that we become a "magnet" for negative events! Because our thoughts are so powerful, we have to be **sure** to remove any statements in our speech or thinking that we don't want to see manifested in our future!

Which negative emotions nag at you like a mosquito bite in a place where you can't reach? When life dumps a truckload of manure on your doorstep, it's still best to take on one problem at a time! For each negative emotion, there is at least one opposite emotion that can replace it.

Hatred	Love
Anger, Impatience	Compassion, Calmness, Patience
Sadness, Guilt	Comfort, Altruism
Greed, Pride	Contentment, Humility
Fear, Doubt, Stress	Courage, Confidence, Love

Hatred

Love is a common dynamic in all organized religions and part of our higher self. Love dissolves negatives and impurities. If your thoughts come from love, act on them.

> *True love is unconquerable and irresistible. It goes on gathering power and spreading itself until eventually it transforms everyone it touches.*
> **–MEHER BABA–**

Many express hate because of an absence of love in their lives. Ironically, people who hate are actually looking for love and acceptance! Love and hate are related, as evidenced by love relationships that quickly turn from love to hate in a heartbeat!

Hatred is really a disguise for hating some aspect of the self that is weak, but the ego directs it outward toward other people, things, or circumstances. Hatred can only be eliminated through love, not more hatred. Hatred is…

- a destroyer of happiness,
- inflexible,
- caused by deeply-rooted past programming,
- an absence of compassion,
- an unwillingness to walk in another's shoes, and
- destructive to self and others.

The antidote to this bitter recipe is flexibility, willingness to understand others, compassion, patience, and of course, love—no small order!

To hate something gives it power over us, and we're strangely obligated to act negatively in order to sustain the hate. Hate infects the "hater's" life like a spreading plague. If you hate your job, your hatred will expand to circumstances surrounding you, your fellow employees, your drive to and from work, and even your non-work hours. The more you focus on what you hate, the more it manifests.

At her job, Susie constantly complains about the rude customers she faces. "It seems like they're just lining up! It's getting worse and worse each week!"

If what we hate doesn't change or go away, then unless **we** change, we'll go on hating it forever, which gives it more power over us than it ever deserves. I can **guarantee** that as long as Susie continues to hate rude people, they'll literally line up until she declares, "You know what? I'm not going to let them bother me anymore." She doesn't have to start liking rude people; she should just no longer feel hate toward them.

What we focus on tends to manifest. Focusing on hate **definitely** creates more suffering. For that reason alone, it's far more beneficial to focus on what we're **for** rather than what we're **against.** Express your views in terms of what you want because if you spend time thinking about what you don't want, then what you **don't** want will grow faster than a cumulus cloud on a hot summer day! What better reason is there to focus on what you love versus what you hate?

When we receive hate from someone, it takes all our resolve not to become kids in a sandbox. "Johnny hit me so I will hit him back harder!" Exhibiting hate toward something or someone only demonstrates one's own supreme idiocy.

When one person mistreats another, it's tempting to believe all people of the same group are that way. This is called **stereotyping.**

"This (man) beat me. All men are brutal slobs."

"This (member of an ethnic group) yelled insults at me. All (members of this group) are bigots."

"This person in New York was rude to me. All New Yorkers are rude."

"This woman lied to me. All women are liars."

The unwanted twin of stereotyping is prejudice, which means to "prejudge." For "haters," it requires Herculean efforts to overcome ill will. Every hateful act or war ever fought was the result of thousands of repeated negative thoughts, words, and actions that accumulated to a breaking point. Will you have the courage to stop hate when it is encountered? We might need to protect ourselves against hate for survival, but we have to be strong and not spread hateful acts or start a world war! The bravest heroes throughout history were the ones who adopted the doctrine of non-violence.

When you point your finger at someone, three fingers are pointing back at you.

Don't allow your emotions to be controlled by outside events. If your past behavior makes Ivan the Terrible look like an angel, vow to do better next time. We need to train the mind so thoughts don't run amok like a stampede of wild horses. Turn your "less than stellar" thoughts into positive ones. For example:

"I hate Angela because she hates me."

Let's give this a little more insight:

"I know Angela is mad at me, but she really hates herself because she doesn't get the good grades I do and her parents recently got divorced, so she hates a lot of things right now. I'll stay away from her, but I hope her situation will improve."

What good could a negative action toward Angela possibly achieve? Only more hate. Not only do we need to reduce negative thoughts, but we also need to trace what caused them in the first place. Perhaps it was a violent movie or someone else's bad behavior. All negative thoughts can be traced to egos "needing" something to be a certain way.

Another hateful party pooper we'll run into are chronic complainers, which are why those "no whining" signs were invented! We've all griped about something, but how **much** for how **long?** Complaining about a long line isn't going to make the line go any faster. Strike up a conversation, or focus on what's good. Give yourself a short "ranting session" once in a while, but then either fix what you don't like or save your time and do something more constructive!

Hatred occurs when someone with a small mind isn't able to control something or someone. When a big ego is threatened, look out! Ego will do **anything** to protect what it thinks it needs. Deeply-programmed hatred can be lethal, but mostly to the hater! We humans can do better. Replace your hateful thoughts. If you'll allow hate to dissipate like the morning fog, you'll gain something far more valuable—your freedom.

> *I have been all things unholy. If God can work*
> *through me, he can work through anyone.*
> *Where there is hatred in me, let me sow love...*
> **-ST. FRANCIS-**

Anger, Impatience

When self-centeredness or the need for control is challenged, another common reaction is anger, which is often associated with hate, impatience, or both. When you feel angry, rational decisions go flying out the window. As with hate, violent crimes resulting from anger can ultimately be traced back to the ego's need for love gone terribly wrong!

Anger is a dangerous emotion. An expression of frustration can be a short-term release, but if you commit an action from anger or hate, you may have to live with the devastating results for a very long time.

> *You will not be punished for your anger, but by your anger.*
> **-BUDDHA-**

Anger is triggered because someone or something has irked a part of us that is weak. Impatience is related to the ego's desire for control, wanting what it wants **right now.** Except in training sessions for those who deal with life-threatening emergencies, impatience arises when something didn't happen **fast enough** to satisfy someone's "need." Instead of recognizing our own weakness, our ego directs the blame to that person or event that ticked us off.

Our clever ego wants us to believe that demonstrating anger or violence is justifiable. It's not. A boss directs anger at an employee for not closing a sale and losing a client, but that temper tantrum reveals the weakness of the one who is angry and does no one any good. Offering concern, disappointment, and a solution or two can be accomplished without anger. Irate people might think of themselves as a **powerful, angry** being (add some of *The Wizard of Oz* thunder). Really? You can well imagine the reaction of others to such anger. When was the last time you heard someone say, "I love how he's **always** losing his temper. So awesome!"

Notice how people look when they're REALLY angry. *Alien vs. Predator* comes to mind! An act of anger might accomplish short-term fear from those subjected to the anger, but it usually generates hate. Most comedies feature a character who displays anger over some situation that is quite laughable, which means if you get angry a lot, people will just laugh at you (behind your back!). At best, people will feel sorry for you.

Violence resulting from anger is often labeled as "courage" or "bravery." In a case of self-defense, such actions may be necessary, but not when revenge or personal vendettas become the motive. With anger, we lose a critical quality inherent in humans: **judgment.** Anger and actions associated with it create only more crises in our lives and others' lives.

Demonstrating anger requires very few brain cells. It takes far more resolve not to react with anger. Exercise patience by delaying an outward reaction so as to not hurt someone, or you'll only end up harming yourself. Anger is sparked by our past programming or a pointless attachment to the future having to be a certain way. Ram Dass says succinctly, in his book *Be Here Now*, that we can only live in the moment we have now. It's up to us to determine the quality of every moment.

This doesn't imply that we are to be meek or passive—not one bit. First, if you've succeeded in delaying an angry reaction, congratulate yourself! Then release the energy from your anger constructively soon because storing it is like con-

suming a poison and keeping it in your body. Flush it out! Work on fixing the problem or do something that will take your mind off the problem.

When I'm angry, I'll go for a long, hard run. It's hard to stay angry when you're physically exhausted! After a run and a nice shower, I'm able to look at a situation differently, or at least not want to torch a small city. With stored anger, each new potentially-angering event is like throwing a burning match into a room filled with sticks of dynamite. A few matches might fall harmlessly, but sooner or later, the whole house is going to blow! How many times have you seen someone blow up over nothing? That's stored anger. The display of temper was really about a sum total of events from the past.

Have you ever noticed how you feel tired after a major dispute? To exhibit or store anger requires tremendous energy, and it is a key contributor to illnesses, such as high blood pressure, degenerative disorders, and insomnia. Whether stored or exhibited, anger will always bring you trouble and suffering (and one helluva blues song!).

If we want peace on Earth, we have to first have peace with ourselves. What causes you to be angry? Who or what did you blame and under what circumstances? As you work on releasing built-up anger constructively, you'll begin to be angry less often and for shorter periods of time. Revisit Happiness Step Four (Letting Go of the Baggage) to help. Rather than fueling more anger, it's far better to work on inspiring people for the better.

An example of an anger trigger:

"Here I am with a deadline on my presentation, and people are rushing into my office like Black Friday at Walmart! I'm getting interrupted constantly. I swear, if there's one more interruption…"

Beware to the next person who walks in! Unless the fate of the entire world hangs on the completion of the report, this situation is the complainer's fault. If this is you and someone is being inconsiderate of your time, exercise the option of telling others that you are pressed to get something done. That will not always satisfy someone's perceived need to talk, but your conversation can be delayed. The problem here is also self-centeredness! Perhaps you've seen this on someone's desk:

Procrastination on your part does not constitute an emergency on my part.

Point well taken, but not all of the time! It could also be that the person posting this sign procrastinates on his or her work as well, creating an inability to allow room for emergencies! Better time management will allow for life's little emergencies that delay our goals. Adversity is a test of our patience and gives us an opportunity to practice it.

Another example:

"I get angry when (so-and-so) talks about me behind my back."

Gossipers want acceptance when they badmouth others, and they usually have no intention of confronting someone with what they're saying. Those upset by gossip about them are also in need of positive reinforcement, and they may not confront the gossiper. There's no communication going on! If you're thinking of  verbally criticizing someone to a third party, ask yourself: "Is what I'm planning to say in the best interest of all concerned, including the person I want to speak about?" If you cannot answer with a resounding **yes** to this question, you're far better off never saying it. With gossip, your ego gets stroked a little, but it's a shallow "victory" that often comes at a price. Gossip nearly always finds its way back to those being gossiped about and is often worse than the original gossip!

If you're the person being gossiped about, ask yourself: "Oh immaculate being of utter perfection, could I possibly have **ever** done anything to bring about one teeny bit of this gossip?" Gossip usually has a foundation somewhere. Regardless of whether you're right or not, ask yourself: "Am I bothered by this gossip because of my need to be liked?" The satisfaction that we're simply doing our best will override our need for positive reinforcement.

We all get angry at times, but controlling it and releasing it safely is paramount. Do you think what angers you now will matter in fifty or a hundred years? With that perspective, you can learn to not allow anger to get the best of you. Stand your ground with calmness and humility combined with common sense. It's far better to be remembered for your compassion than for your bad temper!

 ## Happiness Step Thirty-Seven
Dousing the Fire

Think of a time you encountered or witnessed hatred, and recall how you felt at the time. How could this situation have been handled without hate?

_____

Now, think of a time **you** displayed hatred. What will you do differently next time?

_____

- *Affirmation: I realize hatred wipes out happiness, holds us hostage, and can be lethal.*

Think of when you encountered or witnessed someone else's anger, and recall how you felt at the time. How could this situation have been handled without anger?

_____

WELL I'LL BE A BLUE-NOSED GOPHER

Think of a time <u>you</u> displayed anger and paid for it. What will you do differently next time?

_____

- *Affirmation: Anger is a dangerous emotion caused by our own weakness, not by what happens to us.*

Write your suggestions into your daily planner by scheduling reminders as preventative measures to avoid costly, even life-changing, mistakes!

CHAPTER TWENTY-SIX
SUBTLE TRICKINESS

Sadness

The negative emotions we're investigating in this chapter may appear less dangerous than hate and anger, but they're just as capable of extinguishing our well-being! We begin with sadness, usually triggered by the loss of something or someone important to us or when an event did not go the way we wanted. Anger and sadness can coexist as well. Throw in a little hate, and we have quite a combination! Fortunately, we can control how sad we're going to be and for how long. Sad times may eventually help us grow spiritually, but we don't want to stay there too long! Even on cloudy days, the sun still shines brightly above the clouds.

Not to sound harsh, but prolonged sadness and grief are a disguised form of self-pity, sugar-coated by our ego. Our ego is telling us we do not have enough of something. When we're sad and lonely, we're thinking about ourselves: "Poor **me**. Woe is **me**. **My** life is so hard." It's all about "me" and "I." We portray ourselves as victims, clinging to grievances as signposts of our own identity. We're the star in our own tragic soap opera.

> *Get off the cross. Somebody needs the wood.*
> **–DOLLY PARTON-**

The next time you wallow in your self-pity remember that it is you who literally decides how long you want to be in a bad mood. You **can** control your moods! Have you ever tried to stay in a bad mood? "I'm in a bad (or sad) mood, and **no one** will get me out of it **everrr!**" You'd better hope someone can get you to laugh, because if no one can even get you to irk a smile, then **you win!** And what do you win? Sadness for eternity? Do you really want to go there? Do something about that bad mood!

Many of us miss someone who is no longer in our lives. Losing a loved one may be the toughest challenge of all, but it happens to everyone eventually. Grief has its own timetable, and we shouldn't try to stifle it. Trudging through the stages of grief (denial-anger-bargaining-depression-acceptance), we can still control how **often** we think of that person, the **intensity** of the grief, how **many** memories we trigger on a daily basis, and for how long. It doesn't mean that we don't care or miss that person!

Some people punish themselves by playing memories in their mind repeatedly until it becomes intolerable. Remember, anything constantly repeated is something we'll get really good at. Many who lose loved ones may suffer excessively for months and even years, perhaps out of guilt for things unsaid or undone. Since that can't be changed, there can be no constructive purpose behind continuing the endless suffering when there is no longer anything we can

do to change the past. The ones who have passed on will be taken care of. Meanwhile, **our** lives have to move on.

Out of your teardrops, you water the seeds for new beginnings.

When we lose someone we love, share the positive things about that person with others. For example, you can say, "Joel had such a sense of humor. We were always laughing." Pass that laughter and humor to others in his honor. It doesn't replace Joel, but it helps to continue the gifts our loved ones gave us.

Don't cry because it's over; smile because it happened.
-PROVERB-

Another powerful way to reduce sadness is to stop immersing yourself in self-pity and **go help someone else.** There is undoubtedly someone at least as sad as you.

I wept because I had no shoes on my feet
until I saw the man without any feet.
–OLD PROVERB-

Find someone who is grieving and needs company. Spend an hour with a person who needs a "pick-me-up." There are homeless children, needy families, and addicts—it doesn't matter who you pick to help, but by helping others get out of their misery, self-pity will shrink. It's one thing to have the treasured memories of those we have lost, but it's quite another to cling to those memories to the point to where our quality of life is compromised.

> *If life seems empty, it means there is a great opportunity to fill it with good things.*
> **-WISE SAYING-**

Guilt

We also become sad when we feel badly about something we did or didn't do, so guilt sets in. Just remember there are no brownie points for feeling worthless, not good enough, unloved, or just plain low. Marcia Menter refers to our guilt as "the slough of suckiness," where we wallow in the trough of every bad choice we ever made. If we lie in the pigpen, we may not notice if the gate's been opened! What is it that sucks, exactly? Well, crawl out of the mud pit, and do something about it!

Rather than negative thinking, think about what you want for lunch.

> *What does not kill me makes me stronger.*
> *So, I'd better not let this kill me.*
> **–MARCIA MENTER-**

Greed

One of the most prevalent negative tendencies in today's society is greed. This is a by-product of self-centeredness that is developed to the point where the acquisition of things for the "I-me-mine" school of life matter more than anything else.

Infected with greed, we become self-indulgent to the point where we've forgotten that many others enabled our every accomplishment, not to mention anything we use, own, or consume. When greed dominates, we crave material excess and become aggressive, competitive, suspicious, and jealous. The impact of one's actions on others or the environment is ignored. Economic benefit matters over anything else, including family and spirituality. We devote our time to meaningless activities designed solely for our own pleasure and benefit, with no thought of helping others. We're unable to develop proper relationships because we're too busy lusting after power, fame, and pleasures. Even if we get what we want, we're never satisfied, and we never will be. Then we wonder why we're lonely!

Any bad deeds ever committed ultimately come from an overblown sense of self-importance, which will suck obstacles and misfortunes toward us like an industrial vacuum cleaner!

> *Whatever joy there is in this world*
> *All comes from desiring others to be happy,*
> *And whatever suffering there is in this world*
> *All comes from desiring myself to be happy.*
> **-SHANTIDEVA-**

Wanting happiness for ourselves is a positive thing, but self-cherishing more than caring about others will bring suffering. As soon as we place others before ourselves, the happiness that once was so elusive will come in abundance!

Pride

Pride, greed's "wicked stepsister," is hard to see as a "fault" because it's usually cleverly disguised as something we "should" have. On my Microsoft Word online thesaurus, there are the following synonyms for "pride":

- arrogance,
- conceit,
- smugness, and
- self-importance, with an antonym of "humility."

In *Merriam-Webster's Dictionary,* we find the following definitions:

- inordinate self-esteem: conceit
- a reasonable or justifiable self-respect
- delight or elation arising from some act, possession, or relationship
- disdainful behavior or treatment
- ostentatious display
- a company of lions
- a showy or impressive group (dancers, for example).

While some aspects of pride are good to have, self-importance can masquerade as pride. Who do you prefer to be around: someone who is humble and thinks of others or a member of **stuckonmyself.com**?

People who flock around those with humongous egos are chasing status or power, and they will do <u>anything</u> to get that for themselves, even above all ethical principles.

The Webster definition, "justifiable self-respect," is the best aspect of pride to have. There is a difference between being confident and respectful of self versus being self-centered. "Delight or elation arising over something" is good provided that what we're elated about is something good versus robbing a jewelry store!

In sports, some public displays of pride can reach sickening proportions with excessive showing off, public taunting, and ostentatious celebrations. Hopefully, the pendulum will swing the other way (and bonk a few show-offs in the noggin!). Already there are penalties in sports for taunting. We could use some in everyday life!

The phrase a "pride of lions" demonstrates ferociousness in consuming of prey. Pride can be dangerous. By all means, be proud of your school, your country, etc., but it can be taken too far.

- "I'm proud of my school, so let's go beat up some people from our rival school."
- "I'm proud of my red gang colors. We shoot anyone wearing the colors and symbols of our rival gang."
- "We're proud of our country's leader. Anyone who says anything bad about our leader goes to prison."
- "We're proud of our religion. Anyone who does not worship like we do must be converted, or else…"

Before we join the "I'm With Stupid" club, let's be responsible big boys and girls when it comes to managing our pride so we don't become self-serving, egocentric, and ultimately dangerous.

Low Self-Esteem

The opposite problem of pride lies with low self-esteem. Those with low self-esteem are often introverted or shy, but not all people with a quiet nature are shy. While humility is a virtue, low self-esteem happens when we're ashamed of ourselves for something we've done, the way we look, or how we assume people think of us. These feelings are a by-product of the ego's need for approval. Shame can result in the same pessimism as "Murphy's Law," where we believe the worst will happen to us and we'll never deserve anything good. This gives us the excuse to doubt our abilities and our future.

Immersed in our self-centered self-pity, we obsess over what others think of us, so we give up control of our future and place it in the hands of others, who may or may not have good intentions. Some worry about what others "might" think, whether they care about us or not! "Oh dear, someone might not like me or like what I do." Given our world's 7+ billion people, that's **very likely!** If we try to live our lives for people who don't even know us or for imaginary people who might be critical, a negative future is all ours!

Jealousy

My wife's jealousy is getting ridiculous. The other day, she looked at my calendar and wanted to know who May was.
 -RODNEY DANGERFIELD-

A by-product of pride and self-centeredness, jealousy occurs when:

- someone else has something we want,
- there's something we think we "should" have that others have, or
- we think someone has something he or she doesn't deserve.

When we're jealous, we blow up our own importance. We're unable to enjoy the happiness of others, so we play the "comparison game." We judge what **we** should have **and** what others should have. We may think someone close somehow belongs to us and must conform to our set of rules. Jealousy does accomplish one thing: It increases competition over who can accumulate the most attachments! Still want to play?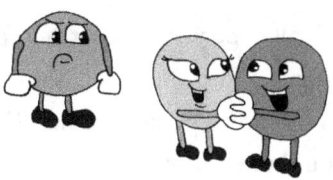

The next time jealous feelings start to creep in, identify their source. The best choices are to…

- recognize what we can improve in the areas where we feel inadequate,
- actively work on our faults that created the jealousy in the first place, and
- do the best we can and stop worrying. No one is perfect at everything!

Jealousy exposes our own perceived inadequacies. Is what you want to improve important enough to make a change or not? Whatever you decide, leave the jealousy behind!

> *As no one desires even the slightest suffering nor is ever content with the happiness he has, there is no difference between myself and others: Therefore, inspire me to rejoice when others are happy.*
> **-BUDDHIST SAYING-**

Happiness Step Thirty-Eight
Overcoming

We all experience negative emotions, but we can work on reducing their intensity and duration. Rank these emotions according to which ones give you the most trouble: "1" is the toughest one for you, and "5" gives you the least problem.

    Sadness   Guilt   Greed   Pride   Jealousy

With your #1 toughest emotion, think of an instance when you saw **someone else** exhibit that emotion. (Note: If you chose sadness, avoid a death scenario unless you refer to how someone is dealing with a loss after a one-year grieving period.)

Was there a way that emotional display could have been eliminated, reduced, or its duration shortened? How?

_____

Think of a time when **you** exhibited this emotion. What will you do differently to eliminate, reduce, or shorten its duration in the future?

_____

Repeat these questions for the other emotions that give you trouble. If you're up to it, do them all, but it's best to focus on one or two at a time.

CHAPTER TWENTY-SEVEN
TURNING THE LIGHT BACK ON

Fear and Doubt

We've talked about fear and doubt a lot—for good reason! This deadly combination can turn our happy, yellow brick road into quicksand. We set out to do something, and a flurry of "yeah, buts" and "what-ifs" stop us in our tracks. Fear produces a resistance to change, uncertainty, and worries about future scarcity.

When we were babies, we had very few fears, doubts, or stresses except for being left alone. As we mature, these feelings are unwittingly programmed into us by people and events that surround us. Good news: if they were programmed in, we can program them back out! Like the scientific method, it's a process.

1. Admit the fear.
2. Identify exactly what it is.
3. Determine its cause.
4. Fix it!

Sounds simple enough, but fear may not always be what it seems.

Monica had been making a good salary as a legal secretary for two years since graduating from the university with a business degree and a minor in theatre. Her first love was acting, and she had landed several major roles in school productions. The civic theatre was holding auditions for *The Lion King*, and their shows were always good. She was torn. Should she try out? A couple of actors from her area had gotten major roles in New York. Monica's parents had always told her there's no future in theatre and that she needed a "real" job. Her boyfriend complained that if she were selected for the production, she would be in nightly rehearsals, and they would never see each other. Another woman who had always gotten the best roles at the university Monica attended was auditioning for the lead part. "I'm rusty," she thought to herself. "I won't get a decent part." But every time Monica convinced herself not to audition, something deep inside tugged at her to try anyway. She still had time to prepare…

Monica's fears and doubts kicked in. "If I get a major part, my parents will tell me I'm wasting my time. Then, my theatre friends auditioning with me will be jealous. If I get a smaller part, there's still a huge time commitment, and my boyfriend won't be happy. What if I fail miserably and I end up shoveling lion poop?"

Monica is not just afraid of failure, she's also afraid of success, which would produce major changes in her life. If she becomes an actress, it would bring chastisement from her family and boyfriend, a change of jobs, and a move to where better opportunities exist. If she doesn't audition, she'll never know how her future life might have been. Her current life is safe and familiar. Does Monica really want to change, or is she just kidding herself? Her answer lies within.

> *Courage is being scared to death…and saddling up anyway.*
> **-JOHN WAYNE-**

If you hang in there, amazing things can happen.

I was looking for my first college-level teaching job in Southern California, but a deep recession seemed to make the chances of getting a job there about the same as being abducted by aliens! Everyone was telling me: "There aren't any jobs out there," and "Hundreds and hundreds of people apply for each job." I'd sent resumes to every university in the U.S. that offered a jazz course, but by May, there were no bites. While grocery shopping, I ran into a friend, and we began talking about jazz teaching positions. Suddenly a young lady walked up, saying, "I couldn't help but overhear you. I'm Debbie, secretary of jazz studies at Mt. San Antonio College, and we're reviewing applicants for a one-year position, and if you apply in the next day or so, there may still be time."

The college was just a **few miles** away! I thanked her and raced home, shattering sound and light barriers to get my materials to the college. Two days later, while I was in the shower, Toni handed me the phone with a request for an interview (there was no FaceTime then, luckily!), and the next day I met Ashley Alexander, a renowned jazz trombonist and educator, who was taking a one-year sabbatical and needed someone to teach that year. He started showing me around, introducing me to everyone and explaining the schedule, and after a while, I began to realize that he wasn't going to interview or audition me at all. I had the job! That happens about as often as palm trees grow in the Arctic! To top it off, Ashley then asked me if my family would like to rent his house a few blocks away at a reasonable rate and watch over his pool, Jacuzzi, and Cadillac collection!

I felt like I'd won the lottery. The job that was "so hard to get" literally fell into my lap! I always assumed it was luck and coincidence, but I later realized that's an extra-thick slice of baloney.

GARFIELD © 1982 Paws, Inc. Reprinted with permission of ANDREWS MCMEEL SYNDICATION. All rights reserved.

Like Odie, I had simply "forgotten" what I wasn't "supposed" to be able to do! Sure, many others with abilities like mine were job hunting. But I've learned...

"Lucky breaks" happen when your unique gifts match the opportunity.

If we continue to offer our gifts to the world, we'll always be provided for.

If opportunity doesn't knock, build a door.
-MILTON BERLE-

Fear and doubt are the two greatest blocks to goal fulfillment. It's not enough to merely recognize this. Absolutely refuse to let fear-based thinking into your mind! Should you prepare for emergencies? Sure! Just eliminate the **time** spent fearing and doubting. Ineffective salespeople worry about low sales and literally manifest them by "making room" for them to happen! The difference between "success" and "failure" originates in thoughts that we literally manifest through our actions.

Pick one of your fears and ask: "Who is it that's afraid? Is it I? What part of me is afraid?" It's not your higher self; that's for sure. Fear is a natural by-product of our survival instinct, but today our minds possess the ability to greatly reduce fear. When we pay less attention to ourselves, fears lessen. Help others overcome their fears, and/or focus on something other than what you're afraid of.

> *Courage is not the absence of fear, but rather the judgment that something else is more important than fear.*
> **-AMBROSE REDMOON,**
> **A.K.A JAMES NEIL HOLLINGWORTH-**

Our frame of mind has everything to do with the quality of our experiences. Our ego wants to impose a "goodness" or "badness" that isn't really there. Have you ever had a really bad day, but then later laughed hysterically about it? Kick your negative thoughts out as quickly as they pop into your mind. All we have is **now**, so you might as well think a positive, constructive thought.

Enter fear's dreaded sibling: doubt. It is a disguised fear of failure, inadequacy, or of success and the responsibility that goes with it. Doubt, armed with supposedly rational reasons why things can't be done, keeps us stuck in whatever current situation we're in. Pessimism about oneself is actually a fear of change, like a jail cell just comfortable enough to not want to escape.

When our music department chair announced his retirement at

UW-Whitewater, a search for a replacement began. The job was heavy in responsibility and high in stress. When several faculty members asked me why I hadn't applied, I thought they were joking, but when a few more urged me to consider the job, it dawned on me they were serious. I realized I had feared the unknown, and it was time to step up to the plate, so I threw my "hat in the ring," and I ended up with the job.

Hit the "delete button" every time doubts appear in your life. If you've been in a life-or-death situation, you had to overcome fear very quickly in order to survive. Congratulations, because you can do this without being in an emergency! Doubt is the ego's attempt to protect an image while it fears a negative result. Replacing fear with love helps give us the confidence and perseverance we need. After all…

The only mistakes we make in life are the ones we don't learn from.

If someone tells you something is impossible, it **is**—for **them!** If you think you can do it, you will, and if you think you can't do it, you won't. Fear and doubt come to everyone, so don't feel badly when they crop up; just place positive thoughts alongside the doubts. Just like you would encourage a child learning to ride a bicycle, give yourself some encouragement and proceed freely!

That the birds of worry and care fly above your head, this you cannot change, but that they build nests in your hair, this you can prevent.
- CHINESE PROVERB-

Stress

Like fear and doubt, stress is another unwanted roommate. We so often hear: "I'm stressed out" or "I'm under a lot of stress." Maybe this is you talking. What is "stress" really? Stress is abandoning your present moment to worry about the future. We're caught in a trap. We want to be "elsewhere," and we wish we were in an imaginary future that we doubt we can have or deserve. And of course, we blame other people and situations for causing our stress.

But stress is not caused by external events; it's a product of our own programmed uptightness. It took time to learn our stress just like we learned our fears and doubts. Where in your mind is the tension? What words or circumstances trigger tension for you? If you're not your own master, who is? Release your tension and those self-debasing thoughts. Stop worrying about anything you can't immediately do something about. Postponing happiness is like chasing a rainbow's end; it's always retreating, and we'll never find it! Enjoy life **now,** not in some unknown future that may not even come because we never know how much time we have, do we?

The other day, I gazed out the window and saw a squirrel munching on this huge nut. I wondered what that squirrel was thinking....

"This nut sucks! It's not as nice as the one my brother got down the street. What will he think when he sees this puny thing? And my tail! It's such a mess today! I wonder if I'll get enough nuts tomorrow. Will it be a cold winter? What if I can't climb the tree as fast as that cute guy over there? That'll ruin my chances of ever getting anywhere with him! Gosh, it's cold. Will it **ever** warm up?"

Some believe stress is a good thing. Incorrect! Stress is an antithesis to happiness and peace, **and** it is a potential killer. Problems and challenges help us grow, but stress is a negative reaction to these challenges. Humans have the ability to feel the way we want at all times! If you have a major meeting to lead, a big game to play, a wedding to be in, or a job interview to go to, be up for it, prepare for it, and be **excited** about it. Rather than sitting there worrying, spend that "stress time" getting ready for your event. Still think stress is good for you? Stress…

- makes performance of any task invariably poorer;
- changes a pleasurable experience (such as eating a delicious meal) into a miserable one;
- spreads like a wildfire through our body, creating heartburn, headaches, muscular tension, sleeplessness, and a host of other miseries;
- when stored over months and years, is a major contributor to obesity, heart problems, strokes, cancer, and other calamities; and
- accumulates in our body and rarely disappears after a night's sleep. There can be fitful dreams or a heckuva stiff neck!

Joy is our natural state. Let's remember babies once again! They haven't learned to allow their thoughts to create worry and stress. Don't fight life; go with the flow.

"Old" thinking: "It's a dog-eat-dog world, and I don't have time to relax."

Makeover: *That's the making of a future heart attack! The tension we experience comes from our **attitude** about our circumstances.*

"Old" thinking: "Well, we're supposed to work hard, aren't we? That brings stress."

Makeover: *Not so much if you love what you do and bring a positive outlook to your challenges. You'll cope better with potential stress, too.*

Stress shows up when we're spending too many hours **not aligned with our higher purpose.** Think of stress as dirt on your windshield that needs washing away.

 ## Happiness Step Thirty-Nine
Washing Away the Dirt

Fear, doubt, and stress only exist if your mind allows them.

- Think of one of your greatest fears.
- Think of one of the greatest doubts you have about yourself.
- Think of something that's bothering you right now.

Envision these three things as a large dark spot about ten feet in front of you. This spot represents what's troubling you the most. Now think of a beautiful white light approaching this dark spot. The white light is your higher self. Think of the white light growing brighter and brighter as it washes over and through the dark spot until only the white light is seen.

As you inhale, imagine taking in the beautiful, healthy white light, and as you exhale, imagine getting rid of all the dark and polluted specks of fear, doubt, and stress.

The unlimited love in your higher self, the white light, can overcome any darkness in your life. Wash away your fears, doubts, and stress, and don't allow them to come back. You can face anything that is troubling you with an attitude of fearlessness, confidence, and inner peace.

Repeat this whenever you feel the dark spot wanting to come back into your mind. Render it useless like a crumb you wipe off your table. After you're through, complete the following affirmations:

- *What I will do differently to overcome my greatest fear is*
- *What I will do differently to overcome my greatest self-doubt is*
- *What I will do differently to overcome my greatest stress is*

Enter your ideas into your calendar SOON!

Collecting Tumbleweeds?

Think of negative thoughts as tumbleweeds blowing in a dust storm. Instead of collecting them, just let them blow by!

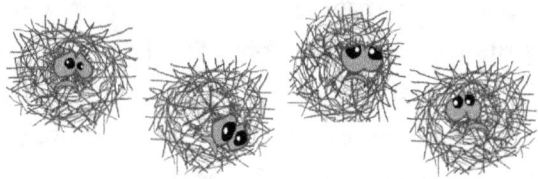

Let's recap what negative thoughts do.

- They prevent us from reaching the goals we want to achieve.
- They repel good things from happening to us.
- They erode our well-being and our health.
- They give us the capability of literally destroying ourselves from within.

The thoughts and attitudes we send out ultimately come back to us. That's why positive thoughts are such a gift! If you send negativity out to the world, it will come back like the worst rerun of *Godzilla Returns*. Most of us wouldn't accept a pile of dung or toxic waste as a present, so why accept negativity from anyone or send it out to the world? If you keep running into negativity, analyze your thoughts and actions. If you are constantly doing and thinking good things, it's only a matter of time before events turn for the better. Before you go back to negative thoughts, remember this simple formula:

Positive thoughts build.	Negative thoughts destroy.
Positive thoughts create abundance.	Negative thoughts create scarcity.

Everything that happens to us is the result of thoughts that were manifested into actions. Refuse to allow negativity from others to have power over you. When the going gets tough, replace your negative thoughts with positive ones.

- Carry a small, smooth rock or other item significant to you in your pocket or perhaps even around your neck. At a low point during the day, look at the object and say, "I am now bringing abundance into my life."
- When the chips are really down, it never hurts to pray for things to get better. They will. All suffering is temporary.
- Realize that the adversity you're undergoing is teaching and testing you. Take a moment to acknowledge that you cannot control everything, and be grateful for what you **do** have.

Worries represent attachments. What is it we hope to own? What do we really need? Is our humanity really about the things we acquire? Every one of us has what we need to be happy and to overcome fears and doubts.

Any overemphasis or obsession with the security, power, and sensation needs listed next will bring about the negative emotions listed below them:

Security

- worry,
- fear,
- anxiety,
- compulsiveness, and
- endless worry about future scarcity.

Power

- anger,
- hostility,
- more compulsiveness,
- fear of loss of power, and
- a need to control others.

Sensation

- disappointment,
- frustration,
- boredom,
- more compulsiveness, and
- feelings of scarcity when our sensations are not gratified.

Is it any wonder why our attachments are enough to keep us in a funk for eternity? Chasing the mirage of the happiness we think they will bring will only create more misery.

Along with trying to reduce our attachments, a long-lasting happiness is also about overcoming adversity. Getting rid of negative emotions and overcoming suffering can be done quickly, but many of us need constant reinforcement by seeking encouragement and inspiration each day. It's like losing weight. Since we put on one pound at a time (or two if you have key lime pie), we can only take it off the same way (and standing on the scale on your tiptoes doesn't count). Each pound represents shedding the weight of past programming that made us miserable. It takes time, commitment, and dedication, but it's worth it.

Negative emotions are only illusions and are powerless unless **we decide** to activate them and make them real. Great spiritual leaders of the world have told us time and time again in many sayings, parables, stories, and teachings that love, compassion, and kindness are the hope for the future of humanity. It's time to heed those words.

CHAPTER TWENTY-EIGHT
WE DON'T HAVE FOREVER...

Our Certain Future

For years, I'd been researching about happiness, but I hadn't gotten around to writing a book. Then, I had three vivid dreams that I'd died before I was ready. The deaths in my dreams were different each time, and while they weren't scary, I felt terrible because I hadn't completed the important things I needed to do! I didn't sense these dreams were foretelling how or when I would die, but they were warning me to get my arse in gear, so I wouldn't have regrets of an unfulfilled life!

> *I am ready to meet my Maker. Whether my Maker is prepared*
> *for the great ordeal of meeting me is another matter.*
> **-SIR WINSTON CHURCHILL-**

We've covered the uncertain future, but what about the "certain" aspects? If you knew you only had a short time left to live, you'd likely make some changes in your life! We don't know if we have six months, six years, or sixty more years, but what **is** certain is our physical demise (and of course, taxes!).

There's a lot we can do without giving up all of our material possessions (well, maybe a few!). Start by asking these questions:

- Is there someone you ought to reconcile with?
- Have you neglected to tell someone you loved him or her lately?
- Is there a person or place you've been meaning to visit and haven't gotten around to?

Let's up the ante. What if you were to die **right now?** Would you have any regrets about words unsaid and deeds unfinished? When death arrives, we'll have no choice, and it will be too late to change anything. We **do** have choices while we're alive! Who would you call if you knew you had one hour to live? When it's our "time," let's not have any regrets.

Many of us behave as if we have all the time in the world to get our life's work done. We **might** live a long life through healthy habits, but that doesn't guarantee us against some other calamity. It's beneficial to care about the uncertainty of when we'll pass on. We want to live to an old age, but some of us will, and some of us won't.

Death is a strange lottery you don't want to "win!" But we don't all live to be ninety, and sometimes the young go before the old. Nobody knows exactly when death will come. That's only depressing if we're avoiding our higher purpose that we've been given to fulfill. Since death is certain, it makes sense to make the most of our lives **now,** in case there is no later.

Being more mindful of death reduces anxiety about it and motivates us to fill our days

with meaning. When death does come, we'll be more prepared. Live your life as if you had six months to live. Then, if you get an "extension," celebrate and keep living that way! In Happiness Step Fifteen, you prioritized your most important wishes. Have you started on them? How about beginning your happier life **right now?**

There **will** be a time when you'll have six months to live. If there's a lot of difference between your "six months to live" goals and your everyday life, I suggest you reconsider your actions. Every time you come in contact with someone is potentially the last time you see him or her, and there **will** be a last time. How do you want that experience to be?

Two certainties:

- Everything changes. Nothing in the material, physical universe remains exactly the same nor will it last forever. Physical objects change in some way every second.
- Every situation we experience is **temporary**, and it will change.

It's easy not to give death much thought until we lose people close to us. In Western society, we typically avoid much talk about death. It's pretty uncomfortable to think about, too, so we anesthetize ourselves against our impermanence. Like an approaching storm, ignoring death doesn't make it go away. Are you ready to focus on your most important goals yet? In order to cement our commitment to a truly meaningful life, we need to look at our future demise more closely.

The Nature of Death

As infinite souls inhabiting the flesh temporarily, we are born, grow, flourish, and then ultimately face decay and demise.

For days after death, hair and fingernails continue to grow, but phone calls taper off.
-JOHNNY CARSON-

Once we go, our mortal perception of time and space will likely undergo a major shift. Most of us sense there's more to us than our bodies. Our bodies age, but our timeless higher self does not. Our birth and death are part of something bigger. There is a part of us that's incapable of dying.

Scientific evidence demonstrates that matter, energy, and consciousness can't be destroyed, only changed. Physical death represents a change of form. For instance, a cloud arises and forms from water vapor in the atmosphere, and that cloud holds water. The cloud becomes part of the weather cycle, and it is released in the form of rain, snow, or sleet (or all three at once if you live in the north!). Or the cloud can evaporate back to vapor. This cycle repeats endlessly, so while the form of water changes, the water still exists. Similarly, we came from a natural state of being, and we ultimately go back to it, so we're always connected to our source! "Something" can't come from "nothing" (though I've tried making that in the kitchen!), and "nothing" can't come from "something." Try to make nothing!

Aging and death are normal. No one can be twenty-one forever, though I attempted that on the softball field. In the U.S., we have a frenzied obsession with youth, which is supported heavily by media and advertising dollars. We turn to young, rich celebrities for advice about anything, yet we often ignore the older generation. While our bright youth have a lot to offer, it's a grave mistake to not turn to our seniors for wisdom. Sadly, the elderly are ignored because of a number of negative stereotypes. Too many die alone with no one really caring for them. And the older you get, the more friends and family members you lose, unless you go first! But, as one greeting card I saw says, "Cheer up. Old age doesn't last that long!"

I play music for seniors often, and many of them are delightful and wise. They usually show a great appreciation for entertainment and don't take it for granted. They drop their need for a facade, saying exactly what's on their mind! Instead of focusing on what is lost as we age, consider aging as an opportunity for spiritual practice.

> After her accident, Toni asked us how old she was, and she first guessed she was twenty-seven! When we told her how old she was, she made a face and said, "That's old!" Then she laughed and said, "I don't want to know how old I am anymore!" She still feels and acts a lot younger than she is, so we just stopped "teaching" her age to her!

Satchel Paige, who was a professional baseball pitcher for twenty-nine years, including a three-inning cameo appearance seventeen days before his sixtieth birthday, quipped:

How old would you be if you didn't know how old you are?

Age is a case of mind over matter. If you don't mind, it don't matter.

How much of our lives are spent trying to accumulate material values and power? We've got to have enough to eat, clothes to wear, etc., but today so many are addicted to accumulating luxury to an astonishing degree! No one in the history of mankind has been able to take any possessions with him at death. It's no coincidence that the great prophets were not rich in material possessions. Our spirituality and effect on others is really all we have. To help jolt us back to reality, let's not hide from some overwhelming evidence…

Turn on the TV, go online, or read the newspaper, and you see death everywhere. You don't even have to go to the obituary section! No one expects to be a victim of a violent crime or an accident. No one "asks" for a heart attack or stroke. So many are here one day and gone the next; their lives ended as quickly as a sandcastle inundated by a huge, crashing wave. These things will **never happen to us**, right?

Visit a cemetery, and read some headstones. Everyone has a birthday and a death day. Some people lived long lives, while others died before any of us would like to. No one knows why the young sometimes go before the old or why "good" people die young. Regardless, when someone we know dies "before his or her time," it teaches us a hard lesson about impermanence.

How long is "long enough" to live?

> *At my age, I do what Mark Twain did. I get my daily paper, look at the obituaries page, and if I'm not there, I carry on as usual.*
> **-PATRICK MOORE-**

We really don't know for sure which will come first: tomorrow or death. We can only hope we'll live long enough to make a difference to others on this planet. We hope for the best, but it's a good idea to prepare for the worst.

Death itself has no compassion. One by one, death picks off each and every one of us like a sniper. When we hear someone passes on, we might think, "It must have been his time." When is your time? Perhaps you've just begun some major project or have unfinished business. Too bad. Death waits for no one to finish anything. None of us can escape it. You may have heard about people who "cheated death," but that's only temporary. Everyone, no matter how great, loses his or her human form. It's not bad or evil; it's just the way things are. All physical objects— molecules, planets, stars, and even galaxies—come and go.

> *What is born will die,*
> *What has been gathered will be dispersed,*
> *What has been accumulated will be exhausted,*
> *What has been built up will collapse,*
> *And what has been high will be brought low.*
> **-BUDDHIST SCRIPTURE-**

At the death moment, our possessions will be meaningless, and all we will have is our spiritual strength and what we can remember about the effect our actions had on people. Reflection on impermanence helps us emphasize something other than the materialism in our lives since we lose all of that anyway. Ram Dass has given a number of talks about "the only dance there is" in life, reminding us that our existence is the sum total of how we've treated **everyone**, including ourselves. If we follow our higher purposes right now, we'll already be more prepared for death! As we realize the fragile and precious nature of each moment we have on Earth, we'll have compassion for all beings.

While we may feel like insignificant specks in the universe, what each of us does in life has more of an effect than we might think. In his theory called "wholeness and the implicate order," physicist David Bohm held a holistic cosmic view that everything in the universe is connected with everything else. Any element in the universe could reveal detailed information about any other element. He has described reality as being "unbroken wholeness in flowing movement without borders." Bohm proposed that the universe behaves like a hologram where time, space, mind, and matter are not only

connected to each other but continuously influence each other. Therefore, each element contains within itself the totality of the universe.

Similarly, in 1982 at the University of Paris, physicist Alain Aspect and his research team's findings assert that subatomic particles (like electrons) can communicate with each other regardless of whether they are a few feet or billions of miles apart. The actions of these particles demonstrate a keen awareness of each other's behavior regardless of distance. The interconnected nature of all things gives us hope that what we do in life **matters** and that there is an existence of some kind awaiting us after death.

If you could live forever, would you really want to? We want a long life with productivity, good times, relationships, etc., but for how long? If everyone lived forever, where would we fit all the newborns? If you occupied your job forever (a scary thought!), how would younger people work? Of course, if we lived forever, we would want perfect health, but what age would we want our bodies to look like? The problems immortality would create are astronomical. The nature of our universe makes death and demise a necessity, so we might as well face it. We really don't want to live forever…we just want to **live.**

CHAPTER TWENTY-NINE
LET'S FACE IT...

Fear of Death

At my age flowers scare me.
-GEORGE BURNS-

To not fear death at all takes some preparation. To never contemplate death grossly underestimates the effect it will have when we genuinely face it. We become afraid because we're not sure what happens after we die. We know the body shuts down, but what happens to the mind or our "spirit"?

We'll fear the death process more if we lack knowledge of who we are. We cling to our name, body, status, etc., which may seem to be what's important to us until death comes and annihilates that illusion like a mirror shattered into a thousand pieces. At that time, we'll no longer be able to hide from our deeper reality, so let's get to know who we are and our purpose sooner rather than later! Then we can transcend any poor concept of self that causes us to fear death.

DR. JOHN C. WEBB

I've never met an atheist on a small airplane.
-UNKNOWN-

Even the notorious dictators Hitler and Stalin were said to be fearful at the very end of their lives, and many hardened criminals on death row become frightened and remorseful. Those who learn they have a short time to live usually make big changes in their lives quickly. They become unconcerned with petty things that don't matter. They know the importance of saying and doing what **does** matter. Perhaps they give things away, spend time with people significant in their lives, or help others if they can. Many who have gone through a near-death experience get the big picture in a hurry, too. Desires for material things are replaced with the wish for more spirituality and purpose.

From those who have had near-death experiences, very few described the event as terrifying; they more often report incredible and delightful experiences. Some common experiences are seeing relatives who have passed on, traveling through a tunnel, seeing life's events like a movie, angelic beings, a beautiful white light, being out-of-body, seeing surgeons work to revive them, and similar scenarios.

My grandfather fell off a barn and nearly died at age seven, but he assured me his experience had been beautiful and that there was absolutely nothing to fear about death. My mother-in-law lay in a coma for nearly two weeks and was given little chance of survival, but she came back to live another year and a half. When she first came out of her coma, she had this incredulous look on her face. She said, "You'll never believe where I've been in a million years." In some cases, people were told it was not yet their time or given a choice as to whether or not to come back.

If this is death, it is easier than life.
-ROBERT LOUIS STEVENSON-

WELL I'LL BE A BLUE-NOSED GOPHER

It is very beautiful over there.
-THOMAS EDISON-

If you feel it'll take a near-death experience for you to activate your higher purpose, then have it—in your mind. If you've had a serious illness or a scary accident, you know how to be thankful for the gift of life!

I think most people expect that some type of review of their life will occur. Whatever we've done with our lives makes us who we are when we die. And everything, absolutely everything, counts.

This existence of ours is as transient as autumn clouds.
To watch the birth and death of beings is like looking at the
movements of a dance.
A lifetime is like a flash of lightning in the sky,
Rushing by, like a torrent down a steep mountain.
-BUDDHA-

We don't want to foolishly dismiss death, nor do we want the realization of death to weigh us down like an anchor in the briny sea. In some societies, death is an occasion for celebration, with full acceptance of the divine timing for each person's arrival or departure in the physical plane.

The traditional New Orleans funeral is a perfect example of viewing life as a celebration, which mixes the somber with the festive. After a serious funeral service, it's time to party with music, dance, and celebrating that person's life. *Laissez les bon temps rouler! (Let the good times roll!)*

Death is simply part of the nature of physical impermanence in the universe. To imagine your own death is not fatalistic, but it will motivate you to improve your life **now,** like Scrooge in *The Christmas Carol*. With belief in a timeless self that goes on after death, there is no need to be afraid. Whatever happened just before your birth didn't involve fear and anxiety, so why should it be any different when you pass on? Fearing death only robs us of our present quality of life. Do the things your heart beckons you to do. Use your thoughts about death to live an abundant life each day. Take the risks involved in listening to your higher self, without thoughts of fear and failure. Then, when death comes, you'll never have to say, "Wait, I haven't really **lived** yet!"

In a strange way, the fear of dying is actually the fear of living. Let's do the meaningful things in our lives while we're healthy **before** our time runs out, especially since not all of us will get any advance warning. If we take the time to truly realize and face our impermanence, we'll be much more likely to be more "alive" until we "die!"

Happiness Step Forty
It's Your Funeral

Do a relaxation meditation, as in Happiness Step One, where you progressively relax all of your muscles. Project ahead to an undetermined time when you have just passed away, and you see your own funeral taking place, but no one can see you. Describe the funeral **exactly** as you would want it to be.

- Who is there?
- What will be said about you?
- How do you feel?

If you get feelings of restlessness or concern about this moment, what do you believe you need to do in order to have this funeral the way that you would like?

No matter what fears and anxieties you may have, envision that you've had a wonderful life and that people will celebrate your life and miss you when you're gone. Make it the best funeral possible—in your mind! Repeat this meditation until you can imagine the "best funeral possible" scenario with no feelings of anxiety or worry.

DR. JOHN C. WEBB

Consequences of Ignoring Death

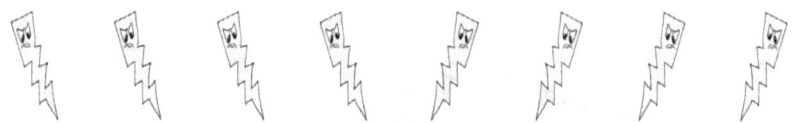

> *My religion is to live—and die—without regret.*
> **-MILAREPA-**

It's easy to put off the meaningful things in life. The notion of a long future stretching out ahead of us tends to lull us away from serious spiritual endeavors. There's always something else to do. You'll start tomorrow, right? But you could die tomorrow, and then all you'll have is regret. Those who say, "I have too much work to do" will always have too much work to do. The truth is that they aren't ready to make any meaningful changes.

We assume our demise will be after some time, but even with ideal circumstances, we don't have as much time for spiritual practice as we think. First, we sleep nearly one-third of our lives. Childhood and adolescence is spent establishing identity. As we become twentysomethings or thirtysomethings, we pursue our careers, intending to begin a spiritual path, but we often don't find the time, intending to begin as soon as this and that get  done. Then more activities crop up like unending blades of grass in a huge meadow. We go through the height of our careers, and before we know it, we're too old or frail to engage in a serious practice of spirituality. If we deeply connect to the fact that our lives are short and waking hours are limited, we can live a more full and meaningful life.

When my parents began a new business, they put off vacations year after year. My dad didn't take a day off for the first five years, and my parents rarely went out in order to save for retirement. Then my mom died suddenly at age sixty-one. All of that hard work and no play for a happier tomorrow that never came was a bitter lesson for our family.

There is wisdom in the cliché that no one on their deathbed wishes they'd spent more time at work. Enjoy your family, loved ones, friends, and even everyone else **now.** There's no guarantee they'll be here tomorrow. Ask the family members of 9/11 victims or of any disaster about savoring moments. Surely as you're reading this, our lives are ebbing minute-by-minute, hour-by-hour. If we're never concerned about our death, we'll continue our meaningless activities unabated. When death comes, none of that will matter, so why spend our lives dedicated to them?

In your mind, go back to that cemetery one more time. What goes on beneath the graves? The flesh rots, the bones crumble, and ultimately, only unrecognizable matter remains. Perhaps you'll be cremated, leaving only ashes. The human body, magnificent as a whole, is only a puddle of fluids and bone material when broken down. We came from the sexual union of our parents and arose into being. We consumed food, water,

disposed of considerable waste, and required a substantial amount of Earth's natural resources. If we live for no purpose, we're simply a manure-producing machine! It would be better to have been born an earthworm! At least they don't harm others or consume much and serve some sort of purpose!

Luckily, as non-earthworms, we possess the ability to contribute to the welfare of others. We know by now that being intelligent or rich doesn't guarantee happiness, freedom, or usefulness. It's far better to do one thing to help others than to have material wealth but do nothing to help others. Seeking excess is the ultimate time-waster, causing our attachments and desires to rise up like a flash flood in a narrow canyon. To be self-serving doesn't bode well for a good future in this life or after! Our purpose here is to grow spiritually and benefit others. If we humans don't do this, who will?

A good time to reflect on the issue of death is during your quiet time, when life-changing decisions can be brought into play. Thoughts about death are only depressing initially, and then they enable us to develop a sincere motivation to **live life to the fullest.** Reflect calmly that death is real and will come essentially without warning. We'll become less obsessed with fame, possessions, and social status. Then watch the "happiness meter" go up!

What if "Dr. Death" were to come knocking **right now?** How would you feel about it? Maybe you aren't afraid, but you might feel it's too soon or that you're "not ready."

If you die in an elevator, be sure to push the "up" button.
-SAM LEVENSON-

Even if death were to come slowly, as in a grave illness, it will be too late to do much. You'll eventually be too weak to complete your business affairs. You'll scarcely be able to move, let alone speak. Others will feel sorry for you, but ultimately, they can only offer you comfort. Then you take your last breath. Who knows how, when, or if you'll see your family, friends, and loved ones again? You will be referred to as "the late (your name here)." If death were to come right now, what would **you** have done differently?

If I Had My Life to Live Over

I'd like to make more mistakes next time.
I'd relax. I would limber up.
I would be sillier than I have been this trip.
I would take fewer things seriously.
I would take more chances.

I would climb more mountains and swim more rivers.
I would eat more ice cream and less beans.
I would perhaps have more actual troubles,
but I'd have fewer imaginary ones.

You see, I'm one of those people who live
sensibly and sanely hour after hour,
day after day.

Oh, I've had my moments,
And if I had it to do over again,
I'd have more of them.
In fact, I'd try to have nothing else.
Just moments, one after another,
instead of living so many years ahead of each day.

I've been one of those people who never goes anywhere

*without a thermometer, a hot water bottle, a raincoat,
and a parachute.
If I had to do it again, I would travel lighter than I have.*

*If I had my life to live over,
I would start barefoot earlier in the spring
and stay that way later in the fall.
I would go to more dances.
I would ride more merry-go-rounds.
I would pick more daisies.*

-NADINE STAIR AT AGE 85-

Enjoy life. Wake up and smell the roses, but don't cling to them. Roses don't last forever. Just move on to the next wonder! A joyous life **is** the best preparation for death. Let's not wait until someone close to us dies or we're close to death ourselves to look at our lives or to show our appreciation to others. Coping with death is most difficult for those left behind who didn't express their feelings to the person **while he or she was alive.**

*They say such nice things about people at their
funerals that it makes me sad to realize that I'm
going to miss mine by just a few days.*
-GARRISON KEILLOR-

Let people know how you feel, preferably when you feel it. You just never know what will happen or when. In other words, don't wait for a funeral to send flowers.

CHAPTER THIRTY
HAVE A GOOD JOURNEY...

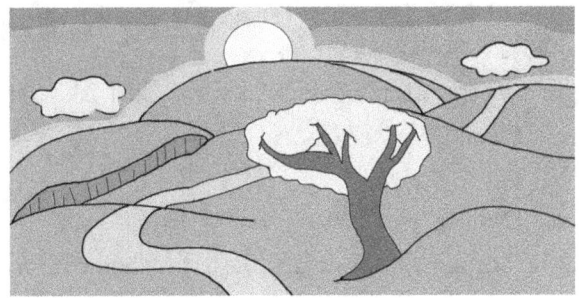

Preparing for Death

The doctor told me I had six months to live. I told him I couldn't pay the bill, so he gave me another six months.
-HENNY YOUNGMAN-

Let's face it—no one wants to think about death unless we see some very compelling benefits. If we embrace our precarious mortality, we'll take more risks to achieve our higher good, with more resolve to get meaningful things done. As long as we have the magnificent gift of life, we can still offer our unique gifts to others. Those who focus on what they don't have in their lives are better off to hope and pray they'll have the opportunity to survive long enough to accomplish their higher purposes. It's time to be proactive about our appointment with the infinite.

Many feel powerless to stop death and shrug. They say, "When it happens, it happens." Others believe their lives don't really matter. To combat this nonchalant thinking, I offer three professorial **howevers:**

- Preparing for death deprives it of having any advantage over you. Don't wait for the hurricane to hit to find out if your levees are going to hold!
- Whatever discomfort is involved in preparing for the inevitable will be far out-

  weighed by the advantages. Ultimately, you'll ask yourself:
  a. Did I live wisely?
  b. Did I love well?
  c. Did I serve humanity well? Did I do some good?
- Your life absolutely does matter—to you and to the many, many people you exist with daily. Fear not death, and trust in the miracles the universe will have for you after death.

Mindfulness deprives death of its strangeness. We need to talk about death to children as well, even at an early age (although in simpler terms). A farmer knows that there's only so much time available before the harvest is brought in. We have a harvest to bring in too, except we don't have the advantage of knowing when the season's over!

The Tibetans take a very active and detailed role in preparing for each stage of death, as explained in *The Tibetan Book of the Dead*. On this side of the globe, few people will take as much time to prepare as the Tibetans do, but we can at least develop awareness, awe, and a sense of destiny about our impending death, as opposed to running from or trivializing it. At least we can hope to gain peace of mind by becoming a bit familiar with the process.

Native Americans often tell the dying to "have a good journey." It's simply smart to make some preparations for that journey. Taking a few moments to experience in our mind what death might be like gives us urgency to making life meaningful **today.** If you're going to give a speech in front of people, you'll want to prepare and practice it a few times, especially if you're "deathly" afraid of speeches! It's easy to say, "Oh well, death happens to everyone." True, but we won't be casual about it when it's **our time.** Since death is certain, it makes sense to internalize what will happen.

We'll be losing our physical body we've occupied for some time. Imagine leaving that body. A lot of us do this when we dream or daydream. It will be far more dramatic at death, so we'll go through several scenarios in meditations. Fear not the death process itself. Whether it's a quick death or not, the real fear is usually of dying before one is "ready."

I used to think that it would be best to die quickly. Now I'm not so sure.

> *I want to die like my father, peacefully in his sleep,*
> *not screaming and terrified, like his passengers.*
> **-BOB MONKHOUSE-**

Those who pass away suddenly suffer little, and everyone says, "At least they didn't suffer!" But everyone is so shocked, and no one had a chance to say goodbye. At least those with an illness or the very elderly have ample opportunities to say goodbye to their loved ones. No matter what, when we lose a loved one, it's NEVER easy—expected or unexpected.

Being with someone who is dying is a profound experience where we can gain much wisdom. It offers us an opportunity to show unconditional love, say meaningful things, make him or her feel better, and in some cases, delay or even deter death. It gives the dying person the same opportunity to say meaningful things, too. One's state of mind at the time of death is quite important. Help your loved ones and friends pass on peacefully. Talk  to them, sing to them, play music, and do whatever you can to make the process a peaceful one, even if they're not conscious.

It's a powerful spiritual practice to meditate about death. Even for the young, a long, prosperous life cannot be guaranteed. None of my semester-long "Practicing Happiness" seminars survived without a student telling me the sad news of the death of a family member or friend. Reflecting on our impending death helps us want to spend our time on what's important in life. We'll be ready to free ourselves from bad habits, and we'll be jolted closer to our true nature and our higher purpose.

Happiness Step Forty-One
Meditations about That Exceptional Moment

Four different meditations are given here. Do these in order, but do only one meditation per session.

I won't sugarcoat the fact that going through the first two death meditations can be quite uncomfortable at first, especially if we're not happy about where we are in life now. The benefit is worth it because we'll be more likely to take care of what's important before death arrives. We don't do these meditations to be depressed or fatalistic, but we do them to bring more meaning to life **while we still have it.**

Do a relaxation meditation, as in Happiness Step One, where you progressively relax all of your muscles and go to your special, favorite place in your mind. Then begin one of the meditations.

First Meditation

Imagine yourself on your deathbed. You've either been ill for some time, or you are old and don't remember those around you. You can no longer take care of yourself. Gradually, as people pay their last respects, your body begins to shut down. It's very important to relax and think pleasant, virtuous thoughts. Hallucinations come and go, and you can no longer speak. Your eyes and ears slowly fail, and soon you lose the ability to move. Your bodily functions gradually stop working as your internal organs shut down. Your body temperature drops, and your breathing slows down and ultimately stops with one last breath. Continue with a positive frame of mind and with no regrets. This happens to everyone, and now it's your turn. As your heart stops beating and the brain shuts down, welcome the change and the end to any suffering you may have been enduring. Imagine incredible beauty and wonder as you let go. You are now clinically dead. As you leave this plane of existence, smile. Reflect on what you've done and what you'll be remembered for. Leave with love and acceptance. Feel good about your life! Think loving thoughts about what will come next for you; there is nothing to fear; it will be wonderful!

Second Meditation

For this meditation, your death is sudden (heart attack, stroke, auto accident, etc.). Repeat the same process as in the first meditation but at a highly accelerated rate. While you are leaving suddenly, you understand that some death scenarios are sudden. You will not be confused or worried because you've taken care of everything you possibly could. Be thankful you didn't suffer for a long period of time. As you leave this plane of existence, think of smiling and reflecting on what you've done and what you'll be remembered for. Leave with love and acceptance. Feel good about your life! Think loving thoughts about what will come next for you; there is nothing to fear; it will be wonderful!

If you don't like how you feel after repeating these meditations, do something about your life while you still can. Your own mind can never be hidden from you. The best way to die well is to live well.

Third Meditation

You realize life is a privilege and ask for the opportunity to age. Imagine aging gracefully. Contemplate how your death is inevitable and how your life is slowly ticking away. You'd like to think you have a lot of time left on Earth, but there's no way of knowing for certain. Reflect on the uncertainty of your moment of death and that it can occur any time, possibly when you least expect it. Realize that you are going to lose all of your status, money, power, and relationships on the earthly plane. Resolve to do something really important with your life while you're alive.

Fourth Meditation

Meditate on impermanence. Change is a natural part of all things that exist in the physical realm. The cycle of birth, growth, and demise is inherent in all physical aspects of nature. Imagine a meaningful life and that you're enjoying the ride! Be comfortable with the idea of life on Earth without you, knowing that someday it's going to happen!

A meaningful life and death is a triumph—a crowning achievement. With a little practice on Earth, you can ensure that the moment of death will be a most glorious one!

Before Birth/After Death

Even if we're prepared for death, we won't accomplish everything we want to in this lifetime, so how do our lives relate to where we've been before and where we might go afterwards? Well, my "expert" answer is: **We don't know!** And, I don't think we're supposed to know, but that's just my opinion. Most religions affirm an existence after this one, so what's next? Whether you believe in reincarnation, heaven, hell, angels, spirits, or anything else, it seems scientifically logical that **there is something out there** for us after we pass on, so we hope for more opportunities to continue doing our work in some way.

Where were we before we occupied our present body? Did we exist in any form at all? Why do so few people remember anything? Assuming that there's some universal intelligence, there's likely a good reason we don't know. Let's say you could remember where you were before here… and you think you have baggage in **this** life? Try taking on the leftover guilt, regrets, and negative emotions from 2,000 lives! If we came to this life to be tested in some areas and we're given all the answers to the test before we take it, how can we evolve? Since challenges often reoccur in life, they could repeat from one existence to the next as well (too much chocolate, **again?**). Hopefully, our daily behavior in this life is what earns our "merit."

I used to think that because of the evil that exists on Earth, we probably did some terrible things to be brought here, but now I see that humans have great potential to benefit our beautiful planet. To be born as a human is a gift that we might not be given again. So maybe we didn't do anything that bad after all!

What happens after we die? Here's one take:

> A jazz trumpet player and a drummer were lifelong friends and had played together for many years. Now elderly, the drummer fell ill and was about ready to pass on. "Hey, man," the trumpet player said, putting his hand on the drummer's shoulder. "I'm gonna miss you, bro, but I was wondering if you could do me a favor. When you get to heaven, somehow let me know if they have a real cookin' jazz band up there 'cause I'm not into playin' a buncha harp music when I get there. Dig?"
>
> "I **dig**, my friend. I'll do what-

ever." And with that, the drummer man passed on to drummer heaven.

Three nights later, the trumpet player woke in the middle of the night to thunder and lightning! There before him was the misty, ethereal figure of his drummer friend. "Hey, you came back! Out o' sight! Is there a hot jazz band in the great beyond?"

The ringing voice of his friend said, "I have gooooood news and baaaaaad news!"

"What's the good news, man?"

"There's a reeeeeaaally **cookin'** jazz band in heaven!"

"Cool, dude! Well, what's the bad news?"

"**You**, my friend, are playing lead trumpet Saturday night!"

For the sake of happiness, it doesn't matter whether you believe in reincarnation, an afterlife, or pure "nothingness" after death. If you believe in reincarnation, your current life is based on your past lives, and what you do will affect the quality of your future lifetimes. Just look around you. We humans are far from the dominant species in terms of population, as I was once reminded when roaches literally moved me out of my apartment. Recognizing that being human **is** rather special and not wanting to be reborn as a Sub-Saharan dung beetle might put more depth and meaning into our present moments, which are all we have.

If reincarnation isn't your thing and you believe in an afterlife, heaven, hell, or other existence, that makes this life **pretty important** because this is the only game in town, so you're creating your future heaven or hell right now! If you believe in "nothingness" after this life or that you'll sleep for all eternity, then be sure you have a helluva good mattress, and make hay while the sun still shines!

If you have a million dollars in your hand right now, don't throw it away and then pray for another million!

Those consumed with self-centeredness with no regard for the consequences of their actions just continue a world without compassion. While we hope for a better afterlife, it just makes sense that no one gets a good future "anything" unless they **earn it!**

Can our loved ones who have passed on still see us or be with us? In some cultures, it's perfectly acceptable to talk out loud or pray to those who have passed on, which can help with the difficulty of losing those we love. Is there any proof that loved ones or angels **cannot** be around us?

When my grandfather passed away, my sister Hilary was three years old. My parents didn't take her to the funeral service, but later that day, at my grandmother's house, she kept pointing to an empty chair, asking who the man sitting there was. No one could see anything, so they asked her what he looked like, and she described him with a red shirt and white beard. My grandfather was buried in a red shirt and had a flowing white beard, and my sister was pointing to his favorite chair where he always sat.

My wife, Toni, to this day, has no memory of being hit by a car except for one day in the hospital, three and a half months after the accident, her speech therapist ran up to me and said, "Your wife just suddenly mentioned that angels were with her when they were loading her onto the ambulance!"

Toni has never mentioned that memory again, but at that time, her vocabulary was still quite limited, and she had not yet relearned about angels, let alone remembered what an ambulance was. Who's to say what **isn't** possible?

Happiness Step Forty-Two
Remember Me!

Write your future epitaph as you want it to appear on your gravestone or appropriate memoriam. (Limit this to a maximum of two concise, very meaningful sentences. After all, a hundred years from now, this will likely be **all** you will be remembered for.)

_____

_____

_____

_____

_____

_____

_____

_____

Project into the future until it's your last day on Earth. What did you stand for? What important things did you accomplish? What do you feel good about? What made you happy? What were you grateful for?

What my life stood for

_____

_____

_____

_____

_____

Important things I accomplished (list at least three)

_____

_____

_____

_____

_____

WELL I'LL BE A BLUE-NOSED GOPHER

What I felt good about in my life

_____

_____

_____

_____

_____

_____

What made me truly happy

_____

_____

_____

_____

_____

_____

What I was grateful for about my life

___

___

___

___

___

You've just been told you have only six months to live. How will you spend your last months on Earth? What will you do?

___

___

___

___

___

Now make sure you DO the things you listed soon!

SECTION SEVEN
Happiness **Matters**!

CHAPTER THIRTY-ONE
PRACTICING HAPPINESS MAKES A DIFFERENCE!

Collective Happiness

The beauty about practicing happiness is that every moment offers us an opportunity to practice! Once, when I was having a cosmic meltdown, my wife (pre-brain injury) pointed to a draft of this very book, looked at me, and said, "Chapter Three!" Ay-yi-yi! Perfect we will never be; we just have to keep doing our best!

Reasons to practice happiness run deeper than any one person though. An individual mind in harmony with nature and the universe has a significant effect on others. Our individual intelligence is greatly dependent on the collective intelligence around us. Similarly, happiness in the home will lead to happiness in the community and beyond. A happier world begins one person

at a time, which will bring about more collective happiness and a shift to a higher consciousness.

It's easy to look up at the stars, marvel at the vast universe, and see ourselves as an insignificant speck that doesn't matter. Well, push that thought away! With the gazillion ways to communicate on social media or (God forbid!) **in person**, our kind thoughts, words, and actions have a powerful potential. What you think and do makes a difference. Others may think what they do doesn't matter, making it easy to complain, not do anything, and then wait for others to do something so they can complain some more!

To best help others, we need to be CEOs of ourselves. We expect our governments to solve problems for us, but politics is all about image and rarely on any substantial action. Politicians face a circus of lobbyists, and if they don't change or dilute their positions, they won't even be elected assistant dogcatcher in Antarctica. We love to bash politicians, but guess what? They are simply a mirror of ourselves and the society **we** created!

Governments will never make anything better if we ignore our responsibilities as **individuals.** Consider the urgent need to undo the serious environmental damage caused by lack of consideration and disrespect toward our planet. This goes beyond politics; it concerns everyone's quality of life. But with each election, our leaders are simply replaced by more of the same people who act on behalf of the special lobbying groups that elected them as opposed to acting on any moral obligation.

In traditional Native American societies, leaders were selected according to honesty, generosity, and moral ethics. The chief was usually the poorest man in the village; he gave away everything to those who were in need. Another essential skill for leadership was to be a good **listener.** When the leader did speak, he spoke softly, using only a few, meaningful words. Wouldn't that be refreshing today?

Even electing **GOD** won't do a bit of good if the general populace remains unscrupulous or selfish. If we as individuals are compassionate, our loved ones, friends, and neighbors will follow. Are **you** ready to lead?

Taking Care of Each Other

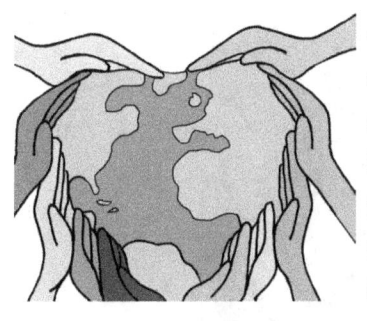

Whether or not our happiness is where we want it, it's a **privilege** to have the opportunity to work on it! Thankfully, we don't have to spend all of our waking hours scrounging for breadcrumbs or fighting off flesh-eating predators! Try talking to someone about happiness if he or she is homeless, destitute, or starving! Only after our basic needs are met are we able to confront the real enemies of our happiness—endless desires for things we really don't need.

In the big picture, the suffering of others ultimately becomes our suffering too. Our future survival is dependent on rich and poor countries working together to solve problems of the environment and the world's

economy. To avert future disaster, wealthy countries will have to make economic sacrifices for the benefit of the Earth. Economic stability is best achieved out of compassion for those who don't have enough to survive. Successful businesses of the future must operate according to what is good for the entire world and our fragile ecology.

Those who don't earn money for a living are often deemed lazy or useless, but unemployment is not negative when people use the free time in a positive way. My wife stopped "working" at the prime of her marketability, which was our choice. Until her accident, she spent much of her time helping others who were less fortunate than her. Stop for a moment. Do you remember when someone was compassionate or helpful to you? Take that gift and do something similar to help others, which will inspire them to do the same. Merely recognizing the need to help others won't cut it. The most significant acts in history (like ending slavery!) arose out of compassion. Kindness has to be the new, necessary "business" of every part of our human community.

It is our collective and individual responsibility to protect and nurture the global family, to support its weaker members, and to preserve and tend to the environment in which we all live.
-HIS HOLINESS THE DALAI LAMA-

Peace—More than a Word

After the 1960s, the words "peace" and "love" together conjured up visions of hippies and flower power. The original hippie movement crashed fairly quickly due to rampant commercialization, pushers selling addictive drugs, and the crimes associated with them. Peace, love, and taking care of the planet have been around since the beginning of mankind, but it takes commitment and courage to live up to those ideals. Or consider the alternative: war, hate, and an Earth devoid of life!

As individuals seeking happiness and a meaningful life on our precious planet, it's necessary that we live in peace and harmony with each other. What happens in one part of the world affects us all. Like it or not, we are truly a global family. We can no longer ignore the rights of all living species because our existence is absolutely dependent on them!

The love and compassion we've discussed in this book needs to apply to **all** daily activities, not just some. Bring love to the workplace, shopping, or exercising. Laws of justice should be guidelines for compassion and love. Too often, there is a difference between the ethical principle of a law and its actual application. Murder is ethically wrong, yet world leaders have advocated wars that were labeled "justified" and "heroic," killing hundreds of thousands of men, women, and children. War is a "legal" excuse to kill for profit, retaliation, and to enforce one's way of life.

Who "wins" a war? Leaders of a country attempt to gain something, which may or may not be obvious to the general populace of either side.

Who "loses" a war? It's anything living that gets in the way of war's carnage: dead soldiers, grieving family members, innocent civilians, animals and plants. Wars create decades of long-term hatred and catastrophic devastation.

It's pretty hard to practice happiness if bombs are flying over your head! It's far better to do anything necessary to prevent the killing. Wars are started by unhappy, greedy individuals lusting after power. Through time, war's cast of characters change roles. Who is the country to hate this year? Time and time again, enemies later become allies, and allies become enemies. An old political cartoon has three prisoners in a Russian jail, discussing Khrushchev, a former leader of the Soviet Republic under the communist regime:

Prisoner One: I'm here because I booed Khrushchev!
Prisoner Two: You're kidding! I'm here because I cheered Khrushchev! (to the third prisoner) What are you in here for?
Prisoner Three: What do you mean? I **am** Khrushchev!

Like happiness, peace can ultimately be achieved—one person at a time. Yet countries go eons without trusting; they are always afraid of what "might" happen. War is too often seen as a solution, but that doesn't make it right.

An eye for an eye only makes the world blind.
-ANONYMOUS-

Human nature is to desire peace and tranquility. Destructive actions go against our basic human nature as stated in these excerpts from the Tao over 2,500 years ago:

WELL I'LL BE A BLUE-NOSED GOPHER

You must not parade your success,
You must not boast of your ability,
You must not feel proud,
You must rather regret that you had not been able to prevent the war.
You must never think of conquering others by force.
For to be over-developed is to hasten decay,
And this is against Tao, and what is against Tao will soon cease to be.

And to him even a victory is no cause for rejoicing.
To rejoice over a victory is to rejoice over the slaughter of men!

Hence, even a victory is a funeral.

When the desires of men are curbed, there will be peace,
And the world will settle down of its own accord.

A man of violence will come to a violent end.

You govern a kingdom by normal rules;
You fight a war by exceptional moves;
But you win the world by letting alone.

Happiness and peace are closely related, so we have to practice both. Peace, like happiness will be accomplished through improving the mental health of each individual, which is why the study of happiness is so important!

CHAPTER THIRTY-TWO
THE QUEST FOR REALITY

Getting Closer to Reality

Practicing happiness and discovering our higher nature is essentially a search for reality. There are over seven billion individuals on this planet, which make for seven billion interpretations in how we see reality! Reality doesn't depend on a viewpoint; it simply **is.** The objects and events that we experience through our cerebral neurotransmitters are interpretations based on our own limited knowledge. We see the world as we **think** it is, filtered through our own personal "stained glass window." The more we clean up our window, the more we'll see the truth. Our thoughts create our reality, which is only restricted by whatever limitations we impose. An open mind helps our search for truth and keeps us from limited thinking.

Look beyond the curtain of memory to begin to discover the true fabric of reality.
-DR. DEPAK CHOPRA-

With the vastness of the universe and our tiny brains, we'll just have to accept that we won't have all the answers about reality in our earthly life. That's a tough pill to swallow, so what do we do about it? Call it God; call it anything you want, but to believe in a higher power beyond our understanding helps us to accept people, circumstances, and events as they occur, even when we don't fully understand the "whys." Whatever you believe, it's best to learn to accept our uncertainty about some things.

Our lives are always a mixture of order and chaos, so by combining our intellect with our faith and intuition, we can at least hope to know **some** things **some** of the time! Every day, technology gets us closer to understanding the nature of the universe, and new discoveries raise more questions about the reality we thought we had. Groundbreaking scientific discoveries have always been accompanied by considerable scientific, political, and religious persecution. It took hundreds of years after Magellan for the general populace to believe that the Earth was not flat! On the other hand, particular viewpoints about reincarnation or heaven and hell have not been scientifically proven, yet that does not deter people's beliefs.

Ideas from science and from religion need to to be more compatible. Scientists have to back down and admit the possibility of phenomena that cannot yet be proven, and religious leaders, in the face of irrefutable evidence, will need to rethink some of their doctrines. If we only concentrate on scientific development, we lose a sense of human value. To blindly accept only faith-related issues is to dangerously bury our heads in the sand.

Many today are understandably afraid of religions. The fault doesn't lie with religious ideals, but from the abuse of power and dishonesty by false leaders or practitioners. The same goes with political leaders. When compassion and altruism become the main motive for religious and political leaders, the world will be a happier place.

Spirituality, ethics, and happiness need to be integrated into our education and not routinely trivialized in favor of more "academic" subjects. Yale University's course, "Psychology and the Good Life," and its online counterpart "The Science of Well-Being" deals with many issues surrounding happiness, and at the time of this writing has been touted as the most popular class in the history of the university. I cheer for more classes of this kind around the world! When we look inward, the outward makes more sense. If we can't tame our minds, all of the knowledge in the world will do us little good.

As we practice happiness daily, we make choices. Some choices are seemingly small and unimportant, yet their sum total becomes very important. If what you're doing right now has no potential benefit for the good of someone else, it's probably not worth doing. Your future and that of others depends on what you're doing right now. Know that whatever happens to you ultimately will help you along your spiritual path.

> *The teachings tell us what we need to realize, but we also have to go on our own journey, in order to come to a personal realization. That journey may take us through suffering, difficulties, and doubts of all kinds, but they will become our greatest teachers. Through them we will learn the humility to recognize our limitations, and through them we will discover the inner strength and fearlessness we need to emerge from our old habits and set patterns, and surrender into the vaster vision of real freedom offered by the spiritual teachings.*
> **-SOGYAL RINPOCHE-**

Spiritual transformation takes time and patience. Like happiness, we already possess the qualities needed for that transformation; we just have to bring them out. To practice happiness is to practice spirituality, and as you merge with your higher self, you will see that the happiness you so richly deserve is already here!

 ## Happiness Step Forty-Three
Making a Difference

I will take a leadership role in the following area(s) in order to bring happiness to others and/or improve a cause that I firmly believe in.

_____

_____

_____

_____

_____

I will do the following compassionate deed for someone in need without expectation of anything in return.

_____

_____

_____

_____

I will do the following to promote peace and non-violence in my life and in the lives of others.

_____

_____

_____

_____

_____

I will do the following in order to ensure that I continue my progress with my well-being and spirituality.

_____

_____

_____

_____

_____

Enter these into your calendars, including daily/weekly/monthly reminders!

Happiness Steps Locator

Happiness Step		Pages
1	Meditations	32
2	Discovering Your True Nature	42
3	The Real You	44
4	Letting Go of the Baggage	56
5	Releasing Negative Emotions from Childhood	60
6	Doing What You Love	63
7	Keeping Score	67
8	Have a Perfect Day	71
9	What Are You Thinking?	79
10	Positive or Negative Thoughts?	81
11	What I Want More of in Life	89
12	Practicing Intuition	97
13	What I Really Want	108
14	The Truth Is…	115
15	Prioritizing…	119
16	Shortcuts! Getting There Sooner	129
17	Follow through with Your Goal!	135
18	Time-Saving or Squandering?	142
19	Movin' On	148
20	Your Now Moments	158
21	Good Riddance to Weak Verbiage!	173
22	A Happier Future	177
23	Energy Check!	185
24	Unclogging the Drain!	212
25	Lightin' the Fire or Chillin' Out?	223
26	Ego Check!	249
27	Happiness Weather Report	252
28	Ego-Squelching Activities	262
29	Facing Adversity	272

30	Morphing Attachments into Preferences	280
31	Don't Worry!	287
32	Just Being	293
33	Erasing Disappointment	296
34	Showing Compassion and Love	301
35	Saying Thanks	307
36	A Little Self-Analysis	309
37	Dousing the Fire	326
38	Overcoming	338
39	Washing Away the Dirt	348
40	It's Your Funeral	365
41	Meditations about That Exceptional Moment	375
42	Remember Me!	381
43	Making a Difference	399

ACKNOWLEDGMENTS

To…

Toni, my wife and soul mate.
You are a beautiful and wise being; you are the greatest gift in my life. You chose to remain with me on Earth in a more limited form after suffering a near-fatal accident—one of the greatest sacrifices one can make. I am blessed every day you share your life with me. I love you; you are the "blue-nosed gopher" of my dreams!

Monique, my stepdaughter and best friend.
The bond you share with your mom is incredible. Thank you for all you've done to make our lives so much richer.

Paul Goode, my favorite son-in-law.
Thank you for being such a caring and integral part of our family unit.

Evalee and James Webb, Mom and Dad.
I couldn't have had better parents. Thank you for your love, caring, and sacrifice so I could have this great life!

Tony and Juanita Jaramillo, the best in-laws I could possibly have had.
Thank you for raising my greatest gift, Toni, and for your love and friendship.

Jim Eggler, super-cousin and retired librarian.
Your meaningful comments, constant encouragement, and support throughout the creation of this book will not be forgotten. I appreciate you!

Stormy, Oreo, and Jessie, our cats.
You kept me company during the hundreds of hours while I wrote this book, and the comfort that bought deserves a dedication. My life would have been so much emptier without you.

Josephine Lee, caregiver and friend for Toni.
Thank you for giving Toni so much more than caregiving. You'll always be family. We love you.

Sarah Bausinger, illustrator.
How you have made my book dance! Your creativity added so much, and I'm sure there are hundreds more smiles from our readers because of your gift of illustration. Not to mention how great you were to work with! Thank you.

Traci V. Bransford, Stinson LLP.
Thank you for so adeptly handling the numerous permissions I needed for quotations and for your constant encouragement and patience. You and your team saved me more than a few aspirins and hopefully any lawsuits!

Sarah Fox, editor, The Bookish Fox.
I cannot begin to explain how much of a difference you have made in improving my manuscript to the point where someone might actually be able to understand it. You are the perfect combination of being so nice yet so brutally thorough. As they say in restaurants, I made an "excellent choice!" Thank you!

Regina Wamba, Creator of Awesome Things, www.ReginaWamba.com
Thank you for turning my crazy ideas into something magical. Your cover design proves you are indeed, a creator of awesome things! Someone might just pick up a copy, and be a blue-nosed gopher!

The Damonza team, www.damonza.com
Thank you for taking on this complex formatting job so willingly. Your timely and high-quality work is noteworthy, and greatly appreciated!

Sarah Kolb-Williams, self-publishing consultant
I so appreciate your expertise in navigating the tricky waters of self-publishing and distribution. Without your prompt, thorough and savvy advice, my book would likely have been lost at sea! And did I say, you are great to work with?

Katharine Bolin, digital marketing strategist, founder of Sweet Reach Media, LLC.
If anyone reads this book, it's because of your sure-fire ability to guide my technically-challenged brain to move faster than a speeding snail. Thank you for the website makeover and marketing ideas. I might just reach a few more readers beyond my living room!

Dr. Forrest Rollins, professor, University of North Texas.
The two graduate education courses I took from you were groundbreaking and captured the essence of the way learning should be. You created the spark that compelled me to discover why happiness can be so simple yet so elusive. You got us students to want to learn for ourselves. Thank you for being a spiritual change agent and creating a paradigm shift in my life!

Andrea LaFave, transcendental meditation teacher, Milwaukee, WI.
The invaluable technique of transcendental meditation was the beginning of a series of positive, profound changes for the better throughout our lives. Toni and I are so grateful for your teachings!

Bob Stone, pipe carrier and sun dancer, Whitewater, WI.
Thank you for sharing your knowledge and humor with us on the red

road. The times we spent with you taught us so much and created vehicles for profound thought. We miss you.

Sam Lone Wolf, pipe carrier and sun dancer, Palestine, TX.
You helped us further understand Native American spirituality and the struggles that indigenous people have had to endure. Thank you for sharing your wisdom with us. Rest in peace, brother.

All my teachers who guided and mentored me at the following institutions and locations. I really can't thank them enough...
Dundee Elementary School, West Dundee, Illinois
Dysinger Elementary School, Buena Park, California
Crescent Junior High School, Anaheim, California
Savannah High School, Anaheim, California
Cypress Community College, Cypress, California
California State University Fullerton, Fullerton, California
The University of North Texas, Denton, Texas
The University of Northern Colorado, Greeley, Colorado

All my students and colleagues at the following institutions and locations. You all taught me how to be a better person.
Mt. San Antonio Community College, Walnut, California
California State University Fullerton, Fullerton, California
Chadron State College, Chadron, Nebraska
The University of Wisconsin-Whitewater, Whitewater, Wisconsin
The University of Texas at Tyler, Tyler, Texas

I thank all of the great contributing authors who have educated and inspired me to write about happiness.

REFERENCES

Academy of Ideas (AI). 2015. "Abraham Maslow: The Jonah Complex and the Fear of Greatness." AI. https://academyofideas.com/2015/03/abraham-maslow-the-jonah-complex-and-the-fear-of-greatness/.

Adrienne, Carol. 1999. *The Purpose of Your Life: Finding Your Place in the World Using Synchronicity, Intuition, and Uncommon Sense.* New York: Eagle Brook, an Imprint of William Morrow and Co., Inc.

Baba, Meher. 1987. *"Eventually It Transforms Everyone."* Ahmednagar: Avatar Meher Baba Perpetual Public Charitable Trust. http://www.avatarmeherbaba.org/erics/catchit.html.

Baker, Dan, and Cameron Stauth. 2004. *What Happy People Know: How the New Science of Happiness Can Change Your Life for the Better.* New York: St. Martin's Griffin.

Ben-Shahar, Tal. 2007. *Happier: Learn the Secrets to Daily Joy and Lasting Fulfillment.* New York: McGraw-Hill.

Bloom, Pamela. 2000. *Buddhist Acts of Compassion.* Berkeley: Conari Press.

Bstan-'dzin-rgya-mtsho. 1999. *Ethics for the New Millennium.* New York: Riverhead Books.

Bstan-'dzin-rgya-mtsho, 2001. *Art of Living, A Guide to Contentment, Joy and Fulfillment.* Translated by Geshe Thupten Jinpa. Thorsons: London.

Bstan-'dzin-rgya-mtsho. 2008. *The Way to Freedom.* Edited by Donald S. Lopez. Dharamsala, H.P.: Library of Tibetan Works and Archives.

Bstan-'dzin-rgya-mtsho, Herbert Benson, Daniel Goleman, and Robert A. F. Thurman. 1991. *MindScience: An East-West Dialogue*. Boston: Wisdom Publ.

Bstan-'dzin-rgya-mtsho, Anne Benson, and Fabien Ouaki. 1999. *Imagine All the People: A Conversation with the Dalai Lama on Money, Politics, and Life as It Could Be*. Boston: Wisdom Publ.

Bstan-'dzin-rgya-mtsho, and Jeffrey Hopkins. 2009. *How to See Yourself as You Really Are*. Bath: Thorndike/Chivers.

Bstan-'dzin-rgya-mtsho, and Donald S. Lopez, Jr. 1997. *Joy of Living and Dying in Peace*. San Francisco: HarperCollins.

Bstan-'dzin-rgya-mtsho, and Donald S. Lopez, Jr. 2008. *Awakening the Mind, Lightening the Heart*. Dharamsala, H.P.: Library of Tibetan Works and Archives.

Cai, Zhizhong. 1995. *The Tao Speaks: Lao-Tzu's Whispers of Wisdom*. Translated by Brian Bruya. New York: Anchor Books.

Capretto, Lisa, Wayne Dyer, and Oprah Winfrey. 2013. "Watch: How to Attract Anything You Want into Your Life." The Huffington Post. TheHuffingtonPost.com. https://www.huffingtonpost.com/2013/07/08/wayne-dyer-art-of-manifestatation_n_3543023.html.

Chopra, Deepak. 1994a. *Perfect Health: The Complete Mind/Body Guide*. New York: Harmony Books.

Chopra, Deepak. 1994b. *The Seven Spiritual Laws of Success: A Practical Guide to the Fulfillment of Your Dreams*. San Rafael: Amber-Allen Publ.

Chopra, Deepak. 1996. *The Way of the Wizard: Twenty Spiritual Lessons in Creating the Life You Want*. New York: Harmony Books.

Chopra, Deepak. 2010. *Ageless Body, Timeless Mind: The Quantum Alternative to Growing Old*. New York: Three Rivers Press.

Cohen, Alan. 1995. *I Had It All the Time: When Self-Improvement Gives Way to Ecstasy*. Des Moines, WA: Alan Cohen Publications.

Cohen, Alan. 1996. *Are You as Happy as Your Dog? Sure-Fire Ways to Wake up with a Smile as Big as Your Pooch's*. Illustrated by Alan Gordon. Haiku: Alan Cohen Publications.

Cohen, Alan. 2002. *Why Your Life Sucks: And What You Can Do about It*. San Diego: Jodere Group.

Cohen, Alan. 2018. "Blissful Innocence." Empowering Caregivers. http://www.care-givers.com/DBArticles/pages/viewarticle.php?id=775.

Csikszentmihalyi, Mihaly. 1997. *Finding Flow: The Psychology of Engagement with Everyday Life*. New York: Harper Collins.

Csikszentmihalyi, Mihaly. 2009. *Flow: The Psychology of Optimal Experience*. New York: Harper Row.

Dass, Ram. 1974. *The Only Dance There Is: Talks given at the Menninger Foundation, Topeka, Kansas, 1970, and at Spring Grove Hospital, Spring Grove, Maryland, 1972*. New York: Anchor.

Dass, Ram. 1978a. *Journey of Awakening: A Meditator's Guidebook*. Edited by Daniel Goleman, Dwarkanath Bonner, and Ram Dev. Illustrated by Vincent Piazza. New York: Bantam Books.

Dass, Ram. 1978b. *Remember, Be Here Now*. San Anselmo: Hanuman Foundation.

Dass, Ram. 2001. *Still Here: Embracing Aging, Changing, and Dying*. Edited by Mark Matousek and Marlene Roeder. New York: Riverhead Books.

Dass, Ram, and Paul Gorman. 1985. *How Can I Help? Stories and Reflections on Service*. New York: Alfred A. Knopf.

Dass, Ram, and Stephen Levine. 1987. *Grist for the Mill*. Berkeley: Celestial Arts.

Denniston, Denise. 1991. *The Transcendental Meditation TM Book: How to Enjoy the Rest of Your Life*. Illustrated by Barry Geller. Fairfield, IA: Fairfield Press.

Dooley, Mike. 2014. *The Top Ten Things Dead People Want to Tell You*. Carlsbad: Hay House, Inc.

Duffy, Prasad. 2002. *Dancing as the Infinite: The Freedom of Our True Self*. San Diego: Master Peace Pub.

Dyer, Wayne W. 1998. *Wisdom of the Ages: A Modern Master Brings Eternal Truths into Everyday Life*. New York: HarperCollins Publishers.

Dyer, Wayne W. 2001a. *There's a Spiritual Solution to Every Problem*. New York: HarperCollins.

Dyer, Wayne W. 2001b. *You'll See It When You Believe It: The Way to Your Personal Transformation*. New York: HarperCollins.

Dyer, Wayne W. 2003. *Getting in the Gap: Making Conscious Contact with God through Meditation*. Carlsbad: Hay House, Inc.

Dyer, Wayne W. 2004. *The Power of Intention: Learning to Co-Create Your World Your Way*. Carlsbad: Hay House, Inc.

Dyer, Wayne W. 2012. *Excuses Begone! How to Change Lifelong, Self-Defeating Thinking Habits*. Carlsbad: Hay House, Inc.

Dyer, Wayne W. 2013. *Change Your Thoughts, Change Your Life: Living the Wisdom of the Tao*. Carlsbad: Hay House, Inc.

Dyer, Wayne W. 2015a. *I Can See Clearly Now*. Carlsbad: Hay House, Inc.

Dyer, Wayne W. 2015b. *Memories of Heaven: Children's Astounding Recollections of the Time before They Came to Earth*. Carlsbad: Hay House, Inc.

Elk, Black. 1988. *The Sacred Pipe: Black Elk's Account of the Seven Rites of the Oglala Sioux*. Edited by Joseph Epes Brown. Norman: University of Oklahoma Press.

Farrer-Halls, Gill. 2001. *The World of the Dalai Lama: An inside Look at His Life, His People, and His Vision*. Wheaton: Godsfield Press, Quest.

Firth, Shannon. 2010. "Sunday Morning Coming Down." FindingDulcinea. http://www.findingdulcinea.com/news/health/2009/april/Sunday-Morning-Coming-Down.html.

Gawain, Shakti. 1989. *Return to the Garden: A Journey of Discovery*. San Rafael: New World Library.

Gawain, Shakti, and Laurel King. 1986. *Living in the Light: A Guide to Personal and Planetary Transformation*. San Rafael: New World Library.

Golas, Thaddeus. 1995. *The Lazy Mans Guide to Enlightenment*. Layton: Gibbs Smith.

Green, Barry, and W. Timothy. Gallwey. 1986. *The Inner Game of Music*. Garden City: Anchor Press/Doubleday.

Hanh, Thich Nhat. 2001. *Anger: Wisdom for Cooling the Flames*. New York: Riverhead Books.

Hanh, Thich Nhat. 2003. *No Death, No Fear: Comforting Wisdom for Life*. New York: Riverhead Books.

Hay, Louise L. 1984. *You Can Heal Your Life*. Carlsbad: Hay House, Inc.

Hesse, Herman. 1951. *Siddartha*. Translated by Hilda Rosner. New York: New Directions.

Hettinger, Eugen. 1964. *Springs of Oriental Wisdom: Confucius, Fu-Kiang, Hakushu, Lao-Tse, Tseng-Kuang*. New York: Herder.

Holland, John. 2005. *101 Ways to Jump-Start Your Intuition*. Carlsbad: Hay House, Inc.

Holy Bible, The, Authorized Version Set Forth in 1611 and Commonly Known as the King James Version. 1940. New York: American Bible Society.

Keyes, Ken Jr. 1975a. *Handbook to Higher Consciousness*. Coos Bay: Living Love Publications.

Keyes, Ken Jr. 1975b. *Taming Your Mind*. Coos Bay: Living Love Publications.

Keyes, Ken Jr. 1980. *How to Enjoy Life in Spite of It All*. St Mary, KY: Living Love.

Keyes, Ken Jr. 1983. *Your Heart's Desire: A Loving Relationship*. Coos Bay: Living Love Publications.

Keyes, Ken Jr. 1986. *Prescriptions for Happiness*. Coos Bay: Love Line.

Keyes, Ken Jr. 1989. *Discovering the Secrets of Happiness: My Intimate Story*. Coos Bay: Love Line Books.

Keyes, Ken Jr., and Bruce (Tolly) Burkan. 1974. *How to Make Your Life Work or Why Aren't You Happy?* Illustrated by L.E. Anderson. Coos Bay: Living Love Publications.

Keyes, Ken Jr., and Penny Keyes. 1987a. *Gathering Power through Insight and Love*. 2nd ed. Coos Bay: Living Love Publications.

Keyes, Ken Jr., and Penny Keyes. 1987b. *Your Life Is a Gift so Make the Most of It*. Illustrated by Ann Hauser. Coos Bay: Love Line.

Keyes, Ken Jr., and Penny Keyes. 1989. *Handbook to Higher Consciousness, the Workbook: A Daily Practice Book to Help You Increase Your Heart-to-Heart Loving and Happiness*. Coos Bay: Love Line Books.

Laozi, and John C. H. Wu. 1990. *Tao Teh Ching*. Boston: Shambala.

LaRoche, Loretta. 2008. *Relax—You May Only Have a Few Minutes Left: Using the Power of Humor to Overcome Stress in Your Life and Work.* Carlsbad: Hay House, Inc.

Leaming, Linda. 2015. *A Field Guide to Happiness: What I Learned in Bhutan about Living, Loving, and Waking Up.* Carlsbad: Hay House.

Maharaj, Nisargadatta. 1992. *I Am That: Talks with Sri Nisargadatta Maharaj.* Edited by Sudhakar S. Dikshit. Translated by Maurice Frydman. Durham: The Acorn Press.

Mahesh, Maharishi. 1995. *Science of Being and Art of Living: Transcendental Meditation.* New York: Meridian.

Manson, Mark. 2016. *The Subtle Art of Not Giving a F*ck: A Counterintuitive Approach to Living a Good Life.* New York: HarperOne.

Martin, Patricia. 1994. *Ancient Echoes: Native American Words of Wisdom.* Glendale Heights: Great Quotations Pub.

Matthews, Andrew. 1990. *Being Happy! A Handbook to Greater Confidence & Security.* New York: Price Stern Sloan.

McGraw, Phillip. 2001. *Self Matters: Creating Your Life from the Inside Out.* New York: Free Press.

Menter, Marcia. 2003. *The Office Sutras: Exercises for Your Soul at Work.* Boston: Red Wheel.

Merriam-Webster. s.v. "pride." 2018. https://www.merriam-webster.com/dictionary/pride.

Myss, Caroline M. 1997. *Why People Don't Heal and How They Can.* New York: Three Rivers Press.

Nachmanovitch, Stephen. 1990. *Free Play: Improvisation in Life and Art.* New York: Jeremy P. Tarcher/Putnam.

Niven, David. 2000. *The 100 Simple Secrets of Happy People: What Scientists Have Learned and How You Can Use It.* San Francisco: HarperSanFrancisco.

Ortner, Nick. 2013. *The Tapping Solution: A Revolutionary System for Stress-Free Living.* Carlsbad, CA: Hay House.

Pell, Sidney, and Bstan-'dzin-rgya-mtsho. 1993. *The Dalai Lama, a Policy of Kindness: An Anthology of Writings by and about the Dalai Lama.* Ithaca: Snow Lion.

Pilgrim, Peace. 1982. *Peace Pilgrim: Her Life and Work in Her Own Words.* Santa Fe: Ocean Tree Books.

Powell, Robert, ed. 1995. *The Ultimate Medicine as Prescribed by Sri Nisargadatta Maharaj.* San Diego: Blue Dove Press.

Prabhavananda, Swami, and Christopher Isherwood, trans. 1944. *The Song of God: Bhagavad-Gita.* Mentor: New York.

Prabhavananda, Swami and Frederick Manchester, trans. 1948. *The Upanishads: Breath of the Eternal.* Mentor: New York.

Prager, Dennis. 1998. *Happiness Is a Serious Problem: A Human Nature Repair Manual.* New York: ReganBooks.

Reps, Paul. 2008. *Zen Flesh, Zen Bones: A Collection of Zen and Pre-Zen Writings.* Transcribed by Nyogen Senzaki. Tokyo: Tuttle Publishing.

Richardson, Cheryl. 1999. *Take Time for Your Life: A Personal Coach's Seven-Step Program for Creating the Life You Want.* New York: Broadway.

Richardson, Cheryl. 2006. *The Unmistakable Touch of Grace: How to Recognize and Respond to the Spiritual Signposts in Your Life.* New York: Free Press.

Richardson, Cheryl. 2011. "Find Your Passion." Martha Stewart Living Omnimedia, Inc. https://www.marthastewart.com/287175/cheryl-richardson-find-your-passion.

Rinpoche, Sogyal. 1992. *The Tibetan Way of Living and Dying*. San Francisco: Harper San Francisco.

Rinpoche, Sogyal. 1995. *Glimpse after Glimpse: Daily Reflections on Living and Dying*. San Francisco: HarperSanFrancisco.

Roman, Sanaya. 1986. *Living with Joy: Keys to Personal Power & Spiritual Transformation*. Tiburon: H.J. Kramer.

Roman, Sanaya. 1989. *Spiritual Growth*. Tiburon: H.J. Kramer.

Roman, Sanaya, and Orin. 1986. *Personal Power through Awareness: A Guidebook for Sensitive People*. Tiburon: H.J. Kramer.

Roth, Ron, and Peter Occhiogrosso. 1999. *Prayer and the Five Stages of Healing*. Carlsbad: Hay House.

Roth, Ron, and Peter Occhiogrosso. 2000. *Holy Spirit: The Boundless Energy of God*. Carlsbad: Hay House.

Rubin, Gretchen. 2011. *The Happiness Project: Or, Why I Spent a Year Trying to Sing in the Morning, Clean My Closets, Fight Right, Read Aristotle, and Generally Have More Fun*. New York: Harper.

Schucman, Helen. 2018. "Lesson 243." Mill Valley: The Foundation for Inner Peace. http://www.acim.org/Lessons/lesson.html?lesson=243.

Schucman, Helen. 2018. "Lesson 281." Mill Valley: The Foundation for Inner Peace. http://www.acim.org/Lessons/lesson.html?lesson=281.

Sharma, Robin S. 2003. *The Saint, the Surfer, and the CEO: A Remarkable Story about Living Your Heart's Desires*. Carlsbad: Hay House.

Sher, Barbara. 1996. *Live the Life You Love: In Ten Easy Step-by-Step Lessons*. New York: Dell Trade Paperback.

Stephenson, Sean. 2009. *Get off Your But: 6 Lessons to Overcome Obstacles and Stand up for Yourself at Work and in Relationships*. San Francisco: Jossey-Bass.

Suzuki, Shunryu, and Trudy Dixon. 1973. *Zen Mind: Beginner's Mind*. New York: Weatherhill.

Tolle, Eckhart. 2007. *The Power of Now*. Novato, CA: Namaste Pub; and New World Library.

Turtle Zen (TZ). n.d. "Two Wolves: A Cherokee Teaching." TZ. Accessed July 31, 2018. http://www.turtlezen.com/twowolves.html.

Virtue, Doreen. 2011. *The Angel Therapy Handbook*. Carlsbad: Hay House.

Ware, James R., trans. 1955. *The Sayings of Confucius*. New York: Mentor Religious Classic.

Watts, Alan W. *The Way of Zen*. 1957. New York: Pantheon Books Inc.

Weiss, Brian L. 1988. *Many Lives, Many Masters: The True Story of a Prominent Psychiatrist, His Young Patient, and the Past-Life Therapy That Changed Both Their Lives*. New York: Simon & Schuster.

Werner-Gray, Liana. 2014. *The Earth Diet: Your Complete Guide to Living Using Earth's Natural Ingredients*. Carlsbad: Hay House, Inc.

White, Russ. n.d. "Quiz." Accessed July 31, 2018. Vedas. https://msu.edu/~rmw/quiz.htm.

Wholey, Dennis. 1986. *Are You Happy? Some Answers to the Most Important Question in Your Life*. Boston: Houghton Mifflin.

Wiederkehr, Macrina. 1995. *A Tree Full of Angels: Seeing the Holy in the Ordinary*. San Francisco: HarperSanFrancisco.

Wilson, Paul. 2000. *Calm for Life*. New York: Dorset Press.

Womack, Kenneth. 2017. *The Beatles Encyclopedia: Everything Fab Four*. Santa Barbara: Greenwood.

ABOUT THE AUTHOR

Dr. John C. Webb served as a professor of music and university administrator for thirty-one years. He taught saxophone and jazz studies at universities in California, Nebraska, Colorado, Wisconsin, and Texas.

Dr. Webb's passion for research about happiness began early in his career when he realized that in an environment filled with brilliant minds and talented people, there was an astonishing amount of unhappiness. In his book *Well I'll be a Blue-Nosed Gopher...Practicing Happiness Now!*, Dr. Webb creates a "practice makes perfect" approach designed to help others discover their own way to improve their well-being. When his wife, Toni, sustained a traumatic brain injury in a serious accident, Dr. Webb retired early to care for her. He shares innovative insights about what we really need to be happy from his wife's perspective. He and his family live in Camarillo, California, where he continues an active writing and performing schedule.

For more information, go to
https://www.drjohncwebb.com

Thanks for reading! If you enjoyed this book, please consider leaving an honest review on your favorite store.

Sarah Bausinger graduated from the University of Texas at Tyler with a bachelor's degree in music education. She is an outstanding bassoonist and is well-versed in all the woodwind instruments. She is currently a band director who teaches grades six through twelve.

At UT Tyler, her artistic abilities became well-known, and after seeing samples of her work, Dr. Webb knew he had found the perfect illustrator for his book. In addition to her skills in designing creative T-shirt logos, programs, and advertisements for her band, she has contributed over 300 innovative cartoons made specifically for *Well I'll be a Blue-Nosed Gopher...Practicing Happiness Now!*

Contact her at sbausjam@gmail.com.

www.ingramcontent.com/pod-product-compliance
Lightning Source LLC
Chambersburg PA
CBHW051416290426
44109CB00016B/1317